SONGS REMEMBERED IN EXILE

SONGS REMEMBERED IN EXILE

Traditional Gaelic songs from Nova Scotia recorded in
Cape Breton and Antigonish County in 1937
with an account of the causes of Hebridean Emigration,
1790–1835

edited by
JOHN L CAMPBELL, LLD St FX, FRSE

tunes mostly transcribed by
SÉAMUS ENNIS

ABERDEEN UNIVERSITY PRESS
Member of the Maxwell Macmillan Pergamon Publishing Corporation

First published in 1990
Aberdeen University Press

British Library Cataloguing in Publication Data

Songs remembered in exile: traditional Gaelic songs from
  Nova Scotia recorded in Cape Breton and Antigonish County
  mostly in 1937.
  1. Folk songs in Gaelic
  I. Campbell, John L.
  784.4'9411

ISBN 0 08 037977 X

TYPESET AND PRINTED IN GREAT BRITAIN
BY BPCC-AUP ABERDEEN LTD

MAR CHUIMHNEACHAN
AIR
AN URRAMACH PÀDRAIG MAC NEACAIL
CEANN-SUIDHE OILTHIGH NFX 1944–1954

ORAN

do Mhgr Iain L Caimbeul agus a Bhean
le
Bean Dhaibhidh mac Pheadrais

Air fonn: Fail ò ro mar dh'fhàg sibh
Cur cùl ri ur càirdean,
Tha sinn uile tùrsach
   'Gar n-ionndrainn a thà sinn.

Iain Caimbeul an t-uasal
Bha suairce 'na nàdur,
Cha n-fhaic sinn mu'n cuairt thu,
   'S gur truagh leinn thu dh'fhàgail.

'S gu bheil do bhean cho fialaidh,
Cho ciatach, 's cho bàigheil,
Tha i cridheil caoibhneal,
   Làn aoibhneis is càirdeis.

Gu robh mise deurach,
Nuair leubh mi 'sa phàipear
Sibh dhol cho fada bhuainne,
   'S nach d'fhuair mi bhith làimh ribh.

Ach gu bheil mi 'n dòchas
Ma's beò agus slàn sibh,
Gun till sibh air a' bhòidse
   Gu 'n còmhlan a dh'fhàg sibh.

'S bho'n a thug sibh cùl ruinn,
'S an dùthaich seo fhàgail,
Mo bheannachd le deagh-dhùrachd
   Bhith dhùibh fad ur làithean.

(Faicibh am fonn air taobh 86 de *Folksongs and Folklore of South Uist*)

CONTENTS

CONTENTS

CONTENTS

CONTENTS

ILLUSTRATIONS

ILLUSTRATIONS

Photographs 1 and 2 are from St F.X. University publicity, 11 is from the *Book of Barra*, 15, 16, 17 and 18 were communicated by the singers or their relatives, and 21 was from the Rev. Malcolm MacDonell. All the others were taken by Margaret Fay Shaw.

INTRODUCTION

S ONGS Remembered in Exile, the title of this book, refers to traditional Gaelic songs from the Scottish Highlands and the Hebrides remembered by emigrants who left the 'Old Country' and departed for Eastern Nova Scotia and Prince Edward Island, but particularly to the Island of Cape Breton, between 1770 and 1830, taking a great deal of their magnificent oral tradition with them. This has always included a great deal of poetry, composed from the late sixteenth century onwards, and Ossianic ballads and chimeric folktales which are even older. The poetry has always been intimately linked with music, and some of the airs may well be much older than the poems. The airs were named after the refrains. The songs were expected to tell a story, and Gaelic audiences expected the story to be clearly told; hence the diction of traditional Gaelic singers is nearly always exceptionally good.

The songs are extremely numerous; many were composed by unlettered bards in the seventeenth and eighteenth centuries and preserved in the first place in oral tradition, from which they started to emerge in printed anthologies compiled from 1776 (the date of Ranald MacDonald's 'Eigg Collection') onwards—some had been taken down in manuscript earlier. The controversy over the authenticity of James MacPherson's alleged translations of the poetry of Ossian, which raged in the last third of the eighteenth century and the first quarter of the nineteenth, aroused keen interest in Gaelic oral literature and a search for ancient Gaelic manuscripts.[1]

Emigration of Gaelic-speaking Highlanders to the New World had begun before 1770; originally to the Cape Fear district of North Carolina, associated with the name of Flora MacDonald, after 1745. Here a Gaelic community put

[1] *See* D. S. Thomson, *The Gaelic Sources of MacPherson's Ossian,* very important in connection with this subject.

1

down roots which lasted until the Civil War (1861–65); the area settled consisted of the counties of Cumberland, Harnett, Moore, Robeson, and Hoke, with its centre at Fayetteville where the last Gaelic sermon was preached by the Rev. J. C. Sinclair, minister of the Presbyterian church of Galatia there from 13 January 1859 to 10 April 1863; he was then transferred to the Presbytery of Mull in Scotland, from where he had come. He used to preach in Gaelic and in English, separate sermons, every Sunday[1].

The American Revolution discouraged further Scottish immigration into North Carolina; by the 1770s it had become diverted to eastern Nova Scotia and Prince Edward Island, and particularly to the Island of Cape Breton, where Gaelic has now been spoken for more than two hundred years by descendants of emigrants from many parts of the Scottish Highlands and the Hebrides, who left their native land unwillingly, and whose nostalgia led them to preserve a great deal of its oral tradition and music. Cape Breton today is the one place in North America where a Celtic language and its literature really has deep roots.

By the 1920s the settlers who had come to Cape Breton in the early 1800s were represented by their grandchildren, themselves now grandparents, and contacts with the 'Old Country' had become only occasional; by North American standards Cape Breton is an out-of-the-way place. That being so, the writer, who had studied Gaelic under Professor John Fraser at Oxford, where he had graduated in agriculture, took the advantage of being in the United States in the early spring of 1932 to visit Cape Breton on a tour of eastern Canada, in order to discover the lie of the land. To reach Sydney, Cape Breton in those days required two nights and a day in the train from Boston. The story of that visit is told in the next chapter of this book.

By the beginning of 1937, the writer and his wife were living on the island of Barra in the Outer Hebrides; his wife had previously lived for some years in a remote crofting township in South Uist collecting traditional Gaelic songs and folklore.[2] In January 1937 they acquired a clockwork ediphone recorder for this study. By the end of July 1937 they had, with the encouragement of the late Miss Annie Johnston, the Rev. John MacMillan, and John MacPherson called 'the Coddy'[3] recorded on wax cylinders 195 songs and stories from thirteen men and seventeen women traditional reciters, including such outstanding persons as Mr Roderick MacKinnon, 'Ruairi Iain Bhàin', and Mrs MacDougall 'Anna Raghnaill Eachainn'.[4] When an invitation came from American relations who

[1] Letter to the writer by the Rev. Frank M. Bain, Galatia Manse, Fayetteville, N.C., dated 13 April 1938.
[2] See *Folksongs and Folklore of South Uist,* by Margaret Fay Shaw, 1955, 1975.
[3] See *Tales of Barra, Told by the Coddy,* 1959 and later revised reprints.
[4] See *Gaelic Folksongs from the Isle of Barra,* published by the Linguaphone Co. for the Folklore Institute of Scotland, 1950.

2

1.   Rt Rev. Mgr P. J. Nicholson, President of St Francis Xavier University 1944–54

2. MacKinnon Hall and University Chapel, St Francis Xavier University

3. The Country of the Barramen in Cape Breton taken from the top of Beinn Bhriagh. In the centre is the Washabuck district and in the distance on the left is the shore of Christmas Island

4. 'Caolas nam Barrach' (Ceap Bretunn). The Barra Settlers' Country in Cape Breton

5. Cape Breton countryside, near Margaree

6.   An abandoned farm. The occupiers had probably moved to Western Canada

7. Farm near Castlebay, Cape Breton

8. Chief Gabriel Syllibuy and Levi Poulette of the Micmac Indians

9. The Bard MacLean's tombstone, Glenbard Cemetery, Antigonish County

10. Wallace MacNeil, Vernon River, Prince Edward Island. Representative of the old MacNeil of Brevig family, Isle of Barra, which emigrated in 1802

11.   General Roderick MacNeil of Barra, 1788–1863, last MacNeil of Barra in the direct male line. Reproduced from a copy in the possession of Mr Donald MacNeil, Castlebay, Barra. The identity of the painter has not been discovered, nor has that of the present owner of the portrait.

  A portrait of General MacNeil's father (also named Roderick MacNeil) by Raeburn was sold at Sotheby's in London in November 1960. The source was the collection of Lady Cathcart Gordon. The portrait is reproduced in Sotheby's catalogue of that date; the identity of the purchaser has not been revealed.

12. Castlebay, Isle of Barra, showing Kismul Castle, herring fishing boats, and in the background parts of the islands of Vatersay and Sandray

13. Eoligary House, Isle of Barra. Built by Colonel Roderick MacNeil of Barra 1763–1822, around the time of his marriage to Jean Cameron of Fassiefern, 1785, when kelp was paying Highland proprietors handsomely. It was described by the famous chemist E. D. Clarke on his visit in 1797, see his life by Bishop William Otter (1824)

summering near Georgian Bay in Ontario to visit in August, it was decided to take advantage of the occasion to visit Cape Breton with the ediphone afterwards. The story of that visit was told in two articles in the *Scots Magazine* in September and October 1938, which are reproduced as the second chapter here, with some necessary revision, with the consent of the editor, which is gratefully acknowledged here. While in Cape Breton we were joined for a time by Professor, as he became later, Angus McIntosh.

The visit of 1937 convinced us that Gaelic oral tradition was very much alive in Cape Breton, and that anyone with suitable training and adequate time could then have made a very large collection of songs and stories from the reciters then living, including descendants of emigrants from districts in the Highlands and Islands now depopulated, which would have been of much interest for dialect and lexicographical studies, as well as for folklore.

The collection we made in 1937 amounted to 43 ediphone wax cylinders. On these cylinders were recorded 90 traditional songs, 5 traditional ballads (mostly Hogmanay ballads), two traditional games, seven local songs, and three original songs sung by their composer, A. J. MacKenzie. Sixty-four of these songs came from singers of Barra or South Uist descent, four women and three men, three of them MacNeils by birth; a further fourteen traditional songs and one local song were recorded from a male singer of Lochaber descent, a descendant of the Bohuntin family, Angus 'Ridge' MacDonald, living in Antigonish County. Three stories were recorded, but one was an amusing composition of A. J. MacKenzie himself, one was said to have come from the pages of *Mac Talla*, and another from an 'English book'.

Some outstanding traditional singers were revealed, particularly Mrs Neil McInnis, Mrs David Patterson, and Mrs J. R. Johnston, with whom we spent some time, but also Mrs MacLean and A. J. MacKenzie, bard and historian of Christmas Island, with both of whom we regretted not being able to spend more time, and Angus 'Ridge'. Fifty-nine of the songs collected in 1937 were chosen for this book, with two games, and an Ossianic ballad recorded from Angus McIsaac at Antigonish on a visit to St F.X. in 1953 was added to make up sixty musical items.

The purpose of the expedition was to record songs brought from Scotland by emigrants from Barra and South Uist, and see how the versions compared; if we could record songs so brought which we had not heard in the 'Old Country', so much the better. Recording songs that had been composed in Cape Breton was not our primary purpose, though we never refused to record them if people wanted to sing them. They receive adequate treatment in other anthologies.

After a brief visit to Prince Edward Island, we left the Maritime Provinces of Canada, and returned to the United States, and eventually to Scotland at the end of January 1938, bringing with us a Presto disc recorder, with which the first electrical recording of traditional Gaelic songs was done on the Isle of Barra in February and March of that year. We also brought disc copies of one of Mrs Patterson's songs and two of Allan Ridge's songs, and some of the Micmac material; we tried to present these to various institutions in Scotland, and found that none of these had provisions for accepting such things! Pre-Second War Scottish academia had very little interest in oral tradition, and as far as Gaelic was concerned, preferred to believe that everything of interest had already been collected by J. F. Campbell of Islay, Alexander Carmichael, and Mrs Kennedy Fraser, and that no further work needed to be done in the field. Excessive interest in it could lead to suspicion of being involved in ultra-Scottish nationalism.

The whole ediphone collection of 1937, Barra and South Uist as well as Nova Scotia material, underwent some vicissitudes after that year, owing to my wife and myself migrating from Barra to the Isle of Canna and undertaking the rehabilitation of a hill farm there, under very difficult conditions; a story which remains to be told.

Although we did have the chance to make an occasional disc recording of the last Canna *seanchaidh,* Angus MacDonald 'Aonghus Eachainn' and of Gaelic speaking persons who came from South Uist to help us (and once to make the only recording ever made of the late Professor John Fraser, who brought his family to live on Canna for a number of months), there was no possible chance to work on musical transcriptions. The words were little trouble, they had been taken down in the field; sometimes texts had been supplied by Miss Annie Johnston (for Barra) or by the Rt Rev. P. J. Nicholson (in the case of the songs of Angus Ridge). Transcribing tunes was too time-consuming to think of.

Ediphone cylinders are apt to deteriorate in storage, being attacked by mould, resulting in scratchy and unpleasant reproduction of sound. By 1946 the situation was getting desperate, and an appeal for help in transcribing the tunes was made to the Irish Folklore Commission, which had been set up in 1926, and which was well aware of the interest of the Gaelic tradition of South Uist and Barra. The late Professor Delargy, head of the Commission, very kindly responded by sending the late Séamus Ennis, the Commission's musical transcriber, to Canna, along with Dr Calum I. MacLean the well known folktale collector, then working for the Commission, subsequently for the School of Scottish Studies, and later to be given a posthumous honorary degree by St Francis Xavier University. While on Canna Séamus Ennis transcribed 147 airs from our ediphone collection including 56 of the airs recorded in Nova Scotia, while Calum MacLean recorded the last surviving Canna *seanchaidh,* Angus MacDonald, and also transcribed the two games and some of the ballads from the Nova Scotian recordings. Séamus Ennis's tune transcriptions are printed in this book by kind permission of Professor Bo Almqvist, head of the Irish Folklore Department, University College, Dublin, which as successor to the Irish Folklore Commission possesses the copyright; Dr Calum MacLean's transcriptions of the two games are included by permission of his brother Dr Alastair MacLean, acknowledged with gratitude.

The persons who have made outstanding contributions to Gaelic literature in Nova Scotia were the Rev. A MacLean Sinclair (1840–1923), grandson of John MacLean (1787–1848), bard to the Laird of Coll, who emigrated to Nova Scotia in 1819, taking two very important collections of Gaelic poetry in manuscript with him, much of which his grandson published in a series of small, inexpensive books, along with genealogical information of interest, to encourage the Gaels of Nova Scotia to take an interest in their language; Jonathan G. MacKinnon (1869–1944) of Skye descent, who founded the paper *Mac Talla* in 1892 and kept it alive until 1904, and later produced a monthly, *Fear na Céilidh,* and made translations and wrote local history; and the Rt Rev. P. J. Nicholson (1887–1965), Professor of Physics at St Francis Xavier University and later President 1944–54, a Gaelic speaker of Barra descent who took a great interest in Gaelic traditional literature, and contributed for many years items from his own collection, and material sent to him by correspondents, to his weekly column in the *Casket* (the paper published in Antigonish), called *Achadh nan Gaidheal.* We were privileged to know Monsignor Nicholson, Jonathan MacKinnon and the Rev. Donald MacLean Sinclair, son of the Rev. A MacLean Sinclair, well, and to receive much encouragement in our work from them.

As the present collection contains so many references to emigration, I thought it would be worth writing a chapter on the causes of emigration which operated between 1770 and 1830, particularly as some very relevant material relating to it survives in the MacNeil letters printed in the *Book of Barra* and in letters at the Scots College at Rome written from Barra between 1826 and 1831, and in legal documents at the Scottish Record Office. I am grateful to the late Rt Rev. Monsignor Clapperton, Rector of the Scots College, for permission to publish long quotations from these letters, and to the authorities of the Scottish Record Office for leave to make similar quotations from the documents referred to in my third chapter.

Apart from the persons and institutions already mentioned, my wife and I have to thank many friends at St Francis Xavier University, which over the years has become our Nova Scotian base and second home, for much encouragement and hospitality, especially the recent President, the Rev. Gregory MacKinnon, and past Presidents, the Rt Rev. Monsignor P. J. Nicholson already mentioned, Dr Somers, Dr Malcolm MacLellan, and the Rev. Malcolm MacDonell; Sister Margaret MacDonell, formerly head of the Celtic Department, Professor

Kenneth Nilsen present head, and John Shaw, who published *Tales Until Dawn,* the Gaelic stories of Joe Neil MacNeil, Big Pond, Cape Breton; Maureen Lonergan Williams of Special Collections in the Angus L. MacDonald library at St F.X.; for encouragement and useful help.

In Scotland I must thank the Scottish Record Office for permission to quote from the Crown Copyright SRO list of CS 96, Court of Session productions, in my third chapter, as well as for many helpful answers to enquiries; Professor Derick Thomson of Glasgow University, and Dr Colm Ó Baoill of Aberdeen University for useful advice on a number of points; the Editor of the *Scots Magazine* for permission to reprint the articles already mentioned, after bringing them up to date; Iain Thornber, Knock, Morvern, for very interesting information about Iain Mac Thearlaich Òig, the MacLean poet from Ardgour with whose song on the unhappy condition of the Highlands after the failure of the '45 Rising this book appropriately ends; and Miss Magdalena Sagarzazu, without whose help in typing the English text, the book would have taken much longer to write.

I must also thank Mr Colin S. Macdonald of Newcastle, New Brunswick, for some useful local information, given in 1939; the singers of the songs printed in this book, for their kind hospitality and interest in our work, sincere thanks are also due to the Gaelic Books Council for a very generous grant of £1200 towards the expense of producing this book; and to the Royal Society of Edinburgh for the very generous grant of £800. Publication has also been assisted by the HIDB as part of HI Light: Year of the Arts.

I must also thank the kind friends who helped in reading the proofs of this book, particularly the Rev. Malcolm MacDonell and the Rev. Canon John MacNeil, both Gaelic speakers. I am indebted to Mrs Kate Chapman for indexing the parts of this book that are in English.

Notes on the Editing

This book follows the lay-out of Margaret Fay Shaw's *Folksongs and Folklore of South Uist,* and the orthography used there and in *Hebridean Folksongs* by Campbell and Collinson; this involves the use of the normal dialect forms of words, especially where rhyme is involved; the practice of folklorists nowadays is to reproduce what people actually say or sing. It also involves the normalisation according to Scottish Gaelic usage, of the Irish spellings and accentation that sometimes occur in Séamus Ennis's transcriptions; Séamus Ennis was a most gifted singer, performer (on the uileann pipes and the eight-keyed flute) and transcriber of traditional Gaelic music, but at the commencement of the work on this collection, though acquainted with several Irish Gaelic dialects, he had not previously worked with Scottish Gaelic. His part in saving this collection, at a time when the Editor and his wife were both very tired and in poor health, is something for which all lovers of Hebridean and Nova Scotian folksong should be deeply grateful.

Ennis did not have time to transcribe the whole collection; some more musical transcriptions were later made by Margaret Fay Shaw and A. Martin Freeman (author of *Folksongs from Ballyvourney*), while the recordings were still playable. The late Dr Calum MacLean, an honorary graduate of St Francis Xavier, who was working on Canna at the same time recording Angus MacDonald (Aonghus Eachainn), made some prose transcriptions, two of which are included here.

With regard to the translations, Gaelic and English differ so greatly in their structures and modes of expression, that at times it is impossible to produce readable English by translating Gaelic poetry literally. There are times when I have felt it necessary to do this by translating Gaelic expressions into English ones which are normally used to express the same ideas, rather than translating more literally. Instances are usually explained in the notes to the songs.

The composition of songs, usually to pre-existing airs, some of great beauty, has been the great means of literary and artistic expression of the Gaelic people of Scotland. It is very important that such songs, which are very plentiful, should not be allowed to die. Because they were expected to tell stories about personalities, events, or the beauty of the Highlands and Islands, to unlettered but intelligent audiences which included passive tradition-bearers who could criticise, the traditional singers were expected to have perfect diction, and normally did so. The songs themselves had a great effect in preserving the Scottish Gaelic language with its enormous vocabulary, as well as memories of the history of the Scottish Gaels and their country, from the late sixteenth century onwards, if not earlier.

The bibliography given in this book is practically restricted to books connected with Canada. Full extensive bibliographies relating to the whole subject of Hebridean folksong can be found in *Folksongs and Folklore of South Uist,* and in Volume I of *Hebridean Folksongs,* with some additions in Volume III. Other sources for songs of which versions occur in all three publications, can also be found in those two books.

J. L. CAMPBELL

Isle of Canna
January 1989

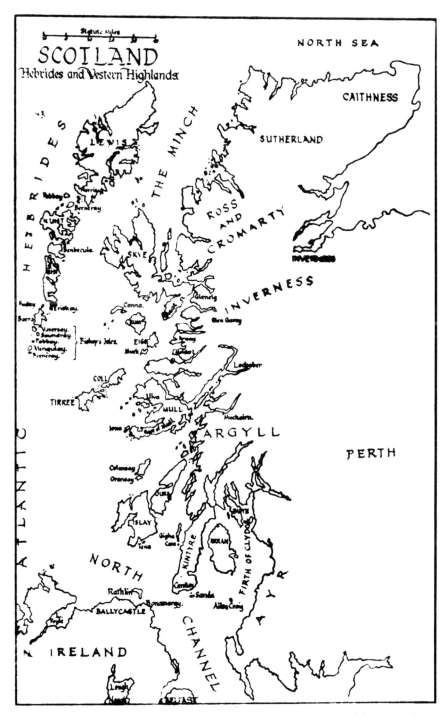

Map 1　The Hebrides and the North-west coast of Scotland.
Reproduced from *The Irish Franciscan Mission to Scotland, 1619–1646* by
Cathaldus Giblin O.F.M. with the author's permission.

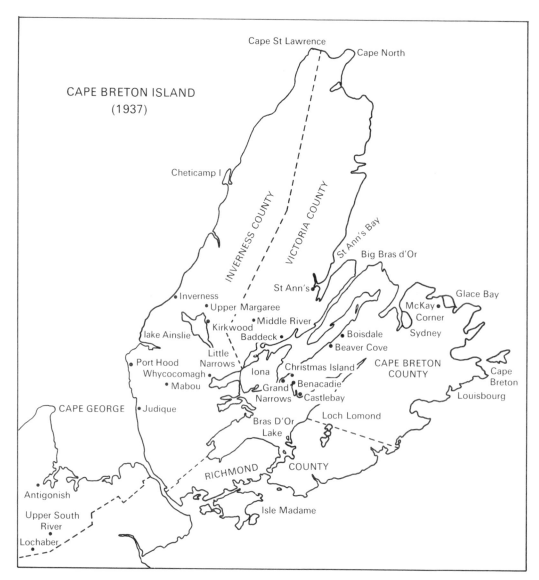

Map 2   Cape Breton, Nova Scotia.

A VISIT TO NOVA SCOTIA, 1932

Monday April 11th. Arrived Sydney, Nova Scotia 7.30 a.m. (having travelled by rail from Boston).* Stayed at the I.R. Hotel.

Called on C. & G. MacLeod booksellers. (Also) Donald MacKinnon, publisher, brother of Jonathan MacKinnon editor of *Mac Talla* (and of) *Fear na Céilidh.* No Gaelic paper here in circulation at the moment but *Fear na Céilidh* may start again.[1]

Search for James MacNeill not successful. At Donald MacKinnon's met the Rev. J. A. MacLellan (who) told me that Gaelic was strongest at North Shore—St Ann's—Whycocamagh[2]—Baddeck—Iona. Must see him again. In the evening called on the MacCurdys, v. hospitable and informative.

The Antigonish *Casket* has a Gaelic column.

Tuesday April 12th. Awful weather. Visited MacLeods and Donald MacKinnon in morning re Gaelic books. Visited Jonathan MacKinnon, editor of *Mac Talla* and *Fear na Céilidh,* in the afternoon, and received much useful information in a long talk.

Mac Talla, monthly,[3] ran from 1892 to 1904, with a circulation of about 1200–1500. It was brought to an end by the boom at Sydney which put up costs of production, wages etc. E.g. cost of printing in 1900 was double that of 1899. Until that time *Mac Talla* paid its way.

---

* Words in brackets are added.
[1] It did not, as far as I know. Eight numbers appeared monthly in 1928.
[2] Pronounced with stress on second syllable, as if written Why-cógama. Skye people. St Ann's—Lewis and Harris; Iona—Barra.
[3] This is wrong: *Mac Talla* appeared as a weekly for the first nine years of its existence, as a fortnightly for the last three.

Predecessor, the *Cuairtear nan Gaidheal* of Antigonish, date uncertain (1852).

Teachdaire nan Gaidheal, founded 1925, and moribund in 1928, ed. James MacNeill.

Fear na Céilidh now edited by Jonathan MacKinnon, monthly, appeared first in 1930 and 21 numbers have been published since. Publication suspended but is to be resumed.[1]

Gaelic in the Schools. Voluntary school were founded amongst the settlers where Gaelic was taught, but in 1864 Provincial schools were started into which Gaelic was not admitted. Lately (about 10 years ago)[2] Gaelic received recognition as an optional subject, but almost complete lack of teachers hinders people from learning how to read and write it.

Gaelic in the United and Presbyterian Churches. About 18–20 congregations in Cape Breton have Gaelic services, and other congregations would benefit if their ministers could use the language. Most of the Catholic congregations are Gaelic. The continuing Presbyterians are largely Gaelic and have three or four ministers all able to preach in Gaelic. They could do with more.

Further Gaelic Communities
Valleyfield, Prince Edward Island. Rev. D. MacLean Sinclair.
Kinross, P.E.I.
Marsboro, Quebec.
Scotstown, Quebec.
Glengarry County, Ontario.
Small colony in west Newfoundland, about 20–30 families.
Loch Lomond, Cape Breton.

Native poet. Kenneth Ferguson, born on the Island (of Cape Breton) of parents born on the Island, has left poems in MS shortly to be published. This will be the first original book in Gaelic by a Nova Scotian.[3] Other anthologies from Scottish MSS (taken to Cape Breton) not the same. Many fleeting poems in newspapers of course.

Gaelic life in Cape Breton is rural, and lacks both a centre and organised leadership. Jealousy between the clergymen of various denominations prevents a strong movement being formed. Sydney largely run by the English for the English. Gaelic ignored though not persecuted.

Much loss of population in recent years, continuous emigration to U.S.A. Farms easy to acquire, many vacant. No farms have ever been divided and few

---

[1] See note to April 11th.
[2] Bracketed in diary.
[3] Not quite correct. There is Alastair MacGillivray's *Companach an Oganaich,* published at Pictou in 1836, the first Gaelic book printed in Nova Scotia.

are actually occupied by descendants of the original owners.[1] No appreciable immigration from the Highlands for 50 or 60 years. No landlords.

Estimated 50,000 Gaelic-speakers in the Maritime Provinces of Canada, but number very hard to ascertain. Existence of Gaelic ignored by the Canadian Government and (the language) not mentioned in the linguistic statistics.

Many settlers came completely ignorant of Gaelic literature and Gaelic scholarship and though not hostile never realised any aspect of their language could be cultivated.

Norman MacLeod and his Ark. Norman MacLeod, son of a Highland father and an English mother, ordained in New York, went to Pictou. Very independent and autocratic. With his congregation, built a ship intending to go to Hamilton, but gale compelled landing at St Ann's, Cape Breton, in 1820.

In 1851 MacLeod heard good news of New Zealand from his brother, so decided to move. He built a ship with some of his congregation, sailed around the Cape of Good Hope, landed in Australia which did not suit him, later went to New Zealand, where he and his followers received a large grant of land. Three or four ships followed from St Ann's at intervals of about a year.

(Here follows a list of addresses. It can hardly have any relevance now, but the following names may be noted.)

Fr Macdonald, Clan Donald, Alberta.

Fr Ronald Beaton, Comox, B.C.

Spent evening with Dr and Mrs W. McK. MacLeod. Mrs MacLeod's parents from Lewis. She knows a little Gaelic.

Twenty-five years ago no merchant in Cape Breton could hope to do business unless he knew Gaelic or at least had a Gaelic-speaking clerk to his store.

Most Cape Breton people are from Lewis, Harris, Skye, Uist, Barra and Sutherland.

Wednesday April 13th. Saw N. MacLeod, born in Island (Cape Breton), fluent Gaelic speaker, both MacKinnons again, and Alexander Matheson.

Jonathan MacKinnon gave me 8 copies *Fear na Céilidh,* and showed me MS of no small interest dealing with the settlement of Cape Breton. Also MS of history of the Highlanders written by himself. Promised to find back numbers of *Mac Talla,* for me.

He informed me that *Mac Talla* had ended $6000 to the bad. Rev. A. MacLean Sinclair was $300 to the bad on his (Gaelic) publications.

He also told me that the descendants of the settlers had preserved the peculiarities of their original dialects e.g. Lewis, Harris, Uist, Barra and Skye.[2]

[1] 'Settlers' originally written.
[2] As I had plenty of opportunity to confirm on my 1937 visit.

He also told me that MacVurich descendants lived in the Island. One, recently dead, was a poet. See *Fear na Céilidh*.[1]

He said to his knowledge none of the settlers had brought any old MSS with them.

Micmac Indian reserve at Whycocamagh. Jonathan MacKinnon gave me his history of Cape Breton, and his translation of Tolstoy's story (Far am bi Gràdh, bidh Dia).

Alexander Matheson aged 81, hale and hearty, told me that his parents came to the island in 1820.

Talked in Gaelic for some time.

He had been punished for speaking Gaelic in school. Quoted 'dìth Bheurl' ort', also a verse composed on the island on a minister beginning 'Thug Antony an turus èibhinn'. (The first means 'may you lack English.)

Mr Matheson possesses a Manx New Testament 1810, and a Scottish Gaelic N.T. 1813.

Visited Scotland in 1901 and 1908. He was post master of Sydney during the boom in 1900 when the entire postal system was disorganised.

He commented on lack of Gaelic scholarship here and amongst many of the ministers.

Thursday April 14th. Visited in the morning, and had lunch with, Rev. J. A. MacLellan at Bridgeport, who gave me a great deal of general information, viz.

Cape Breton

Ingonish an English settlement.

Cape North—still Gaelic.

Bay of St Lawrence—Catholic.

Lake Ainslie and Strathlorne. Minister A. S. MacLean, who has no Gaelic.
  Not preached in United Church, and losing ground.

Grand Mira. Gaelic strong, but little Gaelic preaching.

Fourchu. Scots and French.

Port Hastings. A little Gaelic (Dr D. MacDonald).

Hawkesbury. None (Protestants:) but R.C.s, yes.

Margaree. English.

Margaree Forks. Gaelic.

Mabou, Glendale, Judique. Catholics use Gaelic.[2]

Loch Lomond, St Peter's, Grand River. No preaching in Gaelic.

Gabarus ?

[1] *Fear na Céilidh* I, 54. His name was Lachann MacMhuirich. Died at Loch Blackett, near Sydney, in 1926.
[2] Many Mùideartaich.

Inverness. Gaelic not preached.

River Dennis. Gaelic 1911–20, when he himself was there. No Gaelic since. Only occasionally used in church.

Orangedale. Only occasionally used.

Little Narrows.　　do.

West Bay. Strong years ago, now dead.

Boulardarie. Gaelic strong.

Louisburg—mixed.

Iona—R. C.

Prince Edward Island

Valleyfield. Rev. D. MacLean Sinclair, only Gaelic congregation.

Belfast

Kinross. None now.

Belleview, Brookland, Commercial View. Part of Valleyfield parish.

Antigonish County

Little Gaelic. No Protestant Gaels.

South River. A little.

Pictou County

Two generations ago Gaelic was used. Earliest settlers from Highlands in Nova Scotia. No Gaelic-speaking United Church ministers.[1]

Quebec: 'Eastern townships'

Milan—A. Murray.

Scotstown—J. W. MacLean.

Lake . . . ?—Lachlan Beaton.

Sherbrooke

Ontario: Glengarry district

Moose Creek. Small Gaelic congregation.

Kirk . . . ? Allan Morison

Port Arthur

Fort William—MacLennan

Small Gaelic Sunday School at Lake Ainslie (Cape Breton). He had also assisted a few individuals to learn to read Gaelic.

---

[1] I was told many times in 1932 and 1937 that the formation of the United Church of Canada had been a severe setback to Gaelic, as Gaelic congregations had joined and were then without Gaelic ministers, while Gaelic ministers had refused to join and were left without congregations.

Names

Dr Nicholson ed. (Gaelic column) Antigonish *Casket*.

Dr MacPherson, Antigonish.

Rev. Donald MacDonald, Port Hastings.

Rev. E. Lockhart, Antigonish (United Church).

Rev. Alasdair Murray, Caledonia, P.E.I. (Presbyterian).

Rev. A. D. MacKinnon, Whycocamagh (Presbyterian).

(The last now at Little Narrows, Cape Breton, and may be the only survivor of these persons. J.L.C.)

Examples of English borrowings in Cape Breton Gaelic, given by Rev. J. A. MacLellan:

Well, tha deagh-room agam air an t'ird story: tha e ochd dollars an seachdain room and board.

Bidh sin all right.

Bha i ten o'clock at night nuair a thàinig mi, agus bha mi all in: bha 'n t-uisge a' pouradh, agus bha a leithid de bhare spots air an rathad 's nach b'urrainn dhomh headway a dheanamh.

Tha e smart gu leoir.

Loanwords: Fence—stove—stave—rubbers (rubbers = British 'galoshes')—store (store = British 'shop' (bùth))—yoke—mallet—cabin—corn (i.e. Indian corn, maize)—railway—train—drug-store—post office—cinema—trace (of harness) (treas, pl. treasaichean).

Seòmar not used at all.

Loch not used, but léig (lake) pl. léigeachan. Lochan has survived.

mogaisean—a moccasin (snowshoe). fromh (frõ) an implement for splitting wood.

Money

Tri sgilinn = 5 cents (nickel piece)

Sia sgilinn = 10 cents (dime)

Tastan = 20 cents

Cairteal = 25 cents (quarter)

Dà thasdan agus sia sgilinn = 50 cents (half dollar)

Trì tasdain is naodh sgilinn = 75 cents (three quarters)

Cóig tasdain = 100 cents (one dollar)

Ochd sgilinn diag = 30 cents.

The Gaelic terms are based on the fact that pounds, shillings and pence were formerly used in Canada.

(In a letter dated 30/6/37 the late J. G. MacKinnon, editor of *Mac Talla,* made the following comment on this matter of money nomenclature:

Re-reading your article on Gaelic in Canada, I came across one or two errors, as I thought. The $4.00 pound and 20 cent shilling belonged to a regular currency adopted in Canada after it became British. It was usually called Nova Scotia currency, and fitted the dollars-and-cents of America. The dollars and cents money was adopted in Canada after Confederation, 1867, but for a long time people counted their money in pounds, shillings and pence; and Canada kept a $4.00 note in circulation until a few years ago.)

April 14th (continued) In afternoon, saw J. G. MacKinnon again and collected back numbers of *Mac Talla,* and discussed Scottish history.

J. G. MacKinnon also gave me some Gaelic terms peculiar to the island.

Said farewell to the McCurdys. Discovered local bus driver and policeman Gaelic speakers. First descended from Barra people. Received letter from Fr Rankin.

Friday April 15th. Left Sydney 6.35 for Iona where I was met by Fr Rankin at the station.

Iona population 1200 all Catholic and nearly all Gaelic speaking. I spent a very interesting day with Fr Rankin. In the morning we visited the church, built of stone.[1] Later we called on many parishioners most of whom spoke Gaelic. Nearly all MacNeils and all of Barra origin.

In the afternoon we visited the school, and Fr Rankin decided that in place of catechism I might give an address on Scotland, so I spoke shortly on the growth and aims of An Comunn Gaidhealach and on Gaelic as a bond between Gaels all over the world &c. Afterwards one girl sang 'Fuadach nan Gàidheal' and another sang 'Tha mo rùn air a' ghille'. 'Fuadach nan Gàidheal' said Fr Rankin 'is our national anthem over here'. At least half the scholars (10–17 years or so of age) knew Gaelic. Later we visited the younger school, but here not more than 5 out of 20 admitted knowing it. Then we made various calls. In most families the old people knew Gaelic better than English, and hardly anyone did not understand it. In the evening I saw the Victorian–Inverness *Bulletin* which prints Gaelic poems.

History of Gaelic Singing Contests in Cape Breton
Waulking (milling) Songs
Prize cup offered by Murdoch MacLeod of Little Narrows.

First contest November 1931. 3 teams: Washabuck, Ottawa Brook, Jubilee. Judges: J. G. MacKinnon, Rev. A. D. MacKinnon and Rev. D. J. Rankin, PP. Won by Ottawa Brook. Contest well attended.

Second contest February 11th 1932. five teams entered. Barra Glen won with a local composition. Judges: D. J. MacDougall (Christmas Island), Hugh MacKenzie and Col. M. D. MacKeigan.

[1] Most country churches in Nova Scotia are built of wood.

Third contest. March 19 1932. Six teams entered. Won by Highland hall. Largest crowd that was ever in Iona hall. Method: 6 in a team; 6 stanzas sung with chorus after each stanza.

Fr Rankin gave me some of his books, also a letter to the Rev. P. J. Nicholson of St Francis Xavier College.[1] Altogether a very interesting day. It is long since I spoke so much Gaelic. Left for Antigonish 9.30 p.m., arrived 3.00 a.m. 1½ hours late.

Saturday April 16th. Frightful weather. Pouring rain &c. Afternoon mailed circulars re Gaelic to R.C. priests of Cape Breton, 39 in all.

Called at St Francis Xavier College at 4.30 p.m. on Dr Nicholson. Was kindly greeted and put up for the night and met with great hospitality. Six or seven of the teaching staff speak Gaelic,[2] and Gaelic is taught twice a week.

I had supper in the College and afterwards a long talk with the Rector about many questions. There are two kinds of French in Canada, Acadians and the French of Quebec.

Sunday April 17th. At St Francis Xavier College. Finished circulars, 151 in number, and still must look up the Continuing Presbyterians[3] of Cape Breton and North Nova Scotia.

Talked in Gaelic with the Rev. Hugh MacPherson [Rector of the College] in the morning and afternoon. In the afternoon I visited the Library. They have some fairly good books there viz. Inverness Gaelic Society, Dwelly's *Dictionary,* Irish Texts, *Amhrain Grádha chuige Connacht.* J. F. Campbell's *Tales from the West Highlands,* and others. Advised them to get [Bergin's edition of] *Trí Bior-Ghaoithe an Bháis.* In the evening went around with H. MacPherson DD in car. Gaelic not now used in churches here. Most people above 40 know some. I heard two men conversing in it in the street on Saturday.

Of the 12-15 secular clergy here I suppose at least half know some Gaelic viz: H. P. MacPherson, Rector; Dr Nicholson; H. MacPherson; W. K. Mac...(?); McKay; MacEachern.

Monday April 18th. J. B. Isaac's bookstore in Antigonish contains many good Gaelic volumes. Bought a few. Left Antigonish.

---

[1] Rev. P. J. Nicholson was then Professor of Physics at the College (now University). He was a native speaker of Barra descent. See obituary in *Oban Times* of 16/12/65. He was President of the University from 1944 to 1954.
[2] Out of about 18 at the time, as far as I remember. The staff now numbers about 160 or more and only about six of them know Gaelic.
[3] i.e. The Presbyterians who refused to join the United Church of Canada when it was formed shortly before 1932.

A VISIT TO NOVA SCOTIA, 1932

Tuesday April 19th. At Quebec.

Wednesday April 20th. Quebec to Montreal.

Thursday April 21st. At Montreal.

Friday April 22nd. Went to see T. B. MacAulay, head of a big insurance company, and heard what he was doing for the people of Lewis and peat husbandry. Two kinds of peat, one the peat bog, the other the peat through which water passes. Saw also Dean McKay of McGill University and had a long talk.[1]

Gaelic books printed in Canada:

Leabhar nan Sonn, *Gearr-aithris air curaidhean na craoibhe ruaidhe is air diulanaich iomraiteach la an diugh, le Alasdair Friseal,* Toronto. William Briggs, 1897.

Stratton, Thomas, *Illustrations of the Affinity of the Latin Language to the Gaelic or Celtic of Scotland.* Toronto. Hugh Scobie, 1840.

Rev. A. MacLean Sinclair, *The Glenbard Collection of Gaelic Poetry.* Charlottetown. Hazard and Moore, 1890.

—*Gaelic Bards from 1411 to 1715,* ibidem.

—*Gaelic Bards from 1715 to 1765,* ibidem.[2]

Saturday April 23rd. Arrived at Toronto in the morning and found letters awaiting me there. Went to call on Alexander Fraser[3] and had a good long talk with him. He was born in Inverness-shire and knows the Highlands and speaks Gaelic well, and is well acquainted with the literature and history of the Gaels, but is old and not in good health. (He was the Provincial Archivist).

Sunday April 24th. Saw Alexander Fraser again, and had another talk about Highland music. He and his family very hospitable. Driven around Toronto by one of his daughters.

Monday April 25th. Had a few words on the telephone with Archbishop MacDonald, but he had a cold and I could not see him.

Names of clergymen friendly to Gaelic:

Rev. D. J. Rankin, Iona.

Rev. D. MacLean Sinclair, Valleyfield, P.E.I.[3]

Rev. Donald MacDonald, Port Hastings, Cape Breton.

[1] In Montreal I had a guide the representative of an American company to whom I had an introduction from the head office. This person, who had little sympathy with anything as impractical as Gaelic, was astonished that I was able to get a long interview with such an important person as T. B. MacAulay!

[2] This list omits the first Gaelic book printed in Canada, *Companach an Oganaich, no an Comhairliche Taitneach,* le Alastair McGillevra (Pictou, printed in the Bee Office, 1836).

[3] I did not meet the Rev. D. MacLean Sinclair until my 1937 visit to Nova Scotia.

Rev. J. D. Nelson Macdonald, the Forks, Baddeck, C.B.
Rev. Clarence MacKinnon, Pine Hill Divinity Hall, Halifax.
Rev. Angus D. Beaton, PP, Port Hawkesbury, C.B.
Rev. P. J. Nicholson, St F.X., Antigonish.
Rev. Allister Murray, Caledonia, P.E.I.
Rev. W. B. MacLean, Boylston, Guysborough, Co N.S.
Rev. A. C. Fraser, North River Bridge, C.B.
Rev. Dougald MacEachern, PP, Bailey's Brook & Arisaig, Antigonish Co., N.S.
Rev. A. D. MacDonald, Box 253, New Waterford, C.B.
    (blank)   PP, Inverness.
Rev. John MacKinnon, Baddeck, C.B.
Rev. D. J. Morrison, Whycocomagh, C.B.
    (blank)   Boularderie, C.B.
Rev. Ed. MacKillop, Gabarus, C.B.
Rev. A. C. MacNeil, PP, Glendale, C.B.
Rev. F. MacLennan, 11 Commercial Street, Glace Bay, C.B.

THE 1932 UNOFFICIAL GAELIC CENSUS

The question asked in the writer's private 1932 Census of Gaelic (the language being then ignored in the Official Canadian Linguistic Census) were as follows:

1. How many people in your parish speak Gaelic?
2. How many of the children speak it?
3. Is it used in school?
4. Is preaching done in Gaelic?
5. Is the language declining?
6. Is it becoming corrupted?
7. Are any Gaelic books or periodicals read?

To these questions I should have added another on the numbers of monoglot Gaelic speakers surviving. There were still some living in Cape Breton in the 1930s. Otherwise a great deal of valuable information was sent by my clerical informants, some of whom went to considerable trouble in doing so, for which sincere thanks are due.

The strongholds of Gaelic were at that time Inverness County (except for the Port Hawkesbury area and the Protestant parish of Mabou), Victoria County, and rural Cape Breton County. On the mainland, the Arisaig district of Antigonish County; in Prince Edward Island, the Valleyfield district. The results of the census were summarised in an article published in the *Scotsman* of 30 January 1933.

In Inverness County, replies were received for 15 out of 23 parishes, enumerating approximately 6,980 Gaelic speakers.

In Victoria County, replies for 8 parishes out of 13, enumerated 2,975 Gaelic speakers.

In Richmond County replies for 3 parishes out of 6, gave 230 Gaelic speakers.

In rural Cape Breton County, replies for 8 out of 13 parishes received, gave 1,261 Gaelic speakers.

In urban Cape Breton County, replies for 14 out of 24 parishes received, gave 2,200 Gaelic speakers.

On the mainland, in Pictou County 10 out of 17 parishes gave about 350 Gaelic speakers.

In Antigonish County, 6 parishes out of 13 gave 1,129 Gaelic speakers.

In Guysborough County, about 50

In Prince Edward Island, in eight parishes only, about 250 speakers.

Total number enumerated 15,425 Gaelic speakers. It would not have been surprising if the actual total were twice that figure, especially as some correspondents only estimated percentages. The most impressive were:

Cape Breton Island

	81–100%	61–80%	41–60%	21–40%	1–20%
Inverness Co.	4	3	5	1	5 parishes
Victoria Co.	3	4	2	—	—
Richmond Co.	1	2	—	—	1
Cape Breton Co. (rural)	4	—	2	—	2
Cape Breton Co. (urban)	—	—	—	2	8

Mainland

	81–100%	61–80%	41–60%	21–40%	1–20%
Pictou Co.	—	1	—	—	9
Antigonish Co.	1	1	1	—	6

Prince Edward Island	—	—	—	—	8

As regards Gaelic in church, Gaelic was used or preached every Sunday in only 5 churches on Cape Breton Island, 'often' in three, once a month in six, 'occasionally' in eight and 'once or twice a year' in nine, and 'sometimes' in two. In Prince Edward Island, it was preached once a month in two parishes; in Antigonish county it was preached occasionally in one and once or twice a year in two.

As regards the places we visited particularly in 1937, the following information was given in 1932 in reply to our questions:

Whycocamagh and Little Narrows Inverness Co.
  (Presbyterian, Skye people, Rev. A. D. MacKinnon):
  1. Gaelic speakers, 300–400, 50 per cent.
  2. Some children speak Gaelic, some both, some learn it as they grow older.
  3. Gaelic is not used in schools.
  4. Gaelic services held quite frequently, especially in summer. Preaching done in Gaelic.
  5. Gaelic congregation compares favourably with the English.
  6. Not declined a great deal recently.
  7. Gaelic books read. Provincial newspapers publish Gaelic articles and songs.

Iona and Baddeck, Victoria Co. (R.C., Barra people, Rev. D. J. Rankin):
  1. Gaelic speakers, about 800, 80 per cent.
  2. Children mostly bilingual.
  3. Not used in school much.
  4. Gaelic preached occasionally.
  5, 6. Holding its own.
  7. Some Gaelic books read.

Boisdale, Cape Breton Co. (R.C., Barra and South Uist people):
  1. About 90 per cent speak Gaelic.
  2. About 75 per cent of children bilingual.
  3. In recreation only, about 25 per cent.
  4. Gaelic sermons preached once or twice a year.
  5, 6. Declining slowly.
  7. The monthly *Mosgladh* read.

Christmas Island, Cape Breton Co. (R.C., Barra and South Uist people):
  1. Gaelic spoken by all in parish.
  2. Children bilingual.
  3. Not used in school.
  4. Gaelic preached once a month.
  5, 6. Declining and becoming corrupt.
  7. 'Yes' (not specified).

Arisaig, Antigonish Co. (R.C., Morar people; Rev. D. M'Eachern):

1. Gaelic spoken by about 325 out of about 374.
2. Most children understand it.
3. Not used in school.
4. Not preached.
5, 6. Declining.
7. Only (the monthly) *Mosgladh*.

Lochaber, Antigonish Co. (R.C., Lochaber people):

1. Not spoken at Lochaber, but spoken at Giant's Lake a parish mission (actually in Guysborough Co., near Upper South River), by half the population, about 35 people.
2. Children speak English.
3. Not used in school.
4. Not preached.
5, 6. Declining, but attempt being made to revive it.
7. A few read *Mosgladh*; sometimes Gaelic stories are read at meetings.

Prince Edward Island, Valleyfield Parish
(Presbyterian, Rev. D. MacLean Sinclair):

1. About 100 persons, 25 per cent.
2. A few children bilingual.
3. Not used in school.
4. Gaelic preached once a month and at the Long Communion in July.
5. Gaelic congregation about 30, 'Mostly old people many of whom cannot speak English'.
6. Declining.
7. A few journals and books read.

This was the background to our visit of 1937.

THE 1937 VISIT TO
CAPE BRETON AND
ANTIGONISH COUNTY

Gu bheil mi'm ònrachd 'sa choille ghruamaich
Mo smaointinn luaineach, cha tog mi fonn;
Fhuair mi an t-àite so an aghaidh nàduir
Gun thréig gach tàlant a bha 'nam cheann.

I am alone in the gloomy forest; my thoughts are restless, I cannot sing; I found this place contrary to nature, every talent that was in my head has departed.

John MacLean (1787–1848)

' THE people of this country,' wrote an agent of Clanranald's from South Uist in 1827, when Government assistance for emigration was being discussed, 'will all go to Cape Breton, and nowhere else if they can help it. They are accustomed to live at home almost exclusively on meal and milk and potatoes. The expense therefore of sending them across the Atlantic will be much less than that of transporting the same number of people from England. I am of the opinion that from 30s to £2 would feed a full-grown Highlander for the ordinary voyage to Cape Breton and I should imagine ampill might be freighted for about 40s each passenger. If you substitute molasses for the milk they are accustomed to at home, and lay in a sufficient quantity of good meal for the voyage, I do not think more will be necessary.'

37

THE 1937 VISIT TO CAPE BRETON AND ANTIGONISH COUNTY

Some seventy years before this, the ancestors of the same Highlanders whose transport across the Atlantic Clanranald's agent discusses in 1827 in much the same terms that a West Highland farmer would that of his cattle with MacBrayne's today had repaid the failure of the French Government to provide the Scottish Jacobites with adequate help in 1745 by taking an active part in the capture of Louisburg and Quebec and thus putting an end for ever to the possibility of a French empire in North America. They could never have dreamed of the hardships which their descendants would have to undergo in the selfsame 'gloomy wood' so vividly described by John MacLean, the Tiree-born poet.

Today, Cape Breton appears to a Highland visitor as a land of strange incongruities; a country where one can hear the Gaelic of Lewis, Skye or Barra against a seemingly most inappropriate background of dense spruce forest; a Highland community where there are no lairds; where the descendants of settlers from Skye live beside Micmac Indians, the aboriginal inhabitants of the Maritime Provinces: where the people still refer to themselves as 'Lewismen', 'Skyemen', 'Uistmen', 'Barramen', and so on, although none of them have ever seen these places; where many can describe perfectly, from their grandparents' reminiscing, places in the 'Old Country' which they have never seen. Where, in fact, an inherited nostalgia and old habits and customs have survived in a most astonishing way.

A hundred and more years ago Cape Breton, the mainland of Nova Scotia and Prince Edward Island, the nearest part to Scotland of the American continent, formed the most convenient dumping ground for the unwanted inhabitants of the Highlands. The first settlement in Prince Edward Island was made in 1769; in 1773 the famous emigrant ship the *Hector* landed its human cargo at Pictou. After 1790 settlers on the Nova Scotian mainland set out to find their way to Cape Breton; their numbers were soon swelled by thousands more from Scotland. Unscrupulous emigration agents described the new country in the most glowing terms; but the truth about the 'gloomy wood' became known, largely through John MacLean's poem.

Armed with an Ediphone dictaphone and cylinders for the purpose of recording songs and dialects, and travelling in an English car (a great mistake as it involved endless questioning and made us immediately recognisable in a short time everywhere) my wife and I set out to visit Cape Breton. It was necessary to land at Quebec and drive eastwards, as few liners call at Halifax in the summer. After several days of driving we caught the first glimpse of the wooded slopes of Cape Breton Island across the water of St George's Bay. There is a common impression in Cape Breton that that island resembles Scotland. In fact, Scotland with its bare and often rocky hills and mountains is almost the exact antithesis of Cape Breton, of which the hills are mostly rolling and wooded to the summit.

THE 1937 VISIT TO CAPE BRETON AND ANTIGONISH COUNTY

We crossed the Gut of Canso, a third of a mile wide, by ferry, as both trains and cars then must, and continued towards Whycocamagh from Port Hawkesbury. For miles and miles we passed through dense forest, where a white farmhouse showed from time to time in the middle of a few cleared fields. Sometimes these farmhouses appeared empty and deserted, with conifers springing up again on the fields that had once been so laboriously cleared for tillage. The forest seemed to be alive and to hold the country in its grip, intense, malignant, ever ready to reclaim as its own the land that had been once won from it. Vast areas seem entirely unoccupied.

Whycocamagh is a pretty village situated on an arm of the Bras d'Or lake, which, although actually an arm of the sea, is hardly more than brackish at this distance from it. Here we were to call on Mr. J. G. MacKinnon editor of the now defunct weekly Gaelic paper *Mac Talla,* and generally recognised as one of the leading Gaelic authorities in Nova Scotia.

It is significant of the dispersal of the Gael that this paper published in Cape Breton from 1892 to 1904, had a longer continuous life than any other unsubsidised venture of its kind. I asked Mr MacKinnon about its history.

'I was twenty-three years of age when I started *Mac Talla,*' he said, 'and who knows whether I would have attempted it at all if I had been older. I wrote much of it myself. The late Rev. A. MacLean Sinclair (a descendant of the poet John MacLean, who composed the song about the 'gloomy forest') was a frequent contributor of unpublished songs. Some of the best articles I ever had were contributed by the late Professor MacKinnon (the first holder of the Chair of Celtic in Edinburgh University).

'The best circulation we had was about 1500. There were subscribers in all parts of the world. It fell off in circulation towards the end. There was a mining boom in Sydney. Costs of printing rose, and we eventually ended on the wrong side after having paid our way for several years—longer, I believe, than any other Gaelic paper ever did.'

Mac Talla contains much interesting material, and can also be read as a chronicle of life in Cape Breton forty years ago. In politics it was imperialist and a firm supporter of the temperance movement.

Mr MacKinnon and others told me that Gaelic in Cape Breton was beginning to decline owing to an unfortunate combination of circumstances.

'Many of our people went to the Western Provinces when these were opened up around 1900, and the population has fallen almost continually since that time'—this is true, and there are Gaelic songs composed in Cape Breton which lament it in much the same tone that ours lament the depopulation of the Highlands—'hence the deserted farms you have noticed in coming here. Now, some of these people are beginning to come back, especially from Saskatchewan,

14*a*. Jonathan G. MacKinnon, Editor of *Mac Talla*

14*b*. JLC recording a Gaelic song from J. D. MacKinnon at Kirkwood, Lake Ainslie. Mr MacKinnon's ancestors came from the Isle of Muck

which has been badly hit by drought. But even so, Cape Breton is three parts empty. Land can be bought for next to nothing here. The churches have not got a quarter of the congregations they were built to hold.'

Gaelic, said Mr MacKinnon, had been a permissive subject in the schools since after the War, but no way had been found yet to introduce it into the curriculum. The Premier of the Province of Nova Scotia (Angus Macdonald) was a Gaelic man, and no doubt his administration would have been willing to accede to any united demand, but the difficulty was to hit on a scheme that would get the support of all the different sections and denominations.

I learned from other sources confirmation of these views. There also appeared to be a shortage of Gaelic preachers amongst the clergy of all denominations. Some of these were actually opposed to the language, and often when a minister was an enthusiast he turned out to be a native of the 'Old Country'.

How many Gaelic speakers in Cape Breton? I asked. Mr MacKinnon said that there could not be less than 40,000 or 50,000 in the Maritime Provinces of Canada and that most were in Cape Breton. Practically all the country districts, except those occupied by the Acadians were peopled by descendants of the Highlanders. Lewis, Harris, Skye, Mull, Wester Ross, Moidart, Morar, Lochaber, Uist, Barra, Colonsay and Coll were the districts chiefly represented. There were also a good number of Highlanders in the towns—Sydney, New Waterford, Glace Bay.

Mr MacKinnon told me he was now engaged in translating English books into Gaelic. He had done Van Dyke's *Story of the Other Wise Man*[1] and short stories by Thomas Hardy and Tolstoy. He hoped to do *Treasure Island* and other works of R. L. Stevenson.

I asked about Gaelic songs and stories. 'The songs are still popular and there are many current that were composed in Cape Breton. There are also some excellent fiddlers in this county (Inverness). But the old stories, *sgeulachdan*, have gone quite out of fashion.'

We later visited with Mr MacKinnon a family, MacKinnons originally from the Isle of Muck (*Mucanaich*), where Gaelic singing was kept up, and we heard some of the compositions of Malcolm Gillis, Lake Ainslie, a well-known local bard, and also various songs of Scottish origin. One of the best of the singers was a boy of twelve years.

We visited several families of *Mucanaich* near Whycocamagh and Lake Ainslie, all MacKinnons, and were given a warm welcome everywhere and asked many questions about the Old Country and the Western Isles. Here I may say that the Gaels in Cape Breton have preserved the best traditions of Highland

---

[1] This translation was later published in Scotland.

hospitality. There can be few places where a stranger is received with so much kindness, especially if he has a knowledge of Gaelic.

We asked the people for songs *that had been composed in Scotland*, in particular traditional songs such as the old waulking songs that often embody local history and folk-lore, the authors usually being unknown and the airs very old. Such songs were sung during the process of waulking or fulling tweed by hand. They are rapidly becoming forgotten, and the archaic style of their language, together with the many interesting allusions contained in them (many date back to the seventeenth century) and with the great beauty of many of the airs, as sung unaccompanied under natural conditions, renders them of peculiar interest. We knew many of the old waulking songs that are sung in Barra and South Uist. Were such things remembered in Cape Breton after a separation of over a hundred years?

We were told that some of the descendants of the Barra and Uist settlers living around the Bras d'Or lake (in Gaelic called Loch Mór nam Barrach, 'the Big Loch of the Barramen', from this fact) knew old waulking songs that were unknown around Lake Ainslie or Whycocamagh. We were also told that there was to be a 'milling frolic', which is the Cape Breton term for a waulking party or *luadhadh*, at North River near St Ann's Bay, a district populated largely by people of Lewis and Harris origin. The chance of attending was too good to be missed, and we accepted an invitation with alacrity.

We first spent a few days at Baddeck, noted as the scene of the first aeroplane flight ever made in the British Empire, and now a tourist centre. Alexander Graham Bell, inventor of the telephone, is buried near here on the summit of Beinn Bhreagh, 'Beautiful Mountain'.

The roads of Cape Beton, we soon found, were nearly as bad as those of Barra. Rough gravel, with here and there patches of 'washboard' surface which shook one to pieces. In many parts, particularly in the country districts, the roads consist only of red clay, which after a night's rain, becomes as slippery as wet ice. The roads were lined with wooden fences and flimsy telegraph poles which collapsed after every gale like ninepins. Nevertheless most of the houses seemed to have telephones, and Cape Breton in this respect is far ahead of the Highlands. Party lines are the usual arrangement, and in country districts one may speak to everyone on the same exchange without any charge.

St Ann's Bay is deservedly considered one of the finest beauty spots in Cape Breton. It has a slight resemblance to Loch Linnhe. Halfway down, the bay is nearly closed by a pebble spit that juts out from the west side a considerable distance. Here there is a lighthouse and a ferry reminding one of that at Corran crossing to Ardgour. The hills around St Ann's Bay are higher and steeper than those in the south of Cape Breton.

THE 1937 VISIT TO CAPE BRETON AND ANTIGONISH COUNTY

It was dark when we reached the hall at North River where the milling frolic was to take place. It was crowded, and we were reminded instantly of similar gatherings anywhere in the Western Isles. In feature, manner and speech the people present, at any rate those over twenty-five or thirty years of age, were practically identical with such an audience as one might see in any town in the Outer Isles. The meeting opened with some speeches. There were solo songs and a humorous Gaelic anecdote or two told by a Mr Kenneth MacLeod in excellent Harris Gaelic, which won an instant response. Then began the milling.

In the Outer Isles, where waulkings are still kept up, either spontaneously or as part of an arranged concert, the newly-woven cloth, or a blanket taking its place, is dampened and taken by a number of women who sit around a table (called the *cleith luadhaidh*) and pound and push the cloth to the rhythm of the song, which usually starts in slow time and accelerates towards the end. One person sings the verses, while the others take the chorus.

In Scotland (so far as I have seen) waulking is considered women's work, and the great majority of persons who know the waulking songs are women. But at North River it was the men who sat down round the *cleith luadhaidh* and took up the blanket and started to sing. A great many of the audience stood around the men at the *cleith luadhaidh,* and, taking hands, swung their arms back and forth in time to the music while singing the chorus—a thing I had never seen at home.

A strangely incongruous feature to our eyes was provided by some of the younger folk, who leaned back against the wall of the hall chewing gum while the *luadh* was in progress.

We recognised some of the songs, one of which was *Biodh an deoch so an làimh mo rùin*—'Let this drink be in my love's hand'—but there was so much conversation to be done that we could not pay very much attention to the singing. Everyone wanted to hear about the islands from which their grandparents or great-grandparents had emigrated. Many had heard such vivid descriptions of these places in their childhood from the old people that they could discuss them as something they had actually seen.

St Ann's Bay is associated with one of the most remarkable personalities in the whole history of the Highlander, the late Rev. Norman MacLeod. Norman MacLeod was originally the minister of a congregation near Pictou, on the mainland of Nova Scotia, at the beginning of the nineteenth century. He was a man of iron will and great personality. In those days the settlers were very dependent on their clergy, who often acted in the capacity of lawyer, doctor and schoolmaster, as well as of preacher, to their congregations. (Indeed it is noticeable today that the clergy of all denominations in Nova Scotia occupy a more prominent position in the life of the community than they do in Scotland, owing to the entire absence of anything corresponding to the landed gentry in this part of Canada; and the churches there seem to play a much greater part in the people's lives than is often the case at home.)

MacLeod was intensely autocratic, and he ruled his congregation, which was devoted to him, with a rod of iron. One day he got news that a place called Hamilton, on the Ohio River, was very suitable for a settlement. Although getting there meant a journey by sea to the mouth of the Mississippi and thence up that river, amounting in all to about 2,000 miles, Macleod told his congregaion that they were going there and they must build themselves ships for that purpose. So, although the people had no experience in building ships of any size, the ships were made, and they started out for Hamilton in them. They had not gone far when a severe gale forced them to put into St Ann's Bay for shelter. When the dawn broke, MacLeod looked at the neighbouring country and saw that it appeared pleasant. He told the people that since God's will had brought them to this place, they would stay there instead of going to Hamilton. so they disembarked, cut down trees, cleared land and built themselves houses around St Ann's Bay.

For over twenty years the people remained settled around St Ann's Bay, ruled by Norman MacLeod. Many stories, some possibly apocryphal, are told of his autocratic government and arbitrary punishments. It is enough to say that although often much disapproved of by his fellow ministers in Cape Breton, MacLeod had throughout the devotion and loyalty of his own congregation.

Then, when nearly a generation had passed, MacLeod received a letter from one of his sons praising the climate and opportunities of Australia. He decided that he and his congregation would leave St Ann's and go to Australia. The great majority of them consented as before, although not all were willing to remove on this occasion. Eventually ten or eleven ships were built, and sailed for Australia over a period of years. After arriving, MacLeod decided that he did not like Australia, it was too dry; and so he told his people they would go on to New Zealand, where they settled and where their descendants are living today.

The voyage of MacLeod and his congregation in home-made ships halfway around the world, with practically no knowledge of navigation, and with practically no casualties, is one of the finest incidents in the history of the Gael. As an achievement in migration, it ranks with the march of Xenophon or the journey of the Czechoslovak legion through Siberia after the World War.

After leaving St Ann's Bay, near where we visited the Rev. D. Gillis, who was probably the only native of St Kilda living in Cape Breton, and who had a congregation largely composed of the descendants of Lewismen, we decided to make for the Barra settlements around Grand Narrows and Iona on the shores of the Bras d'Or lake.

The Iona and Boisdale peninsulas, joined by a single-track railway bridge at

Grand Narrows, about half a mile across, are largely inhabited by the descendants of the Barra emigrants who left Scotland around the beginning of the nineteenth century. The victims of the notorious evictions from Barra in 1851 went to quite another part of Canada, apparently in the Province of Ontario. Many of the local place-names testify to the original home of the inhabitants. The Gaelic name for Grand Narrows is *Caolas nam Barrach,* 'the Barramen's Strait'; Iona was first called Sanndraigh (Sandray), after the island of that name in the Barra group; then there are in the neighbourhood Barra Glen, Macneil Vale, Castlebay and Boisdale. Altogether there cannot have been less than two thousand Barra people in this district; and there are other settlements, such as Big Pond and Barra Head on the Bras d'Or lake; and others again in Prince Edward Island, and, derived from these, a not inconsiderable community living in Boston (which I soon learned was to the Maritime Provinces what Glasgow is to the Highlands and Islands).

We were not long at Grand Narrows before getting to know many of the people on both sides of the strait. On the Iona side Fr Rankin, the parish priest of Iona, a well-known historian and genealogist of the Highlanders in Nova Scotia, kindly introduced us to a number of his parishioners who would be likely to be interested in our work, while at Grand Narrows, Benacadie, Christmas Island, Beaver Cove and Boisdale we were fortunate to make the acquaintance of many good Gaels, some of whom were related to friends of ours in Barra (fourth or fifth cousins).

At Christmas Island we had the luck to meet Mr D. J. MacDougall and Mr A. J. Mackenzie, both strong upholders of the old tradition. Mr Mackenzie is the author of the *History of Christmas Island*, which contains the genealogy of many of the settlers' descendants, and he has also composed some excellent Gaelic songs. At a *ceilidh* in his house we heard these and other Gaelic songs composed in Cape Breton. I recollect a witty one about a man who started a forest fire (it was often easiest to clear land by burning the trees, but this was a dangerous practice) composed by a direct descendant of Clanranald's bards, the MacMhuirichs from South Uist. Mr Mackenzie told me a great deal about the experiences of the early settlers in that district of Cape Breton.

'It is difficult to get the young people to believe', he said, 'the hardships that their great-grandparents underwent in settling this country. As you know, the islands they came from are nearly all treeless; and here they found trees growing right down to the water's edge, and they had to clear the forest and build houses and cultivate the land without a knowledge of woodcraft and without adequate tools.

'The first Barramen who came to the Grand Narrows district did not immediately settle there. They had already settlements on the mainland of Nova

Scotia. In the spring, after the ice had broken up, they used to set out by boat for St Peter's (the isthmus between the Atlantic and the Bras d'Or Lake, now cut by a canal). At St Peter's, they had to unload their boats and drag them across the isthmus (half a mile) and then load them again. When they first came here, they cut down the trees and cultivated potatoes amongst the stumps. In those days the Bras d'Or lakes were full of fish, and potatoes and fish were the greater part of the people's food. Cod and mackerel were the fish mostly caught. In the autumn they lifted their crops and went home the same way they had come. After a while they built houses around here and settled permanently. Travel was all by water in those days: the roads were not made for many years afterwards; that is why all the early settlements were made around the shores of the Bras d'Or lakes. In the winter the lakes would often be frozen for weeks at a time, and could then be crossed by sleigh.

'The first houses built by the settlers were made of logs with the spaces between the logs stuffed by moss. Their early difficulties were very great. They were often desperately short of seed, implements and stock; the winters were much longer and colder than those they had known at home, the summers were short and very hot. There were bears which killed sheep and pigs, and mosquitoes and other pests to which they were unaccustomed. It was years before they attained any degree of comfort, or before money circulated in any quantity in the country. But they were sustained by the knowledge that they were free from the galling restrictions and petty tyranny of factors and ground officers in the Old Country.'

It would have been interesting if any of the old log houses of the early settlers had been preserved, but although we asked in many places about them, nobody knew of any that had been left. The modern wooden farmhouses in Cape Breton are similar in type to those seen in other parts of the Maritimes and in New England. Incidentally, we saw no trace anywhere of Highland cattle.

At the *ceilidh* in Mr Mackenzie's house we heard for the first time since coming to Nova Scotia one or two of the old type of song composed in Scotland. Mr Mackenzie himself knew a number of waulking songs, some of which he kindly recorded for me; and at his house that night we had the fortune to meet Mrs Patterson, Benacadie, an excellent singer, with whom we later did a good deal of work.

In so far as the majority of the readers of this article may not be interested in the study of Gaelic folk-songs, I shall not attempt to describe in any great detail the songs we recorded, or their relationship to the songs we have heard sung at home. It is enough to say that the identity of the tradition, over a hundred years of complete separation, was astonishing. There was hardly any of the old Barra songs known to us, of which the opening line and chorus when sung did not evoke such a response from one or other of our friends as: 'I've never heard that song since my mother died, Many a time she used to sing it.' And in this manner we were able to awaken memories that led from one thing to another, and, I am convinced, were able to obtain material which would have taken a complete stranger to the tradition months instead of weeks to have dug out. There were quite a few old songs our Cape Breton friends sung to us that we had not heard at home; but on going through them with my Barra friends, I find that most of them had heard them at some time or another. There were some songs of which the better versions came from Cape Breton and others of which the Old Country versions were superior.

We had many songs from Mrs Patterson, Benacadie, and some from Mrs MacLean and Mrs J. R. Johnston at Beaver Cove. The singer with the best knowledge of these old waulking songs we met was Mrs Neil McInnis, at Glace Bay; and we owed this meeting to the kindness of Mr J. A. Macdougall, a well-known Gael in Cape Breton, who read the Gaelic address to the Governor-General when he visited Sydney that autumn. Mrs McInnis had an uncommonly good knowledge of the words of these songs.

We made several visits to Sydney, the principal town of Cape Breton, where we were very hospitably entertained by many good friends. Sydney stands on a fine harbour. Around it, and at Glace Bay, are the industrial and mining areas, the most important in the Maritimes. Their development, which took place around 1900, changed the entire character of the district almost overnight. A great many people came then from all parts of Europe and from the U.S.A., so that the Highlanders in Sydney are only a section of the population. The Sydney daily paper, the *Post Gazette*, prints once or twice a week several columns in Gaelic, probably more than any other newspaper in the world; the Gaelic editor was Mr James MacNeil.

After a visit to the ruins of Louisburg, razed to the ground and its inhabitants deported to France on its second capture by British and American troops in 1758, we returned to Whycocamagh by the road south of the Bras d'Or lakes through St Peter's. This part of Cape Breton, as well as Arichat Island, is inhabited by the descendants of the Acadians, whose small farms resembled more closely the crofts of the Western Isles than any others we saw in Canada. We regretted not having had the time or the opportunity to get to know any of these people. There had been some intermarriage between the French and the Catholic Gaels in Canada, but we found no trace of French influence among the Barra settlements in Cape Breton at any rate. I have heard of villages in the Province of Quebec that are bi-lingual in French and Gaelic, but this point needs investigation.

The purpose of returning to Whycocamagh was to leave our farewell with Mr J. G. MacKinnon, who throughout our stay in Cape Breton had taken the greatest interest in our work and had expressed the desire to see our collection before we left the island. We also hoped that he would introduce us to some of the Micmac Indians who live beside Whycocamagh: we wanted to record the Micmac language if possible and anything the Indians would sing to us.

The Micmacs orignally possessed, or hunted over, the whole of the Maritime Provinces and the Gaspé Peninsula of Quebec. They also landed in Newfoundland and practically exterminated the Beothuks, the aboriginal inhabitants (extinct since 1819). The Micmacs are still spread over this area in small groups settled in reservations. There were and are seven territorial divisions of the Micmac nation, each with its chief; but the chiefship of the whole nation resides with the chief of the Cape Breton division, and the present chief, Gabriel Syllibuy, lives at Whycocamagh.

Mr MacKinnon took us to see the chief, an intelligent, middle-aged man, who quickly understood what we wanted and agreed to make a record for us. Next day we went to his house and, in the presence of a large audience, this was done. He recorded in his own language his grandfather's account of how he was spearing out eels in the Bras d'Or Lake when he saw the arrival of the first Scottish settlers in that district, how they landed and the Indians made friends with them and so on. When this record was made, and had been replayed and listened to with appreciation, Chief Syllibuy introduced a neighbour, Mr Levi Poulette, who sang the plain-song hymns that the Indians use in their church services (they were converted by French priests in the eighteenth century). These hymns Mr Poulette rendered remarkably well. They were less willing to sing secular songs for us, but Levi Poulette and John W. Poulette sang a short song which, they said, was sung after the making of a treaty between the Micmacs and the Mohawks, the words of which were Mohawk; at any rate, not Micmac, and not intelligible to them.

We enjoyed recording the Indians; they possessed noticeable spontaneity and enthusiasm, and were glad to help us. They are remarkably faithful to their language: the community at Whycocamagh could not have numbered more than two hundred (there are only 4000 Micmacs altogether), but all kept up their mother tongue. A French priest, Père Pacifique, had worked amongst them for many years and is the author of a most interesting work on their place-names and traditions, entitled *Le Pays de Micmacs*.

This was the end of our work in Cape Breton; but we had yet to visit Antigonish County on the neighbouring mainland, a district mostly settled by the descendants of emigrants from Moidart, Morar and Lochaber. We left Whycocamagh for Port Hawkesbury, and after rashly trying a piece of back-country road from Melford to Judique, on the east coast, which took us through some fine country but which was often so much like a bog that we despaired of ever getting off it again, we finally emerged with the car covered in red mud, reached the ferry and left Cape Breton where we had spent six crowded and exhausting, but most interesting and enjoyable weeks.   Antigonish is only fifty odd miles from the ferry, so we were not long on the way. It is the seat of the Catholic College of St Francis Xavier,[1] and the centre of the diocese of Antigonish, which comprises Cape Breton Island and the neighbouring mainland counties of Antigonish and Guysboro. This college has initiated an adult education movement which is having a most remarkable effect in regenerating the economic life of the Maritime Provinces, which for some time past has been in an unhealthy condition. I had heard allusions to this movement while in Cape Breton, and had decided to learn something about it at its source.

Here it is relevant to discuss a question that has often been put to me: how does the condition of the Highlanders and Islanders who emigrated to Cape Breton compare with that of those who stayed at home?

It is often said by apologists for the Clearances that, granting that these were sometimes carried out with regrettable incidents, they were nevertheless a 'good thing' in so far as they ultimately resulted in the emigrants becoming much better off than they would have been at home. I have already said something about this from the point of view of the original settlers. It remains to compare the condition of a present-day Cape Breton farmer or fisherman with that of a Highland or Island crofter in 1937.

The average descendant of the cottars and tenants-at-will who emigrated to Cape Breton had, I suppose, a small farm with about ten or twelve head of cattle and twenty to thirty sheep. (Incidentally, there seems to be no trace of either Highland cattle or blackfaced sheep in the island.) He very probably had a telephone on the local party line. He may have a car, but is more likely to have a trap. In any case his local roads are exceedingly likely to be bad. He owns his farm outright, but is liable for taxes upon the land he owns. Of course, the conditions of the farmers vary considerably. Many of the fishing communities appeared to be less well off than the farmers. In general, one could say that the descendants of the cottars and crofters who left the Western Isles over a hundred years ago have attained the status of small occupier-owner farmers in Cape Breton. It is difficult to compare their condition with that of the present-day crofters of the north-west coast of Scotland, for that itself is far from uniform. In addition, various amenities such as differences in climate, social services, communications and opportunities for outside employment would have to be taken into consideration. Climate and communications (except the telephone) are, in my opinion, worse in Cape Breton than in Scotland, social services

---

[1] See the next chapter for the subsequent history of this College, now an important University.

probably fewer, but opportunities for outside employment in other parts of Canada and the U.S.A. probably better *in good times*.

That the economic condition of Nova Scotia was far from satisfactory was proved, firstly, by a long record of emigration from what was never anything but a very thinly-populated province, to the United States and Western and Central Canada. It was very evident that many of the young people we met thought much of the time when they would be able to go away to Boston. 'Toronto is too far away, and you must know French to get on in Montreal,' they said. (It was difficult to understand why emigration from Scotland to Canada was being encouraged when the Canadians themselves could not keep their young people from going to the States. Such emigration would strengthen ultimately the States, not the Empire.) In the second place, although the population of Nova Scotia is largely rural, the Province was recently importing no less than $12,000,000 worth of foodstuffs a year from Central and Western Canada. A tourist could guess something of the kind from the number of times he found eggs from Ontario and meat from the Western Provinces served by Nova Scotian hotels. Thus there was a very strong resemblance in the present-day economic conditions of rural Nova Scotia, comprising Cape Breton, and the Highlands and Islands of Scotland; and it was these conditions which the leaders of the St Francis Xavier movement set out, in 1928, to cure.

I was fortunate enough to find Dr M. M. Coady, one of the chief leaders of the movement, in Antigonish at the time of my arrival there, and he was kind enough to explain the movement to me at some length.

'Our movement is first and foremost educational,' he said, 'designed to supplement the conventional education of school and college which is too much based upon the idea that the young man of more than average ability must seek his livelihood by leaving the community in which he was born and brought up. We try to teach people to think for themselves how to make the best use of the opportunities that exist *at home*. It has been proved by experience that plans for co-operative effort are unlikely to succeed unless the people are first educated to work them properly.

'How did we begin? We started around 1928, when it was decided to form an organised department here for this work. The method we adopted was this. Professor Macdonald or myself, or others of our helpers, would go into some fishing village or farming community known to be backward and depressed—in debt to the local merchants, exploited by middlemen, and so on. We would hold a mass meeting and tell the people what things were really holding them back; it was surprising how often these things were not clearly realised. We would tell them of what had been done by people like themselves by co-operative effort to better their conditions. Eventually, we would get the people into a neutral state of mind in which they would be at least prepared to give our plans fair-minded consideration.

'With this end in view, a study club would first be formed in the district and would elect a leader, who would keep in touch with us and serve as a channel for literature and communications. We supply these study clubs with books and pamphlets and run a bulletin appearing every month. A whole winter at least would be allowed for weekly, informal meetings for discussion and for study before any plan would be attempted. By then the probability is that the members of the study club will have thought out a scheme suitable to their local conditions. It may be a 'Credit Union', or a co-operative sawmill, creamery, lobster-canning factory, or some such venture. We encourage the formation of Credit Unions similar to those first devised by Raifeissen, by which the savings of such communities can be pooled for lending for productive purposes; for credit is one of the most difficult things for a poor man to obtain on reasonable terms.

'Opposition? Yes, there has been opposition from interested parties, mostly from the 'big small man' who has a hold over the local community; but such persons are coming to see that things could not have gone on forever as they were, and they have discovered that our coming, although it may break their power over the community, does not necessarily mean they will be put out of business.

'There are today over fourteen hundred educational groups in the Maritime Provinces studying various aspects of co-operation, and their leaders are able to attend courses and conferences here. there are now thirty thousand people in our movement, and it is growing all the time. By last year there were ninety Credit Unions in Nova Scotia, thirty-five co-operative canning factories, twenty-five co-operative stores. We have yet to find a community so down and out and broken spirited that it cannot respond to our teaching, and the effect, in giving such communities a feeling of pride and achievement in having successfully co-operated for the common good, has been most remarkable. Our movement is spreading to Newfoundland, and I believe that the British Commission Government there is apportioning a large sum of money to promote the St Francis Xavier movement in the island. I may say that the movement is undenominational, and is supported by clergy and laymen of all churches here, and by people of all four races, Scots, English, Irish and French. It is based upon a spirit of Christian co-operation, and faith in the ability of the common people to regain control of their economic destinies'.

I left this interview with Dr Coady feeling profoundly impressed. Here at last seemed to be something which, if properly understood and applied with allowance for local differences, might very well prove to be the solution of the economic troubles of the Highlands and Islands. If only we had leaders of the personality and calibre of Dr Coady, Professor A. B. Macdonald and the Rev. James

Tomkins! If only the British Governments would do for the Highlands what it was doing for Newfoundland! Let us hope that the time will come when teachers from St Francis Xavier will assist in the economic regeneration of the Highlands and Islands.

While at Antigonish I had the pleasure of meeting various members of the College staff, Highlanders and old friends; for nearly half of these, including the Rector, Dr H. P. MacPherson, are Gaelic speakers. The neighbouring district is, as already mentioned, settled mostly by the descendants of emigrants from Moydart, Morar and Lochaber; one sees clearly how heavily the Clearances fell upon these old Jacobite strongholds for there must be far more *Muideartaich* and *Moraraich* in Nova Scotia than in Moidart or Morar.

Our 1937 expedition to Nova Scotia concluded with some recordings made at Arisaig in Antigonish County from Miss Flora Macdougall, the Rev. Fr D. MacEachern, and ?? MacGillivray, the airs of which were not transcribed by Seamus Ennis; and finally by a very important session with the late Angus 'Ridge' Macdonald at Upper South River. Angus 'Ridge' was a grandson of Allan 'Ridge' a descendant of the *Sliochd an Taighe* branch of the Keppoch MacDonalds, who emigrated to Pictou County in 1816 and later moved to Inverness County in Cape Breton. The 'Ridge' after which he was nicknamed was in Cape Breton. Fr Allan McDonald of Eriskay also belonged to this branch of the Keppoch family, and would have been related to Angus 'Ridge' in some way. We recorded fifteen songs from Angus, of which twelve are published in this book, and another, with Ennis's transcription of the tune, was printed with translation in Sister Margaret MacDonell's *The Emigrant Experience*, pages 58 and 190. Allan 'Ridge's' songs, where not local, belong to the Lochaber tradition.

From Antigonish County we crossed over to Prince Edward Island by ferry from Pictou in order to call on Wallace MacNeil at Brevig Farm, Vernon River. Wallace, who lived there with his wife and daughter, was a direct descendant of Roderick MacNeil of Brevig who was nominated by Colonel Roderick MacNeil of Barra who died in 1822 as his ultimate heir if all his other descendants failed. Roderick of Brevig had emigrated in 1802 (see page 69). Wallace was not a Gaelic speaker, but was a keen player of Highland music on the fiddle. We had a great welcome in his household, from which we departed on a route that took us back to New York and thence to Scotland.

Scots Magazine (September/October 1938, revised)

THE 1953 VISIT

IN the spring of 1953 the writer, along with the Rt Rev. Kenneth Grant, Bishop of Argyll and the Isles, and the Very Rev. Canon E. MacInnes, from South Uist, was honoured with an invitation to attend the centenary celebrations of St Francis Xavier University at Antigonish, Nova Scotia, and to accept, along with Bishop Grant, the honorary degree of LL D. St Francis Xavier University, despite its name, is an institution of strong Scottish Highland associations. Here is his account of that visit.

We flew across the Atlantic by BOAC, and after landing at Gander we changed planes and flew over the desolate wastes of Newfoundland (resembling the Moor of Rannoch prolonged *ad infinitum*, with some spruce and birch added), and across the Cabot Strait to Sydney, Cape Breton, where we were welcomed by several members of the faculty of St Francis Xavier. My companions remained for two days in Cape Breton, while I was driven to Antigonish, 125 miles from Sydney and across the Gut of Canso, through spruce forests and along the shores of the Bras d'Or lakes, the inland sea that penetrates the heart of Cape Breton Island. Eventually we reached our destination at Antigonish. In order that the background to these celebrations should be appreciated, it is necessary to say something about the history of the University.

In 1852 the Rev. Colin MacKinnon, son of emigrants from the Isle of Eigg, was appointed Bishop of the Diocese of Antigonish, which comprises the three easternmost counties of the mainland of Nova Scotia and the four counties of Cape Breton. By 1852 pioneering days in Nova Scotia, which had begun with the arrival of the ship *Hector* at Pictou in September 1773 with emigrants from the Highlands of Scotland, were drawing to a close. In these eighty years many thousands of Scottish Highlanders and Islesmen, some lured by the exaggerated accounts of emigration agents, others expelled by the Highland Clearances, had made their way to the country of the *coille ghruamach* (gloomy forest), and, facing great hardships, had built themselves houses and cleared land of trees to make farms. The first and second generations of Canadian-born Gaels were growing up, and it was now necessary to organise education, and particularly higher education and education of the clergy, among them.

The blow of the evictions had fallen particularly heavily on the ancient Jacobite districts of the Highlands in those gloomy years after the failure of the Rising of 1745, which saw the replacement of the old tacksmen (tenant farmers related to the clan chiefs, who had proper leases and raised cattle) by Low Country sheep farmers; the failure of the kelp industry, which had been so profitable to the lairds between 1770 and 1815, and in which so many of their small tenants-at-will had been employed as a condition of their occupancies; and finally the eviction of so many of these small tenants in the Clearances made to create big sheep farms, in their turn often later to become deer forests.[1] Districts like Lochaber, Glengarry, Knoydart, Morar, Arisaig, Moidart, Rum, Eigg, Muck, Canna, Barra and South Uist, were in some cases almost entirely denuded of inhabitants, so much so that in many cases the Nova Scotian descendants of the old population are far more numerous than those found in Scotland today. Within the Diocese of Antigonish (a corruption of the Micmac Indian place-name *Naligitgonietjg*, meaning 'broken branches')[2] today about two-thirds of the souls composing the Diocese, some 80,000, are of Highland and Hebridean descent, whereas in the Diocese of Argyll and the Isles, from which the ancestors of most of these came, there are today but 12,000. Names like Chisholm, MacDonald, MacGillivray, MacNeil, MacInnes (in Nova Scotia spelt MacInnis and pronounced Maginnis), Fraser and MacKinnon abound in eastern Nova Scotia.

Bishop MacKinnon's plan for an institution of higher learning in his Diocese came into effect a hundred years ago, and, while a building was being prepared at Antigonish, he established a small college at Arichat in Cape Breton with a handful of students. In 1855 the institution was moved to Antigonish and dedicated to St Francis Xavier out of gratitude for a very timeous grant from the French Mission Society.

From the time that initial difficulties had been overcome, the story is one of uninterrupted expansion. In 1866 the Nova Scotian Government conferred upon the University the right to grant degrees. By 1889 it had 106 students. By 1893 it had produced 2 bishops, 55 priests, 19 seminarians, 1 judge, 2 Canadian senators, 5 Canadian MPs, 19 lawyers, 19 physicians, and many teachers.

[1] See the following chapter. Removal of cattle and intensive grazing by sheep were naturally followed by the deterioration of the land.
[2] Père Pacifique, *Le Pays des Micmacs*.

When I first visited St F.X. (as it is always called) in 1932, there were about 200 students, and more than half the teaching staff of about 18, including the then Rector, the Rt Rev. Monsignor H. P. MacPherson, were Gaelic speakers. In 1953 the student body numbered about 900, including students from all over North America, and the teaching staff numbered about 60; great expansion had taken place under the Presidency of the late Monsignor P. J. Nicolson, a native Gaelic speaker from the Beaver Cove district of Cape Breton, contributor of a weekly Gaelic column in the local paper the *Casket* of Antigonish, president from 1944 to 1954, who gave the writer and his wife the greatest encouragement.

Since his time the University has grown steadily under his successors, the Rev. Dr H. J. Somers (1954–64), the Rev. Malcolm MacLellan (1964–70), the Rev. Malcolm MacDonell (1970–78), the latter two both Gaelic speakers; the present holder of the position is the Rev. Gregory MacKinnon, of Isle of Eigg descent.

The list of distinguished alumni is a long one; it included the late Rt Hon. Angus L. MacDonald, premier of Nova Scotia—which as a Canadian province has a far greater measure of Home Rule than does Scotland. Amongst those now living are the present Prime Minister of Canada, the Rt Hon. M. Brian Mulroney; the Hon. Mr Justice Gerard LaForest, member of the Supreme court of Canada; the Hon. Allan MacEachen, senator and sometime deputy Prime Minister; the Hon. Frank McKenna, premier of New Brunswick; the Hon. Vincent MacLean, leader of the Opposition, Nova Scotia; Dr Larkin Kerwin, President of the National Research Council of Canada; not to mention a large number of persons prominent in the Church and in industry, the latter both in Canada and the U.S.A. The late Hon. Lauchlan Currie, Chief Justice of Nova Scotia, and a descendant of the MacVurichs of Stilligary, bards to the MacDonalds of Clanranald for generations up to 1730, was another very prominent alumnus.

At the present time St F.X. has an enrolment of between 2800 and 3000 students, and a teaching staff of about 200. Of the 28 priests in residence, five can converse in Gaelic, two of them fluently, and of the lay faculty and sisters, perhaps twelve or thirteen. The teaching of Gaelic dates from 1891, and was revived by Monsignor Nicholson's successor Dr Somers in 1958, when the late Calum I. MacLeod, son of John N. MacLeod, well known as the contributor of the Gaelic column in the *Stornoway Gazette* for many years, became the head of the Celtic Department, in which he was succeeded on his decease in 1977 by Sister Margaret MacDonell, trained in Celtic at Harvard, who retired in 1986, to be succeeded by Dr Kenneth Nilsen, the present holder of the position.

St F.X. is now the largest English-speaking Catholic University in Canada. It has gained a great deal of publicity through the 'Antigonish Movement', begun in 1928, with which the names of Dr M. M. Coady, Dr A. B. MacDonald, and the late Rev. J. J. Tompkins are associated. This movement was a successful attempt to counteract the economic depression that came over the fishing and farming communities of Nova Scotia after the First War, by practical adult education in co-operative methods given on the spot by men from the University who travelled to these communities themselves and organised discussion and study groups amongst the people, and trained leaders in co-operative methods. So successful has this movement been that representatives of poor or backward lands all over the world go to St F.X. to study it.[1]

The Convocation began on 18 May, when the baccalaureat sermon was preached by Bishop Grant—'So let your light shine before men that they may see your good works and glorify your Father who is in heaven' (Matthew v.16). On 19 May the Alumni banquet took place; at this Mr J. T. Hackett, QC, later recipient of an honorary degree, spoke on the constitution of Canada, and Mr Justice Hector Y. MacDonald a Gaelic-speaking alumnus, also to receive an honorary degree, recalled the great figures of the University. On 20 May the graduating class received their degrees, and the five honorary degrees were bestowed, being given by the Most Rev. J. R. MacDonald, Bishop of Antigonish and Chancellor of the University.

The degrees were given in the University Auditorium, which is under their new Chapel and can seat about a thousand persons. Mr K. Smith, QC, chairman of the National Harbors Board of Canada, himself the recipient of an honorary degree, gave an eloquent address upon the necessity of protecting spiritual values in education. Bishop Grant's citation was read in Gaelic by the President, Mgr Nicholson.

During this visit the writer gave a broadcast talk on the Antigonish radio station on the late Fr Allan McDonald of Eriskay, 1859–1905, and his work as a priest in South Uist and Eriskay, and his famous folklore collection; this talk was later expanded into a booklet on the subject published in Edinburgh in 1954. He also had the opportunity to record on wire some more songs from Mrs David Patterson, whom he and his wife had recorded in 1937, and to make some interesting recordings from the late Angus MacIsaac, aged 77, of Moidart descent, living in Antigonish, including some verses of the Ossianic ballad *Teanntachd Mhór na Féinne*, 'the great straights of the Fians'; it is included in this book. It was of great interest to find such a thing preserved in the Gaelic tradition of Nova Scotia.

Scots Magazine (October 1953, brought up to date)

---

[1] See the preceding chapter here, also *MacLean's Magazine* of 1 June 1953, 'How St F. X. saved the Maritimes'.

INTO EXILE:
EMIGRATION FROM BARRA
TO CAPE BRETON 1790–1835

Bho nach fuiling iad beò sibh
Ann an crìochaibh ur n-eòlais,
'S fheàrr dhuibh falbh d'ur deòin as
Na bhith fòdha mar thràillean.
Iain Mac Fhearchair

Translation

Since they won't put up with you living within your familiar bounds, it's better for you to leave of your own accord, than to be oppressed like serfs.
John MacCodrum (1693–1779)

Ri linn Ruairi an t-seachdamh Ruairi,
Thig an cuaradh air gach neach;
Mac na baintighearna caoile bàine,
'S minig[1] a bhios ann ri a linn,
'S mi-niarach a bhios ann ri a linn;
Bidh Ciosmal 'na ghàrradh bhiastan-dubha,
'S 'na niod aig eunlaith nan speuran.
Fiosachd Mhic a' Chreachaire

Translation

In the time of Rory, of the seventh Rory (MacNeil of Barra)
Misery will befall everyone,
Son of the slender fair-haired lady,
Pity whoever will live in his time
Unhappy whoever lives in his time;
Kishmul Castle will be an enclosure for otters,
And a nest for the birds of the skies.
The Prophesy of Mac a' Chreachaire

---

[1] Dialect for *mairg*.

1 THE KELP INDUSTRY FAILS

Since the forebears of so many of the singers and tradition bearers represented in this book came from the Isle of Barra, this important subject can be discussed with reference to that island, especially as important and unpublished documents and letters survive to illustrate it, even though the papers of the the old MacNeil of Barra family, which ended with the death of General Roderick MacNeil of Barra in 1863, have disappeared.

Various things have to be considered in relation to this; the personalities of General MacNeil (1789–1863), last chief of the MacNeils of Barra in the direct line, and of his father Colonel Roderick MacNeil of Barra[1] (*c*.1755–1822); the Scottish laws of succession to entailed estates, and the legal obligations which they imposed on their heir of entail towards his younger brothers and sisters and widowed mother; the complete lack of security of tenure as regards the small tenants on such estates, who could be compelled to perform various services as a condition of retaining their holdings, which could be very burdensome; and the ultimate failure of the kelp industry, which had been started in the Hebrides in 1775 by that enterprising tacksman and dealer, Alexander MacDonald of Boisdale, nicknamed in Gaelic 'Alasdair Mór nam Mart' 'Big Alister of the cows' (he was a famous cattle-dealer), who had advised Prince Charles Edward to return to France after he landed on Eriskay in 1745; one of Alister's sons-in-law was Hector MacNeill who came from Campbeltown in Kintyre to Canna as Clanranald's tenant in 1781.

In his *Travels in the Western Hebrides from 1782 to 1790*, the Rev. John Lane Buchanan, AM, who did not by any means spare oppressive lairds and tacksmen (big tenant farmers) from unfavourable criticism, wrote of Colonel Roderick MacNeil of Barra that he was the laird of Barra and the lesser adjoining islands, and said that

> Mr MacNeil generally resides on his estate, an extensive property, which he manages with equal humanity and prudence. He encourages all kinds of improvement, exercises justice amongst his tenants, and protects them from those oppressions, which are too common in other parts of the Hebrides. This gentleman has no tacksmen, except some of his own near relations, who are of too gentle and generous a disposition to abuse the confidence placed in them by their chief, by trampling on a poor, but kindred people.

Barra's heir, also called Roderick, who later became a General in the British Army, was of a very different character, as will be seen.

Kelp is defined by the *Oxford English Dictionary* as: '1. a collective name for

---

[1] The style 'The MacNeil of Barra' is quite unhistorical, and was never used by the old chiefs of the MacNeils of Barra themselves.

large seaweeds (chiefly *Fucaceae* and *Laminariceae*) which are burnt for the sake of substances found in the ashes. 2. the calcined ashes of seaweed used for the sake of the iodine etc. they contain; formerly much used in the manufacture of soap and glass.' Kelp brought fortunes to Hebridean landowners between 1770 and 1815; Edward Daniel Clarke, chemist and discoverer of the element cadmium, traveller, collector, professor of minerology at Cambridge University, wrote very penetratingly in his little-known account of his 1797 Hebridean tour, that the islands were chiefly occupied in the manufacture of kelp; cattle and kelp constituted, in fact, the chief objects of commerce in the Hebrides.

The first toast usually given in all festive occasions is a 'high price' to kelp and cattle. In this, every islander is interested and it is always drunk with evident symptoms of sincerity. The discovery of manufacturing kelp has affected a great change among the people; whether for their advantage or not, is a question not yet decided. I was informed in Canna, that if kelp keeps its present price, Mr MacDonald, of Clanranald, will make £6,000 sterling by his kelp and Lord MacDonald will make not less than £10,000.

But the neglect of tillage, which is universally experienced since this discovery was made, is already sensibly felt; and promises to overbalance the good which is derived from it. The lands lie neglected and without manure; and if naked rocks are to succeed corn fields and the labourers desert the pursuits of husbandry to gather sea-weed, the profits arising from kelp to individuals will ill repay the loss occasioned to the community at large, by the defect of those necessaries they are accustomed to derive from their lands.

The best kelp is usually supposed to be that which is manufactured in the island of Barra. Mr MacNeil, the laird of that island, informed me he got last year twelve guineas a ton for his kelp. The rainy season has this year damaged vast quantities of that which he is preparing, not with standing which, as far as I could learn, he will be able to send 300 tons to the Liverpool markets.

The great scarcity of barilla, arising from the war with Spain, has considerably augmented the speculations of all the western islanders, with regard to their kelp, which is expected to bear a very high price.

The manufacture of kelp is conducted by the following process: the sea-weed is first collected and dried. The usual mode is to cut a portion of kelp annually from the rocks, taking it from the same place only once in three years. After the kelp has been dried it is placed in a kiln prepared for the purpose, of stones loosely piled together, and burned. After it is consumed, and the fire is to be extinguished, a long pole pointed with iron is plunged into it and it is stirred about; the result of the burning being, by this time, a thick glutinous liquid, which runs from the kelp in burning. As soon as this liquid cools, it hardens and the operation is at an end. It is then shipped off to market. The usual expense of manufacturing kelp is about two guineas a ton for the labour; if it is sold on the shore, which is generally the case, and estimating the kelp only at eight guineas a ton, the proprietor clears six.

The manufacture of kelp was in full swing in the Hebrides by 1785, the year that Colonel Roderick MacNeil of Barra married Jean, daughter of Sir Ewen Cameron of Fassiefern. Two years later a duty of £5 5s. 0d. a ton was imposed on barilla, a Spanish product made from similar seaweeds. This, and the wars of the French Revolution, drove up the price of Hebridean kelp; the price of black cattle from the Highlands also rose. The lairds, many of whom had been compensated by the London Government for the loss of their hereditary jurisdictions, supposedly reserved to them permanently by Article XX of the Act of Union with England of 1707, had 'never had it so good'. The average cost of making kelp, work imposed on their small tenants as a condition of retaining their holdings, was £2 5s. 0d. a ton; freight and other costs came to £1 5s. 0d. a ton; returns could come to as much as £22 a ton; their revenue from kelp could come to as much as double their land rent.

The consequence of such prosperity with such small labour costs could be recklessly generous marriage settlements and testaments, and reckless running into debt. In the last quarter of the eighteenth century Colonel Roderick MacNeil, who had succeeded his grandfather as a child after the death of his father at Quebec in 1759, built the three storied mansion at Eoligary, with its walled garden, possibly in connection with his marriage to a baronet's daughter, almost certainly with borrowed money. His feudal protectiveness of his tenants is attested by the Rev. Edward MacQueen, Church of Scotland minister on Barra from 1774 to 1813, in his report on Barra for the *Old Statistical Account of Scotland* (1794); he tells how a number of Barra folk had gone to Glasgow around 1790, invited by David Dale, father-in-law of Robert Owen, to work in his textile factory, but repented of their choice; others prepared to emigrate to North America, sold their possessions (i.e. their livestock) and spent the proceeds, 'so that they would have been destitute in their native country; but Mr MacNeil, the proprietor, not only gave them, and such as returned from Glasgow, lands, but likewise money enought to purchase a new stock of cattle, and all the other necessary implements of husbandry. The spirit for emigration is now happily and totally suppressed.'

The point that must be noticed is that as long as the kelp boom lasted, early emigration from the Hebrides to the New World was voluntary.

The stimulus was, for the tacksmen who formed the middle class, growing frustration; for the tenant-at-will, the almost intolerable insecurity of his tenure, and the onerous and ill-paid work of kelp-gathering and burning, compulsorily attached to it. And both were inspired by the hopes born in the 'common man' by the success of the American revolution, with its spirit of independence and egalitarianism.

In his paper 'Highland Emigration to Nova Scotia and Prince Edward Island from 1770 to 1853' read before the Nova Scotia Historical Society on 4 November 1932, C. S. MacDonald lists no fewer than 46 ships that carried emigrants from the Highlands and Islands during that time. In his *History of Christmas Island* A. J. MacKenzie mentions particularly emigrant ships in 1802, 1813, 1817, 1821, 1822, 1825, 1833, that brought Hebridean immigrants to his district, mostly from South Uist and Barra. Professor J. M. Bumsted in his *The People's Clearance, 1770–1815*, prints interesting lists of names in passenger lists in appendices—one of which was previously printed in the *Casket* of Antigonish 38 years earlier. He lists no fewer than 114 ships which between those dates carried 14,987 emigrants to Canada from Scotland, of whom 11,883 or 79.3 per cent were from the Western Highlands and Islands.

In 1805 the Rev. Fr Angus MacDonald, a member of the Glenaladale family, was appointed parish priest of Barra, where he remained for twenty years. By an exceptional piece of good fortune the letters he received from time to time from Colonel Roderick MacNeil of Barra and his successor, also called Roderick, Major in the Second Life Guards, whom we will distinguish by calling by his later title 'General' here, were preserved on Barra. The letters began in November 1805. Kelp was still flourishing. There was no word of emigration until 6 June 1816, when Colonel MacNeil wrote:

The Revd. Mr. Angus M'Donald
Barra

Liverpool the 6th June 1816

My Dear Sir,—It is now some considerable time since I heard from you. Reports have of late come to me, of spirit of Emigration from your Parish: but having no hint from you on the subject, I paid little attention to them. Matters, however, are now so far settled: a considerable number having signed (as it is called) with a Mr. Fraser.

It is no doubt distressing to my feelings, that People to whom I am so much attached, should leave me: but if it was for their good, I should regret it less.

From the terms, this man has made with the people, I must think, they are far too high: freights and provisions are very low. I have not a doubt much better terms, could be made: this very day, I learn, that Vessells are going out to America in ballast. The saving of two, or three pounds, for each passenger, would amount to a very large sum for a family. Were it agreeable, I would with pleasure do all that was possible to save the small means of those people, and so, let their situation be better, when they get to America. Mr. Fraser, acts as a job to get money, and his profits would be better in the pockets of the Passengers.

I shall make the proper enquiry, and be prepared in a few days to write you by Post, what they are.

I am not quite decided, as to going home this season: but, if I can be of use to these people whether my own business requires it or not, I will not hesitate to go.

The People may be quite easy as to their signing with this man: he has no legal claim on them. The mark, if not before a Justice of Peace, and two witnesses, is of no avail. I shall be anxious to hear from you.—With my best wishes, I am, Yours truly

Roderick M'Neil

If I recollect, some of the people lost money by this very Mr. Fraser, some time since—John M'Kinnon late of Nask.

Please say where the Emigrants wish to go in America.

'Mr. Fraser' was Major Simon Fraser, an emigration agent; such people were then very unpopular with the Hebridean proprietors for depriving them of labour for the kelp, and became notorious amongst the people for persuading emigrants, on whose passage fees they got commission, that Nova Scotia was a land flowing with milk and honey, and then dumping them to fend for themselves in the spruce forests of Canada after they landed.

Emigration continues to be a subject mentioned in subsequent letters, Colonel MacNeil pointing out that Fraser had no legal claim on the people who had signed with him to embark, unless their marks had been made before a JP and two witnesses, but he wrote that he could not do anything for those who were redemptioners, i.e. who had bound themselves to pay for the cost of their passages from their earnings after landing. On 28 May 1817 Colonel MacNeil wrote:

I am sure you are heartily tired of Emigrants concerns: the loss of so many very decent people, is much to be regretted: at the same time, those that remain, will in time, be much better: this reflection always offers us something consolatory when one reflects, he has seen for the last time, those he has been accustom'd to from early infancy.

Colonel MacNeil, who had succeeded his grandfather as a small boy after his father had been killed at Quebec fifty-eight years earlier, was the last proprietor of Barra to express regret at the emigration of his tenants. Unfortunately the reflection he expresses was not to be fulfilled. In a letter written on 27 December 1818, he mentions another emigration agent, a William MacMillan, who was trying to get customers. In the same letter he remarks that his 'loss this year is very great from neglect, I cannot say how much, as to deficiency of kelp: I fear I have suffered loss, as to farming also: for some time a doubt has been on my mind. Had a late person indulged in drink to your knowledge?' In September he had written that he 'feared we would be short of kelp this year, but the price will make up in some measure'. The identity of the person who was in charge is uncertain.

In this letter Colonel MacNeil alludes to the process of the enclosure of arable land on Barra, unfenced and held by ancient custom in runrig, periodically reallotted amongst the small tenants, by individual crofts, which must have been going on at the time.

> It seems to me desirable, that all the hay grounds, and as much as possible of the ground for labouring, were divided, in large portions, so as to encourage the clearing of stones, enclosing, etc . . . should anything of the kind be done, to any considerable extent, and represented to me: the division should be permanent to any one, who clear'd or enclosed.

He alludes again to this in his letter of 27 December 1818. It is not known what terms were attached to the tenure of the crofts so created, but it is likely that these included services to be performed for the estate at kelp-making, and perhaps at fishing, and that these would come to be reluctantly performed, to the rage of Colonel MacNeil's successor, as will be seen. Many of the small tenants must have disliked the break-up of the old townships.[1]

In November 1821 Colonel MacNeil wrote that he was more anxious for the success of his then factor Major MacDonald, in kelp than in farming (the letters were written from Liverpool, where the kelp was regularly shipped).

In fact, by 1821 the boom in kelp prices was collapsing. The fall began in 1814, when trade with Spain revived, including imports of barilla. A further blow was the removal of the duty on salt in 1817; soda could be made from salt by the Leblanc process, invented in 1787, the development of which was delayed by the execution of Leblanc in the French Revolution, and then by the Napoleonic Wars. In 1822 the duty of £11 a ton on barilla, fixed in 1819, was reduced to £8; it was further reduced to £5 a ton in 1823, the same year that the Leblanc process was introduced into Britain by James Muspratt, at Liverpool.

Colonel Roderick MacNeil of Barra died at the beginning of May 1822. His death brought into effect the Deed of Entail he had constructed in 1806 and his Deed of Settlement of 1820. The first was designed to make sure that Barra would remain forever in the possession of heirs belonging to his family; the second includes his will; both incorporate the marriage settlement he made in 1785, when kelp was flourishing. The marriage settlements of landed proprietors in Scotland were a legal device for avoiding the Scottish law of inheritance; a man could only dispose of one-third of his property freely (no cutting off of heirs with a shilling in Scotland!); his widow had the right to another third, and the last third fell to his legitimate children. To avoid the division of landed estates that this would have produced, the custom had been adopted of the prospective widow agreeing to a marriage settlement which gave her and her unborn children the

---

[1] See *The Creation of Crofts and New Settlement Patterns in the Highlands and Islands* by James B. Caird, in Vol. 103 of the *Scottish Geographical Magazine*.

right to money settlements for which the heir to the estate would be legally liable, in return for the prospective bride's surrendering her right, and her future children's rights, to their respective thirds on her husband's decease. Incidentally the legal documents (Register of Tailzies, Book 60, folio 47, recorded 28 June 1822, and Public Records of Scotland 5/63, registered 7 May 1822) reveal that Colonel MacNeil did not have complete confidence in his heir's financial discretion.

Succession in Barra could not have come at a worse time for his heir, whom we will call (General) MacNeil here to distinguish him from his father, though he did not actually reach that rank until 1846. For his father's Deed of Succession imposed the following obligations upon him. He had to pay

1. His brother Ewen £5,000 unless he has succeeded to the estate; if he does succeed, Ewen is to repay this to the trustees of Entail with interest.

2. His five sisters, Ann, Louisa, Catherine, Jane, and oddly named 'Ewen Cameron', annuities of £200 a year each, as long as they remained unmarried, and a dowry of £500 each when they did marry; Ann was already married, in 1818 to John Campbell of Achallader; Jane was to marry in 1828 (General) MacNeil's father-in-law Lt. Colonel Charles Brownlow of Lurgan in Ulster who became Lord Lurgan in 1839. The other sisters remained unmarried. (General) MacNeil had married Lt. Colonel Brownlow's daughter Isabella in the summer of 1818, who brought a £6,000 dowry.

3. His natural half-sister Catherine MacNeil, an annuity of £50.

4. His cousins Marion MacLean and her brother Lachlan MacLean, a joint annuity of £20 a year, as long as either of them was alive.

5. Any obligation incurred to his (the General's) wife Isabella Brownlow under the obligations of their post-nuptial contract in the event of her widowhood, was to be an obligation of the estate.

His father's trustees were to have complete powers of management for the purpose of liquidating the Colonel's debts, for which the sale of the estate of Ashfield in Knapdale was not expected to produce sufficient funds. The heir of entail (the General) was to get only half of the free rents of Barra, the other half was to be used as a sinking fund to liquidate his father's debts. Various other restrictions were imposed.

Thus the obligation was laid on the heir of paying immediately £5,000 to his brother and £800 a year to his then unmarried sisters plus two small annuities of £50 and £20, totalling £5,000 down, plus £870 a year, with the further prospect of providing dowries of £500 each to his four sisters if and when they married, and this at the moment that the price of kelp was collapsing. The only way to save the situation would have been for him to persuade the other beneficiaries to sacrifice all or part of their interests, and this they must have refused to do, for on 27 October 1823 he wrote from London to Fr Angus MacDonald:

> My Dear Sir,—Believe me your well meant advice so far from offending gave me pleasure; you were not aware how matters stood—no man aware of the (to me) ruinous nature of the Deeds executed by my late father could conscientiously advise me to submit to them. With reference to his actual income and enormous debt, they were, to say the least, absurd; I was literally tied to the stake, having no alternative but to reduce them, or consign myself and family to penury—all that man could do, I did, to avoid the expense and vexation of a Lawsuit—I proposed arbitration, and offered provisions to the younger children far beyond my ability, as admitted by several of the Trustees, and all to no effect—evil counsel prevailed. In those of whom, from near connection I had the right to expect justice, if nothing more, I found only duplicity, and a want of candour quite incredible.

The remainder of General MacNeil's connection with the Isle of Barra was spent in a permanent state of rage,[1] attempting frantic money-making schemes with all the pressure of his position as laird of numerous tenants-at-will bound to perform various services as a condition of their tenure, could bring. On 20 March 1824 he wrote asking Fr Angus MacDonald to 'effect a *great* diminution in the number of Holydays . . . my anxious wish is to make the people industrious and comfortable, but they *must* work or they will not do for me'. He added significantly, 'You are the only person connected with my property, from whom I have experienced a friendly disposition during the time it was in other hands, this I cannot easily forget.'

On 10 May the same year he wrote again from London to complain that instead of being willing to fish for him, the Barramen preferred to take their fish to Glasgow and trade them for necessities, or dispose of them to strangers on the coast 'for inferior and dear tobacco, and other articles in barter'. He makes it clear that his strictures apply not only to his tenants but to their 'sons, grandsons and nephews'—who were fed and housed by his tenants,

> In short they are fed and housed on my land and pay me not a shilling. I trust you will now perceive that I know what I am about well enough to see the absurdity of the idea of what you call the spirits of the young lads being dampt, and dampt by what, by having the means of prosecuting useful industry supplied to them by their Landlord instead of having to paddle a distance for them. And now my dear sir let me request you will immediately on receipt of this tell all your parishioners, that

---

[1] The report on his later bankruptcy reveals that he suffered from gout.

although sufficiently disgusted with the manner in which you say my first attempts have been met, *I will persevere*. Any one of my tenants who chooses to take his fish to Glasgow, or dispose of it in barter to strangers on the coast is of course at liberty to do so. But then again they must recollect that I have an equal right to dispose of my lands as I may think most advisable; and they much deceive themselves if they think that opposition or obstacles (and I anticipate some) will turn me from what I conceive the best course—you will tell them all that any man who does not comply with my terms shall be turned off my Lands, and any of the young men who think it proper to voyage to Glasgow may there remain, for I pledge *my word* they shall never again eat a potato on my property, be they ever so penitent. As to holidays I shall be very explicit; many of them are dispensed with in Catholic countries, this I know from having been a good deal abroad. The Bishop has power to dispense with many of them; particularly those that happen during the kelp and best fishing seasons might be omitted. They are peculiarly grievous in the summer and although I have the greatest respect for the Catholic faith I think it hard that I should suffer loss, and I must candidly tell you that if I don't experience *real and effectual* cooperation from the Bishop, and yourself, I will bring in *Protestant tenants*. If my plans cause you any loss in your own pocket say so candidly and I will make it up to you.

You will let it be distinctly understood that all my prohibitions as to the tenants and fishermen apply to this year as well as years to come.

Yours faithfully

R. MacNeil

The correspondence continues in a crescendo of angry frustration. On 7 February 1825 General MacNeil wrote:

I have little dread of emigration. I certainly shall in all the various ways in my power (and they are not few) oppose it—You may tell Alex McIntyre Tailor (*if he has signed*) that although not another man in Barra should sign, I will (after taking the uttermost farthing due to me, and that without giving any time) land him in Arisaig—the very few not in arrears are all liable for delapidations on their property, that part of it in their hands. I saw how matters stood while at Barra—*some* who did not relish any change at first, because they did not understand it, held out emigration *in terrorem*—*others* again, to my knowledge, encouraged Mr. McNiven with the view of introducing Protestants into the shoes of the deluded Roman Catholicks. I myself dont like a divided house, and would much prefer rowing in the same boat with the natives of the soil, and I have no doubt, if industrious, they may become a very comfortable and happy tenantry, it is quite clear to my mind that if not, it will be entirely attributable to inveterate sloath and pig headedness.

On 30 July 1825 General MacNeil wrote to Fr Angus again from London:

I am sorry for the poor fellow at Brevick. I have sent very conclusive orders touching the contumacious Widow and others. I think it but fair candidly to tell you that the conduct and tone of the good people of Barra whom every days' experience teaches me cannot be depended upon, from their fickleness, idleness, and stiff-necked prejudice, has produced in my mind a decided revolution. Every man my good sir has a right to do the best he can for himself in his own affairs—if one set of servants (tenants at will are nothing else) won't do, the master must try others. I cannot afford the slow operation of waiting till John or Thomas or Hamish are pleased to be convinced that Macneil, after all, was right and could not have meant to cheat and ruin them. No, Mr Angus, I see my way sufficiently clear before me, but to ensure myself an ample harvest (which if I live I have no doubts of) I must have fishers and kelpers who will cheerfully do my bidding . . .so if you mean to keep your flock together look to it. I can easily fill up the vacancies . . . I will thank you to read aloud verbatim the following proclamation, after service, on the very first Sunday after receipt, and *at Borve*. I have sent Mr. Stewart [his new factor] a copy, that those who may not be at Mass may not pretend ignorance. Believe me my dear Sir (though out of humour) Sincerely your friend

R. MacNeil

Proclamation

1st. You will tell the kelpers, that they have earned my utmost displeasure. They have not obeyed my orders—nor the orders of those by me set over them, which I consider as disrespectful to me, as it is disgraceful to them. However as they have worked so shall they be paid.

2nd. Say to the fishermen that their audacity and base ingratitude has quite disgusted me. That if they do not within eight and forty hours after this proclamation, bend their energies to the daily prosecution of their calling as fishermen, I shall turn every man of them off the Island were they steeped to the ears in debt—tell them also that since they have shown themselves so unworthy of that interest, which in my heart I felt for them, I shall follow out my plans without in the most trifling degree consulting their feelings or prejudices.

3rdly. Say to those who are about to emigrate that I sincerely wish them well through it, and assure those who have signed and repented that their repentance comes too late—So help me God, they shall go, at all events off my property, man, woman, and child. Tell the people once for all, that I shall consider any act of inattention to the orders of my factor Mr. Stewart as an impertinence to myself. Nor shall any one who dares even to hesitate to obey him and Mr. Parry (in both of whom I have the greatest confidence) remain on my property should his, or their character been so good previously. Lastly I shall exert myself to the utmost to crush all the disreputable trafficking and smuggling which has been too long tolerated.

R. MacNeil

'Tenants at will are nothing but servants.' In fact, very little more than serfs. This is the condition to which Highlanders and Hebrideans were reduced in the early nineteenth century through the operation of *laissez-faire*, when a man could be deprived of his thatched house (made by himself) and his piece of land and his common grazing rights, if any, if he refused to perform the onerous conditions on which he was allowed to occupy it at all. No wonder what Professor Bumsted called 'The People's Clearance' was taking place by the only practical means of escape, emigration to North America.

Another angry letter written from London followed on 8 August 1825, where Fr Angus MacDonald is accused of not helping to promote General MacNeil's schemes, 'What then, I repeat, am I to think—why, one of two things—either you are not free from prejudice yourself, or your feelings lead you to encourage it in others.' He concludes,

> However, as I have already made known to all concerned, I shall now look to my interest without any further regard to obsolete prejudices. You will do well to advise your friends at Sandra,[1] and all the Leaders as they are termed, to mind well what they are about, if they wish to remain at Barra. They are of little or no importance to me, whatever may be their value to you and if I don't on my arrival find them heart and hand engaged in fishing, I pledge you my honor they shall tramp, and the Land shall be this ensuing spring occupied by strangers. I am fully determined to hear no more of supposed Grievances—the only aggrieved person in the Island is the proprietor, and on my word, he will find a remedy. He may be thwarted, opposed, and disgusted, but not easily defeated in his endeavours to improve his property, and humanize his tenants. Pray don't take the trouble of writing again, as I leave here in a few days, and I shall soon be with you.
>
> I hope you see John Bull regularly and that your health continues good. Mrs. MacNeil is quite well, and all the family—I remain dear Sir, Very truly yours
>
> R. MacNeil

2 MACNEIL OF BARRA GOES BANKRUPT

On 1 February 1826 the names of every person immediately or remotely concerned with an interest in Colonel MacNeil of Barra's 1806 Deed of Entail and 1820 Deed of Settlement was listed in a 'Decree of reduction and Declarator to a certain extent; and Interim Decree'. This is a document of great genealogical interest, which has been surprisingly ignored by the Clan MacNeil historians, and which was never produced before the Lord Lyon when the question of the arms and succession of the MacNeils of Barra was under consideration in 1915. The names are as follows:

[1] A small island south of Barra, now uninhabited.

1. 'Colonel Roderick MacNeill (*sic*) now of Barra, Major in the 2nd Regiment of Life Guards, eldest son and male heir of provision in general to the deceased Roderick Macneill late of Barra; AGAINST' his daughter and only child, Caroline Elizabeth Florence; Ewen Cameron MacNeill (his brother) 'at present residing in Edinburgh'; Ann (his eldest sister) 'widow of the late John Livington Campbell of Achallader'; John and Jane their children; Lucy or Louisa MacNeil, his second sister; Catherine, his third sister; Joan or John his fourth sister; Ewen Cameron MacNeil his fifth sister, daughters of deceased Roderick MacNeil of Barra.

2. Margaret MacNeil, his sister, 'spouse of Donald MacNeil tacksman of Watersay' (the island immediately south of Barra) 'for his interest' and their children Ewen or Hugh, Ann, Flora, Marion and Jean;

3. Roderick MacNeil present or lately tacksman of Braewick and his lawful children, resident in the island of Cape Breton, or elsewhere near or on the continent of North America, and his sons Roderick, Gallian, and Lachlan, and his daughter Margaret, 'all now also abroad'. (The late Wallace MacNeil, Prince Edward Island, claimed this Roderick MacNeil as his ancestor.)

4. Mrs Catherine MacNeil otherwise MacDonald, illegitimate daughter of the deceased Roderick MacNeil of Barra, and her husband James Macdonald (who was the late Barra's agent at Liverpool) for his interest.

5. Miss Marion MacLean and Lachlan MacLean her brother, both residing at Eoligary in the Island of Barra 'and the tutors and curators of such of the said defenders as are minors'.

Also parties to the action were the trustees of the deceased Sir Ewen Cameron of Fass[ie]fern, Bt; Sir William Macleod Bannatyne, retired Senator of the College of Justice; Donald Cameron of Lochiel; John MacNeil of Colonsay; Duncan MacNeill, advocate; Patrick Robertson, advocate; Duncan Cameron of Fassfern ws; Captain Peter M'Donald merchant in Liverpool; Major James M'Donald of Askernish in S. Uist.

General MacNeil was presumably unable to get his numerous relations who had an interest in the entailed estate of Barra either to abandon or modify their claims. He struggled on for a number of years trying to make money out of Barra by various means, but in the not so long run bankruptcy and the sale of the estate were inevitable. The sale took place in 1838; nevertheless, in the 1850 edition of *Burke's Landed Gentry* the General is still described as 'MacNeill, Roderick, Esq of Barra in the shire of Inverness, Chief of the Macneills, m. 20 June 1818 Isabella-Caroline, dau. of Charles Brownlow Esq. of Lurgan in co. Armagh, and has an only child, Caroline-Elizabeth-Florence. Colonel Macneill, who is a magistrate and deputy-lieut. for Invernessshire, s. his father in 1822.' His 'seat' is described as 'Barra House, Inverness-shire'.

In his account of his family, he refrains from invoking its mythical history. He traces his ancestry to 'Nigellus Oge', grandfather of the Roderick MacNeil who witnessed a charter by Donald, Lord of the Isles, to Hector MacGillean of Dowart in 1409, saying simply that 'the dominion of this chief (i.e. himself) has been in the family for upward of four hundred years, though tradition assigns a much older date as the period of their occupancy'.

Very interesting evidence on subsequent condition and events on Barra subsequent to 1825 comes from letters in the library of the Scots College in Rome, where Fr Angus MacDonald became Rector in late 1825, from his successor as Parish Priest of Barra, the Rev. Neil MacDonald; Hugh MacNeil of Vatersay (General MacNeil's nephew), and Fr John Chisholm, parish priest of Bornish in South Uist. Constant themes in these letters are the great difficulty Fr Neil has in collecting church dues owed to Fr Angus owing to the poverty of the people; General MacNeil's attempts to deprive Fr Neil of his house, chapel and glebe in order to bestow them on the Church of Scotland minister, the Rev. Alexander Nicolson (apparently to save the General expense; refused by Mr Nicolson); emigration, the General's schemes for making money, especially by fishing; by the creation of a soap and glass making factory at Northbay (Bahierva); the seizure of cattle, horses and sheep from the small tenants against rent owed or due in future; the difficulties of the MacNeil of Vatersay family, with whom, although related, General MacNeil was on very bad terms—Hugh MacNeil refers to him as a 'monster of ingratitude' (25 February 1827); the constant background is poverty and oppression; even after the duty was taken off barilla, the Barra people were not allowed to cut any kelp to manure their holdings (4 March 1831).

By the time that Barra was sold, under sequestration, in 1838, the price of kelp, in which all hands were employed for about two months of the year, at a wage of only £1 15s. or £2 a ton, was down to £2 10s. a ton or so, £4 a ton at the most (*Old Statistical Account*).

General MacNeil actually became officially bankrupt in 1836; for the period of this correspondence, he was certainly still involved with the management of Barra, which he visited several times. As regards emigration, Hugh MacNeil wrote on 25 February 1827 that the colonel blamed his family (Vatersay) for the tenants leaving Barra, which he denies. 'Those emigrants that Engaged with Col. Frazer (*sic*) have been sadly disappointed as he was unable to send them off to America and I am told that the poor wre(t)ches are going about from place to place looking out for some place to rest themselves in. They have been most shockingly used by both Col. Fraser and MacNeil.'

He goes on to say that his own family has 'suffered as much hardship from (General) MacNeil of Barra', who, he says, did everything in his power to injure them in every respect, and as for abuse they 'got that in abundance from him in some of his letters to my mother (the General's aunt) and as to giving them any help, he has sworne against giving them anything'. They have left Barra and gone to live on the Isle of Man. Hugh himself had gone to work in a draper's shop in Liverpool in partnership with his nephew. 'The means were furnished us by our Best friends Mr. and Mrs. (James) MacDonald.'

By the autumn of 1827 things were desperately bad in Barra. On 7 October Fr Neil Macdonald wrote to Fr Angus in Rome,

It will ever be remembered here, the year 1827, to the latest posterity, as a memorable one—After the numbers you have seen enlisting to the different American Agents only half of them could have gone, either for want of sufficient money on their part or want of the fidelity of the Agents—These then in a late season of the year lost before and behind,[1] as they say—It was too late to commence sowing their seed and upon their friends they must live,—impoverish themselves and their families of the little money they had, if they had any, which like fools they deposited in the hands of these demi-gods or Agents—These were sure steps to bring upon themselves and others poverty and starvation—The consequence was that people were actually starving, fainting away in different parts of the island—Had it not been for the cockles of Trà-Mhore,[2] there would have been hundreds dead this day in Barra—350 (?330) were counted one day there—The barrel of potatoes were sold at 6/- and everything else in proportion—during which misery which happened to be at the time of collecting the dues I made absolutely nothing of it and had to lay out part of your £13 to keep myself and the rest from being forced to go to Trà-Mhore too—It is to be feared that the next seanson (*sic*) will be little better for want of seed in the proper time, and for want of money to buy seed where it could be had . . .

To crown the whole poverty and starvation succeeded and obliged those that could do it to procure themselves and their families food from the mainland—Not many weeks ago, I have actually seen in this very farm cattle taken away by the factor and ground officers in a violent struggle between both parties, after the factor and his men were assured that every penny of the rent would be paid at the term—and cattle too that the poor people had no idea of selling to any other drover, and even taken from their very house where they were concealed—Such scenes are scenes of horror—to add more to their misery North Uist and Tiree people (Protestants) are daily flocking in . . .

He adds that the General has been the loser in a legal action with the Minister, and will have to build him a manse and give him a glebe. But he ends that the General had lately been at Eoligary and frequently invited him there—no word of house or chapel being asked for! 'As far as I think he would not be much behind his father was he to remain in the Country and not be so easily advised (*sic*) and

[1] The Gaelic proverb, *Chaill iad rompa 's nan deoghaidh.*
[2] The Tràigh Mhór, the famous cockle strand at the north end of Barra.

that by people that never saw the property.' General MacNeil was only a partial absentee. The proprietor who succeeded him in 1838 was to be a total one.

In July 1828 Fr Neil wrote to his predecessor that (General) MacNeil had given him notice to quit his house at Whitsuntide without delay, countermanded soon afterwards by the order that he was to stay there until the General arrived on Barra—when nothing more was said about it! He said that the General had gained a plea over his brother (the record of this case is said to run to a thousand pages!) and now was full of new plans and ideas for the estate, meaning to set up a glass and soap works at Bahierva (Bagh Hiarabhagh, otherwise North Bay). Since his arrival the system of taking cattle 'by main force' from the people had been given up so far. 'The fishermen and he are at variance, for their having given a part of their fish away to procure provisions' (Previously Fr John Chisholm had written from Bornish (4 February 1827) that they had hesitated about fishing for him, as they had little confidence in him.) There had been no emigration in 1828 so far 'except Malcolm MacNeil from Mingalay and Allan MacArthur'.

Fr Neil's next letter was not written until 12 January 1830. The General and his wife had come to live at Helensburgh; he had no more interest in the fishing since the herring bounty had been withdrawn (it continued at 4 shillings a barrel until 1826, but was reduced by a shilling each year afterwards, ending in 1830). The glass and soap factory at North Bay was expected to be ready (if ever) in the spring. Ewen his brother did not much approve of the General's 'great undertakings'. It was reported that Ewen's uncles (presumably of the Fassiefern family) 'would yet relieve the estate for him.' They never did. Fr Neil continued:

> At Eoligary, for all they can do, they have starvation, owing to the number of servants they keep about the house—Each jeualous (sic) of one another; each undermining one another—MacPherson and Clark, with Parry at their heads are continually collecting the tenantry's cattle—The Col: has at present, grazing at different places upwards of 600 head of cattle—The Col:, as is said, means to send away all the N. Uist men; at least he ordered last year a whole list to be made of them—and Parry is my authority for the above.
>
> There is no incitement for emigration here just now, for very bad accounts have of late been received from America—McNiven, the flying d---l, will become this year a complete bankrupt—Poor unfortunate Fraser (?) is long ago knocked up—He is either still in prison, or in the begging way . . .

He remarks that next year a lighthouse was to be erected at Bernera (Barra head).

Things became worse in the summer of 1830. On 4 March 1831 Fr Neil MacDonald wrote that 'the poverty of the people is beyond description', and sending the news of the death of Donald MacNeil of Vatersay, who was certainly not the Inspector General of Army Hospitals who, the clan historians allege, died on Jersey in 1824. After giving an account of various of Fr Angus's former parishioners who had died since he last wrote, he says:

I am almost afraid of committing these thoughts or matters to paper alone as I am (*sic*), much more to send them abroad, were I not certain of having your confidence on such subjects—Our great laird thought it not sufficient to send a horde of ground officers, and constables,[1] once or twice through the country in taking up the cattle, horses etc, but must needs go himself at their head—This was done truly in style—The very calfs were demanded at last, and hurried to Eoligary—Some had been left with one horse only, others with none at all—Not content with all this he had given strict orders that every sheep in Barra should be killed—The whole have been killed with the exception of a very few kept by the N. Uist people who resisted him in all his unheard of measures, for which, it is reported they are to be sent off—In complying like others with this severe edict, I had from 30 to 34 which is about the number told me by Anny Mcdonald you possessed—Now the number put down by you to me is 50—I cannot conceive where the mistake lies—Parry is removed to Castlebay with no authority, but taking care of the books—No settlement took place since the spring of 1827—all Parry's fault—McPherson who was grieve at Eoligary in your time, but became a great man afterwards, had been disgraced and discharged—His place is filled by another who is not much better—Duncan Clark will, in all appearance be out next term—

Hugh McNeil Watersay has put up a shop at Castlebay by the assistance of Ewen Cameron McNeil (the Laird's brother), he has besides the public houses in the country for which he promised the Laird to pay £200 a year—There was a time in which he could realise his promise, but not now—Peter Robertson in Borve is likewise to be sent off the country.

Mrs. McNeil of Barra was here with himself, from whom and from her brother-in-law (i.e. Ewen Cameron MacNeil) I received the greatest kindness—The Laird himself, thought I attacked him for his severity towards the poor tenantry, and even went so far as to mention to him that he would prove himself to be Rory VII [Ruairi nan Seachd Ruairidh, in whose time as chief an old Gaelic prophesy foretold that great hardship would come to the people of Barra][2] treated me with more than usual kindness, by keeping me constantly down at Eoligary—The works at Bahierva are now complete, but it is the universal opinion that they never will turn out to any advantage [they never did]—In fact, the managers have already involved the poor Laird in a lawsuit in which he is to launch out £1300—The duty is taken off the Barilla and soap—Even though this is the case, the poor people of Barra are not allowed to cut any kelp ware for their lands—and a [page torn] thing, any hardly came ashore here this year—The whole country is besides threatened with privation—Most of your cronies are all well—Poor Neil Bane is removed to Mingalay[3] with 18 or 20 head

---

[1] Not police constables but estate officials who regulated the crofters' common grazings.
[2] Quoted on p. 57.
[3] The largest of the small islands south of Barra.

of cattle—He is not pleased—It is reported that the poor creatures will at Whitsunday be sent elsewhere, except Neil Campbell, who will have no more allowed him than one cow . . .

3   EPILOGUE: EVIDENCE TO THE CROFTERS' COMMISSION IN 1883

Untrained in business and facing a falling market in kelp and cattle, General Roderick MacNeil of Barra failed; his estate was sequestrated on 7 October 1836. The Repertory of the Sederunt books dealing with the case at the Scottish Record Office reads as follows:

MACNEIL, Roderick of Barra, Colonel (then), soda manufacturer, Bahirva, Barra. Sederunt books 1836–37, no. 4274; 1837–39, no. 4275; 1839, no. 4276.
Trustee, Charles Murray Barstow, accountant, Edinburgh. Soda works run in conjunction with Harold Littledale, Liverpool. Inventory of articles of soda works; livestock (very inferior); farm implements, household furniture (some hidden). Rental of estate of Barra. Report on estate by Charles Shaw—advises sending two-thirds of the population to America, so that land can be let for grazing; bankrupt raised rents of tenants he employed in soda works; some tenants employed in kelp and fishing; tenants miserably poor, can only provide for selves till February; estate suffers from sand drift (it still does, 1988). Trustee's account of management of estate. Roup of estate, but bidders unable to pay; land at Barrahead sold to Commissioners of Northern Lighthouses. Creditors in London, Liverpool, Manchester, Ireland. Medical report on bankrupt's gout.[1]

The trustee's suggestion that two-thirds of the population of Barra be transported to America almost reminds one of Stalin contemplating the transportation of some tiresome minority to Siberia. Truly the prophesy about the seventh Ruairi was fulfilled in the years following the death of Col. Roderick MacNeil of Barra who died in 1822; the miseries of the island culminated in the potato famine of the 1840s and the evictions made by General MacNeil's successor in 1851. In the circumstances the survival of the magnificent oral traditions of the island was almost a miracle.

The letters to Fr Angus Macdonald end early in 1831; unfortunately he died the same year. General Roderick MacNeil was forced to sell Barra to pay off his creditors in 1838; MacLean Sinclair says he got 180,000 Canadian dollars for it, then about £36,000. His financial troubles, and the hardships they and the Government policy of *laissez-faire*, imposed on his tenants, do not present a pretty picture; they illustrate the reasons why the grandparents of the Gaelic

---

[1] A condition which prevented him from travelling to Edinburgh. It may well have accounted for his bad temper at times.

traditional singers whose songs we recorded in Cape Breton in 1937 left their ancestral homes to settle in Cape Breton under very great difficulties.

Later on General MacNeil was to find his eulogisers. In his long article on 'Grazing and Agrestic Customs of the Outer Hebrides' printed as Appendix XCIX to the Report of the Crofters' Commission in 1884, Alexander Carmichael wrote (p. 457) that General MacNeil 'was adored by his people, who, with the fidelity of their race, ruined themselves in trying to save him from ruin. They gave him their all', while Charles Fraser MacKintosh, MP, himself a member of the Crofters' Commission, writing in his *Antiquarian Notes* (1897, p. 332) says that General MacNeil 'was singularly kind to the people, and his and his family's name are held in reverent respect to this day'. No doubt by comparison with Col. Gordon of Cluny, who purchased the island from him in 1838, who was a total absentee, responsible for the atrocious eviction of 1851, described in *The Book of Barra*, the memory of earlier oppression had faded by 1884.

Nevertheless, there was circumstantial evidence of the forced taking of cattle and horses and the commandeering of sheep for slaughter described by Fr Neil MacDonald, given at a sitting of the Crofters' Commission at Castlebay, Barra, on 26 May 1883, by John MacPherson, Cottar, Bentangaval, aged 68, so born in the same year as Waterloo, and twelve years old in 1827. Examined by Sir Kenneth MacKenzie, he was asked:

Q. Why did you not get it? (i.e. the land his father had had).
A. I was too young at the time, and my mother was put out.
Q. Could she not pay?
A. She could pay it, and more than that.
Q. Why was she put out?
A. She was put out (of the holding) on account of not being pleased with them for taking the sheep from her at the time of the great wrong that was done by Colonel (i.e. General) MacNeil.
Q. He took the sheep from you?
A. Yes.
Q. And she made objection to that?
A. Yes. She had more sheep than any crofter that was in Barra and there were plenty at that time. There were no big farmers in the island at all, and the hills were full of sheep belonging to the crofters, and my mother had more than any of them. She had about one hundred sheep on the hill, and all these sheep were taken away over to Vatersay by Colonel MacNeil's orders. I saw the constable [not the police constable, but an estate grazing officer] and foreman take them away, and owing to my mother objecting to that the croft was taken from her. She had two cows, and a mare and a foal, and a colt and a few other beasts. A while after that, and after the croft was taken from her, there was a call put out again that there was to be an account given to the Colonel, and the constables came round and every

one gave them a cow. Let him be tenant or cottar the cow was taken from every one in Barra, after the sheep were taken away.

Q. Do you mean that the cow's grass was taken away?

A. The cow itself, from everyone in Barra, was to be taken away. So many constables came for the cows and took them away, but my mother objected to giving a cow. She had two of them, and they were on another man's grass on tethers and the constables went and took one and the tether along with it. There was a sister of mine in the family at the time, and I was quite young at the time, and we met them with the cow coming up the road. My sister ran at one of the constables and hurt him on the knee, and took the cow from him. We could run better than they, and the cow ran well, and ran back to the house; she knew the house—and in she went, and my mother took a stone, and put it at the back of the door to keep it fast. The constables came to the door, and tried to break it open to get the cow. I got above the lintel of the door with a stick in my hand, and knocked off the hat of one of them with the stick. They went away and told this to the factor—the Colonel [General] was not at home—and told what we had done to the constable, and how the man was harried, and all by trying to take the cow away from us. The factor gave them an order to take all she had from her then—to come and take every cow and horse that belonged to her. That factor's name was Macrae, Askernish. I was about twelve years old at the time.

Q. Were the cows taken on account of arrears of rent?

A. There was no settlement required to be taken or given.

Q. But were the people generally in arrears to the Colonel? [the General].

A. I did not think they were. It did not look like that. They would take whatever they liked at any time. There was never any settlement for years at all.

Charles Fraser MacKintosh, MP was one of the Commissioners present while these answers were given.

It was not the business of the Crofters' Commission to investigate into the financial affairs of the entailed estates and their owners in the course of their enquiries, but as we can see here, they were often fundamental to the hardships of the Highland tenantry. It was from this kind of background that the Hebridean emigrants came to Nova Scotia.

THE SINGERS AND THEIR SONGS

JONATHAN G. MACKINNON *MAC TALLA*, 1870–1944
Whycocamagh, Skye tradition

Jonathan MacKinnon was born at Whycocamagh, or Hogamah as the Gaels call it, a pretty village on the east side of the Bras d'Or Lake in Cape Breton; the village is inhabited by the descendants of emigrants who came from the Isle of Skye around 1825, and Jonathan MacKinnon was a Skyeman by descent. He told the writer that he was descended from Tearlach (Charles), the twenty-fifth chief of the Clan MacKinnon.

When he grew up, he became a schoolmaster, and when he was twenty-three years of age, he started publishing *Mac Talla* as a weekly paper, wholly in Gaelic. It came out so for eight years, and for another four years as a larger version fortnightly. It was read by Gaels not only in Nova Scotia, but also in Scotland and in other parts of the British dominions where Gaelic-speaking emigrants had settled. Unfortunately from *Mac Talla's* point of view, Sydney, the chief town of Cape Breton Island, was the scene of a mining boom after 1900; costs rose steadily and *Mac Talla* ended in 1904 $6,000 in debt.

The first number of *Mac Talla* had appeared on 1 May 1892. Unfortunately the entry for *Mac Talla* amongst the Gaelic periodicals listed in the Rev. Donald Maclean's *Typographia Scoto-Gadelica*, stated that 'this was a weekly Gaelic newspaper published in Sydney, C.B., by J. G. MacKinnon a native (*sic*) of Bernsdale, Skye. With the above number [that of 24 June 1904] the paper ceased on the death of the editor.' This was an astonishing error, as the Rev. Donald MacLean was a Skyeman himself. Unfortunately its appearance in an authoritative volume led to MacKinnon becoming practically forgotten in Scotland.

In fact, he was very much alive. In 1928 he produced a well edited, well printed monthly called *Fear na Céilidh*, and later translations of Tolstoy's *Where Love is, God is*, William van Dyke's *The Other Wise Man*, and Thomas Hardy's *The Three Strangers*. He was understood to be translating Stevenson's *Treasure Island* into Gaelic at the time he died. In 1915 he had published in English *Old Sydney, Sketches of the Town and its People in Days Gone By*.

Jonathan MacKinnon also contributed the article 'Na Gaidheil an Ceap Breton' to *Cape Breton, Canada, at the Beginning of the Twentieth Century* (Toronto, 1903) by C. W. Vernon, pp. 71–81. As Professor C. W. Dunn says in his book *Highland Settler* (Toronto, 1953), 'At a time when the Gaelic-speaking people were becoming ashamed of their own language, the paper (*Mac Talla*) elevated it in their eyes to a position of prestige. Jonathan G. MacKinnon had no cause to feel that his toils and trials had been in vain. Few men could have done more for the language and literature in the New World than he did, and only one—the Reverend A. MacLean Sinclair—did as much.'

Jonathan MacKinnon gave us the greatest encouragement in our recording of this collection of old Gaelic songs in Cape Breton and Antigonish County. In the opinion of the writer, he was a man who, had he had the required academic training, could have filled a Chair of Celtic at any university with great distinction.

1 ANNAG A GHAOIL, HAO ILL O

Annag a ghaoil, hao ill ó,
Hao ill o ro bha ho o,
Annag a ghaoil, hao ill ó.
An cuala sibhs' mar dh'éirich dhòmh? (*dà uair*)

Annag a ghaoil, hao ill ó,
Hao ill o ro bha ho o,

Annag a ghaoil, hao ill ó.

Mar a dh'fhalbh iad leis an dròbh,

Bhrist an t-acair, shrac an seòl,

Chaill mi m'athair is m'fhear pòsd',

5. Chaill mi mo thriùir bhràithrean òg.

Uisd a nighean, sguir dhed' bhròn,

Fhir an taighe, faigh an stòp!

Translation

Refrain: Anna, love, hao ill ó
Hao ill ó ro, bha ho o
Anna, love, hao ill ó.

Did you hear what happened to me?
Now they went away with the drove?
The anchor broke, the sail was torn,
I lost my father and my spouse,
5. I lost my three brothers young
Hush, girl, cease from sorrow,
Goodman, get the stoup.

Recorded from Jonathan MacKinnon, *Mac Talla* at Whycocamagh on 10/9/37. Tune and words transcribed by J. L. Campbell. Compare *Hebridean Folksongs* I XXXVIII, pp. 154 and 338.

COMHRADH

(Eoin Mac Fhionghuin *Mac Talla* agus Niall D. Mac Fhionghuin, Ceap Breatunn)

A. Tiugainn a dh'iomain.
B. Dé 'n iomain?
A. Iomain a' chamain.
B. Dé 'n caman?
A. Caman iubhair.
B. Dé 'n t-iubhar?
A. Iubhar adhar.
B. Dé 'n t-adhar?
A. Adhar ian.
B. Dé 'n t-ian?
A. Ian nidein.
B. Dé 'n nidean?
A. Nidean phreilleach.
B. Dé 'm preilleach?
A. Preilleach eich.
B. Dé 'n t-each
A. Each mór, blàr, buidhe.
B. Dé 'm buidhe?
A. Buidhe ghor^{a}m.
B. Dé 'n gor^{a}m?
A. Gor^{a}m na mara.
B. Dé 'm muir?
A. Muir eisg.
B. Dé 'n t-iasg?
A. Iasg dubhain.
B. Dé 'n dubhan?
A. Dubhan air^{i}gid.
B. Dé 'n t-air^{i}gead?
A. Air^{i}gead a ghoid mi a ciste mhór, bhuidhe
mo sheanamhar. Ma dh' innseas tusa
do dhuine a chunna tu riamh, bheir mise
or^{s}t e, bheir mise or^{s}t e.

Translation

CONVERSATION

(J. G. MacKinnon and Neil D. MacKinnon)

A. Come to play.
B. To play what?
A. To play shinty.
B. What shinty?
A. A shinty of yew.
B. What yew?
A. A yew of the air.
B. What air?
A. Air of birds.
B. What bird?
A. Bird of nest.
B. What nest?
A. Nest of hair.
B. What hair?
A. Horse hair.
B. What horse?
A. A big, white-blazoned, yellow horse.
B. What yellow?
A. Bluish yellow.
B. What blue?
A. Blue of the sea.
B. What sea?
A. Sea of fish.
B. What fish?
A. Fish of hook.
B. What hook?
A. A silver hook.
B. What silver?
A. Silver which I stole from the big yellow chest of my grandmother.
  If you tell anyone you ever saw, I'll beat you for it, I'll beat you for it!

Recorded from Jonathan MacKinnon, *Mac Talla* and Neil D. MacKinnon, at Lake Ainslie, Cape Breton, in 1937. Words transcribed by Dr Calum MacLean.

  Compare version of 17 lines in John Shaw, *Tales Until Dawn*, p. 390 from Alasdair Kennedy. See also Roger Hutchinson *Camanachd!* pp. 45, 46, versions from Islay and Jura.

HECTOR MACKINNON
Ainslie Glen, Isle of Muck tradition

2   DEAN CADALAN SÀMHACH

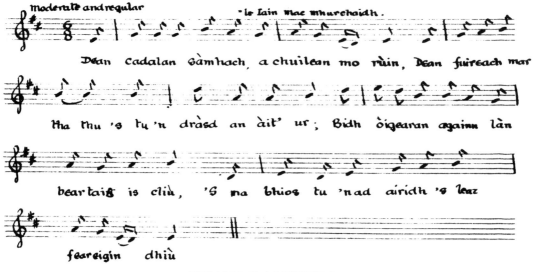

DUANAG ALTRUIM
Le Iain Mac Mhurchaidh

Fonn: Dean cadalan sàmhach, a chuilean mo rùin
Dean fuireach mar thà thu, 's tu 'n dràsd an àit' úr;
Bidh òigearan againn làn beartais is cliù,
'S ma bhios tu 'nad airidh, 's leat feareigin dhiù.

5.   Gur h-ann an America tha sinn an dràsd
Fo dhubhar na coille nach teirig gu bràch;
Nuair dh'fhalbhas an dùldach, 's a thionndas am blàths,
Bidh cnothan is ùbhlan is siùcar a' fàs.

'S ro-bheag orm fhéin cuid de 'n t-sluagh a tha ann,
10.   Le'n còtaichean drogaid, 's ad mhór air an ceann;
Le'm briogaisean goirid, 's iad sgoilte gu 'm buinn;
Cha n-fhaicear an t-osan, 's e bhochdainn sin leam.

82

THE SINGERS AND THEIR SONGS

Tha sinne 'n ar n-Innseanaich cinnteach gu leòir
Fo dhubhar nan craobh cha bhidh h-aon againn beò—
15. Coin-alluidh is béistean ag éigheach 's gach fròig;
Gu bheil sinn 'n ar n-éiginn bho'n thréig sinn Righ Deòrs'.

Mo shoraidh le fàilte Chinn-tàile nam bó,
Far an d'fhuair mi greis àrach, 's mi 'm phàisde beag, òg;
Bhiodh fleasgaichean donna air am bonnaibh ri ceòl,
20. Is nionagan dualach, 's an gruaidh mar an ròs.

An toiseach an fhoghair bu chridheil ar sunnd,
Gheibht' fiadh as an fhireach, is bradan a grunnd,
Bhiodh luingeas an sgadain a' tighinn fo shiùil,
Le'n lasgairean tapaidh nach faicte fo mhùig.

Translation

Sleep quietly, my beloved child,
Stay where you are, you're in a new land,
We will have youths now full of wealth and renoun,
And if you are worthy, you'll have one of them, too.

5. 'Tis in America where we are now,
In the everlasting darkness of the woods:
When the winter is over and warmth returns,
Nuts and apples and (maple) sugar will grow.

Little I like some of the folk who are there
10. With their coats of drugget and big hats on their heads,
With their short trousers, split to the base,
Hose are not seen, that's a pity for me.

We are like Indians surely enough,
In the gloom of the forest no one will survive,
15. With wolves and beasts crying in each nook;
We are in trouble since we abandoned King George.

My best wishes and welcome to Kintail of the cows,
Where I was brought up in my childhood when I was young;
There were brown-haired youths on their feet to sing,
20. And curly-haired girls, with cheeks like the rose.

At the beginning of autumn we were heartily glad
Deer were got on the moor and salmon
Boats fishing herring came under sail,
With able young men, none of them churls.

Recorded at Ainslie Glen on 10/9/37 from Hector MacKinnon, whose ancestors came from the Isle of Muck. Tune transcribed by Séamus Ennis, text communicated by Mgr P. J. Nicolson.

See Margaret MacDonell, *The Emigrant Experience*, p. 42. Séamus Ennis' transcription of the tune from our ediphone recording is printed on 190. Sister Margaret MacDonell says that the poem was made by John MacRae 'Iain Mac Mhurchaidh' who emigrated from Kintail in Scotland to North Carolina around 1774. it was one of the earliest Gaelic songs made in North America.

Notes

Lines 10–13.   This describes the clothing of the English settlers.

Line 15.   King George III. The American revolution began in 1776. Many of the Gaelic-speaking Highlanders who had settled in North Carolina, did not support it. In Scotland Bishop Forbes, the Jacobite compiler of *The Lyon in Mourning*, wrote in 1775, 'War is now lighted up in America. God only knows where it will end R[ebe]l against R[ebe]l, tho' it be melancholy to think' (Vol. III, p. 362).

SE 95; Mode E, pentatonic 2:6.

NEIL MACKINNON
Ainslie Glen, Muck tradition

3   C'ÀIT' AN DIUGH A BHEIL MO DHÌLSEAN?

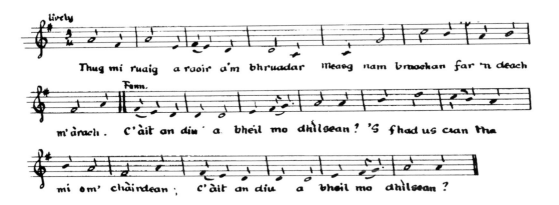

Thug mi ruaig a raoir a'm bhruadar Measg nam bruachan far 'n deach m'àrach. C'ait an diu' a bheil mo dhìlsean? 'S fhad us cian tha mi o m' chàirdean; c'àit an diu a bheil mo dhìlsean?

Seisd: C'àit an diu a bheil mo dhìlsean?
'S fhad' is cian tha mi o m' chàirdean;
C'àit an diu a bheil mo dhìlsean?

Thug mi ruaig an raoir am' bhruadar
Measg nam bruachan far 'n deach m'àrach.

Bha mi 'n dùil gun d'rinn mi triall
Gu Abhainn Mhiadhonach nan àrdbheann.

Mi, ar leam, am measg nan eòlach
A bhiodh geanail, còir mu'n fhàrdaich.

'S math mo chuimhn' air na bha fuireach
Mu na mullaich ud ri m' là-sa.

Gheibhte Domhnallaich an uair sin.
10.   Do'm bu dualach a bhith bàigheil.

Clann Ghill' Fhinnein, gile chìt' ann,
Gillean Sìne, cha robh tàir orr'.

Gheibhte Caimbeulaich mo rùin ann,
Do'm bu dùthchas Earraghaidheal.

85

THE SINGERS AND THEIR SONGS

Thriall an linn ud, mar bu dùth dhaibh,
'S sinne ruith air chùl an sàiltean.

Na tha an diu a' cnàmh fo'n fhòd dhiu,
Fàth mo bhròin a bhith 'gan àireamh.

Ach nuair thig oirnn amm ar caochlaidh,
20.   Chì sinn luchd ar gaoil a dh'fhàg sinn.

Translation

Refrain: Where are my faithful friends today,
Far am I from my relations,
Where are my faithful friends today?

1. Last night in my dream I made a journey amongst the banks where I was nurtured.

2. I hoped to make an expedition to Middle River of the high hills.

3. I felt myself amongst acquaintances, who were cheerful kindly around the fireside.

4. Well I recall those who were staying around those hill-tops in my days there.

5. There were Macdonalds there then, who by nature were kindly.

6. MacKinnons would be seen there, Sheena's lads, of no reproach.

7. My beloved Campbells would be there, whose hereditary home was Argyll.

8. That generation has departed, as was natural, with us running behind their heels.

9. It is the cause of my sorrow to be numbering those of them who are today lying beneath the sod.

10. But when the time comes for us to die, we will see the beloved folk who have left us.

Recorded from Neil MacKinnon, Lake Ainslie, on 10/9/37. Tune transcribed by Séamus Ennis. Words communicated by Mgr P. J. Nicholson. Composed by Rev. Calum Campbell to the tune 'Tha no bhreacan-sa fo'n dìle', 'My plaid is under the flood'. On the effects on a Cape Breton community of emigration to Boston and to western Canada, see *Gesto Collection*, p. 31. Said to have been printed in *Mac Talla* in the 1890s, but I have been unable to find it.

SE 91: Mode ? D, Mixolydian.

MRS J. R. JOHNSTON (née Margaret MacNeil)
Beaver Cove, Barra tradition

We met Mrs John R. Johnston on 24 September 1937 when we stopped at a gasoline filling station at Beaver Cove on the east side of the Bras d'Or Lake. She was in charge. Conversation soon developed, especially when we learnt that her husband belonged to the MacIain clan (the descendants of the dispossessed MacDonalds of Ardnamurchan), like our friend and adviser Miss Annie Johnston, so well known to folklorists visiting the Isle of Barra. When we told her we were collecting old Gaelic songs, she very kindly offered to record some, and invited us to her house, which was quite near by.

In his book about the Beaver Cove district, the Rev. Fr Allan MacMillan describes John R. Johnston as the third child and third son of 'Seumas Iain Ruairidh' Johnston (out of twelve children) Seumas's father having been Iain Ruairidh, who was born in Scotland (and presumably on the Isle of Barra) in 1803. These Johnstons were related to Monsignor P. J. Nicholson through common descent from Fearchar mac Dòmhnaill 'ic Caluim, who was the father of Ruairi who emigrated from Barra around 1806. Annie Johnston and her brother Calum on Barra were considered to be relations, but the precise relationship was uncertain.

According to Fr Allan MacMillan's book, our John R. Johnston was married to Margaret MacKenzie, and they had an adopted daughter, Anastasia, living with them. This does not accord with words on the back of her photograph, given to me by Mrs Johnston: 'Mrs J. R. Johnston, née Margaret MacNeil.' I have been unable to find a reference to a Margaret MacKenzie married to a Johnston in A. J. MacKenzie's *History of Christmas Island Parish*, where MacKenzie families are recorded particularly. My wife and I remember Anastasia, but understood she was Polish.

Mrs Johnston recorded two songs for us, 'A Cholla mo rùin' and 'Port na h-eala (Mo chasan dubh)' on 24 September 1937, and when we recorded her again, along with Mrs MacLean on 1 October she sang ten more. Like her namesake, Annie Johnston on Barra, she excelled at 'little songs' and *puirt-a-beul*. The traditional songs she recorded, apart from those printed in this book, were: 'Port Iain Uilleam', 'Danns, a chlann', 'Uan aig na caoirich uile', 'Crodh an Tàilleir', 'Thuirt an luchag bha 'san toll' and 'Nighean aig a' mhuilleir mhòr'.

15.   Mrs J. R. Johnston, née Margaret MacNeil, Beaver Cove

The locally composed songs she sang were 'Port Mary Anne' and 'Oran an Teine', the last by Lachlan Mac Mhuirich (Currie), Am Bard Ruadh, about a forest fire that got out of hand when a Cape Bretoner was clearing land to sow. This last was also recorded from Mrs Patterson.

It is a great pity that these recordings cannot be played today, and that we did not do more work with her while we were in Cape Breton. There is a version of 'Crodh an Tàilleir' in *Folksongs and Folklore of South Uist*, page 150.

4   THA BO DHUBH AGAM

Tha bó dhubh agam, tha bó dhubh uam, tha bó dhubh agam, tha bó dhubh uam Tha bó dhubh agam, tha bo dhubh uam, Tha trì bà dubh air an leacainn ud shuas.

Tha bó dhubh agam, tha bó dhubh bhuam,
Tha bó dhubh agam, tha bó dhubh bhuam,
Tha bó dhubh agam, tha bó dhubh bhuam,
Tha trì bà dubh air an leacainn ud shuas.

Translation

I have a black cow, I've lost a black cow,
I have a black cow, I've lost a black cow,
I have a black cow, I've lost a black cow,
There are three black cows on yon slopes above.

Recorded on 1/10/37 at Boisdale. Tune transcribed by Margaret Fay Shaw; words transcribed by J. L. Campbell. A lullaby.

Version in *Amhrain Anna Sheumais* (n.d.), p. 2, with tune.

5 AN TARBH BREAC DEARG

An tarbh breac dearg, an tarbh a mharbh mi,
An tarbh breac dearg, an tarbh a mharbh mi,
An tarbh breac dearg, an tarbh a mharbh mi,
Tarbh buidhe, buidhe, buidhe,
Tarbh buidhe, buidhe, a mharbh mi.

Translation

The speckled red bull that did for me,
The speckled red bull that did for me,
The speckled red bull that did for me.
A yellow, yellow, yellow bull,
A yellow, yellow, bull that did for me.

Recorded at Boisdale on 1/10/37. Tune transcribed by Séamus Ennis, words transcribed by J. L. Campbell. A lullaby.

SE 62; Mode Hexatonic, D, no 6.

6   MO CHASAN DUBH

Cu bhi cì, cu bhi cò, Cu bhi cì, cu bhi cò; Cu bhi cì, cu bhi

co, Cu bhi cuan cu bhi cò. Cu bhi cuan, cu bhi cuan, cu bhi

cuan, cu bhi cò; Cu bhi cuan, cu bhi cuan, Cu bhi cuan, cu bhi

cò. Mo chasan dubh, mo chasan dubh, Mo chasan dubh'S mi

fhìn bàn; Mo chasan dubh, mo chasan dubh, Mo chasan dubh'S mi

fhìn bàn.

Cu bhi cì, cu bhi có,
Cu bhi cì, cu bhi có,
Cu bhi cì, cu bhi có,
Cu bhi cuan, cu bhi có,
Cu bhi cuan, cu bhi cuan,
Cu bhi cuan, cu bhi có,
Cu bhi cuan, cu bhi cuan,
Cu bhi cuan, cu bhi có.

Cu bhi cì, cu bhi có
Cu bhi cì, cu bhi có
Cu bhi cì, cu bhi có
Cu bhi cuan, cu bhi có.

Mo chasan dubh,
Mo chasan dubh,
Mo chasan dubh,
'S mi fhìn bàn.

Mo chasan dubh,
Mo chasan dubh,
Mo chasan dubh,
'S mi fhìn bàn.

Cu bhi cì, cu bhi có,
Cu bhi cì, cu bhi có,
Cu bhi cì, cu bhi có,
Cu bhi cuan, cu bhi có,
Cu bhi cuan, cu bhi cuan,
Cu bhi cuan, cu bhi có,
Cu bhi cuan, cu bhi cuan,
Cu bhi cuan, cu bhi có.

Translation
Ku vi ki, ku vi ko (*three times*)
Ku vi kuan, ku vi ko,
Ku vi kuan, ku vi kuan,
Ku vi kuan, ku vi ko,
Ku vi kuan, ku vi kuan,
Ku vi kuan, ku vi ko.

Ku vi kuan, ku vi ko (*three times*)
Ku vi kuan, ku vi ko.

My feet are black,
My feet are black,
My feet are black,
And I am white.

Recorded at Beaver Cove on 24/9/37. Tune transcribed by Séamus Ennis, words translated by J. L. Campbell.

A lullaby. This song was also sung by Miss Annie Johnston on the Isle of Barra. *See Gaelic Songs in Nova Scotia*, p. 142.

See reference to the Swan's song, and other versions in *Carmina Gadelica* II, 276–8. *See also* song number 35 here, line 10.

SE 96; Mode G, Hexatonic, no 7 (4 only in introductory bar).

MRS M. B. MACLEAN (NÉE CATHERINE NICHOLSON)
Beaver Cove, Barra tradition

Alexander Nicholson came to Cape Breton from the Isle of Barra in 1835; his Gaelic patronymic was Alasdair mac Iain 'ic Phadraig 'ic Sheorais. I believe the family originally came to Barra from the Isle of Skye. Alexander had two sons George and Hector, who married sisters, Catherine and Bridget, daughters of Roderick Johnston, who was born in Barra and brought to Cape Breton by his father, also called Roderick, who emigrated as an elderly man. The sisters' line of descent was Catriana (or Bride) nighean Ruairidh 'ic Ruairidh 'ic Fhearchair.

This Fearchar or Farquhar married a widow, Sarah MacVicar, daughter of Roderick Shaw, probably the Roderick Shaw who is mentioned in the account of Barra in the *Old Statistical Account of Scotland*, as tacksman of Allasdale, who is said there to have mortified £100 towards the subsistence of the poor on Barra. Ninety years earlier the Presbyterian Synod of Argyll had made 'A Representation of the most deplorable state of severall Paroches in the Highlands both in the Western Isles and continent within the bounds of the Synod of Argyll in which places the Reformation never obtained, 1703'.[1]

The representation includes, amongst other items, 'A list of children under Popish Parents Tutors or Curators in the conjunct Paroch of South Uist and Barray.' The list includes 'Donald Shau in Barra' with three young children and 'Angus Shau of Ballenicreige' with one child. Ballenicreige (= Baile na Creige) is a township on the west side of Barra, adjacent to Allasdale, and perhaps then including it. An earlier generation may be represented by the Alexander 'Shein', possibly a misreading of 'Shau', who was schoolmaster on Barra in 1675.

Apart from this 'mortification' of £100 on behalf of the sustenance of the poor of Barra, there was a Shaw legacy of which the terms are now unknown; in a letter dated 19 May 1825, General MacNeil of Barra, who had succeeded to the estate three years earlier, asked the Rev. Angus MacDonald, parish priest of Barra, for its history. Unfortunately his reply is lost, with other MacNeil of Barra papers. But it is clear from what Monsignor P. J. Nicholson told the writer, that through their connection with the Shaws from their descent from Farquhar Johnston and

[1] See *Maitland Miscellany* III, 424–31, a genealogical source which seems to have been overlooked by the historians of the *Clan MacNeil*; also *Tales from Barra, told by the Coddy*, p. 35.

Sarah MacVicar, née Shaw, that George Nicholson and his wife had some claim on it, which was eventually successfully pursued.

Catherine, Mrs M. B. Maclean, was thus Monsignor P. J. Nicholson's double first cousin. It was through him that my wife and I obtained an introduction to her on our recording trip in 1937. She had a fine voice, and it is our regret that we did not have more time, or spend more time, working with her.

7 AILEIN DUINN, O HÌ SHIUBHLAINN LEAT

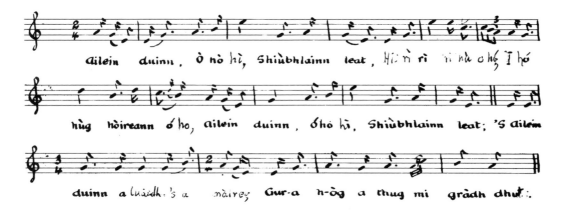

Fonn: Ailein duinn ó ho hì, shiùbhlainn leat,
        Hi rì rì ri, hù o hó, i hó hùg hoireann ó ho,
        Ailein duinn, ó ho hì, shiùbhlainn leat.

        'S Ailein duinn, a luaidh 's a nàire,
        Gura h-òg a thug mi gràdh dhut,

        Gura h-òg a thug mi gràdh dhut,
        Nuair a bha sinn beag 'nar pàisdean.

Translation

Brown-haired Allan, o ho hi, I would go with thee.
Brown-haired Allan, my love, my darling
I was young when I first loved you.
I was young when I first loved you,
When we were but little children.

Recorded from Mrs MacLean, Beaver Cove, on 1/10/37. Tune transcribed by Séamus Ennis; words transcribed by J. L. Campbell. The singer probably knew more verses. See *Hebridean Folksongs*, I, 44–7, and *Folksongs and Folklore of South Uist*, pp. 258–61, for full versions of this fine lament, with notes, and other versions of the air.

C#, mistakenly entered in the key signature, has been deleted. F#, which does not occur in the scale, has also been removed from Ennis's transcription.

SE 102. Mode Hexatonic ?A, no 6, ? E, no 2.

8 'S A MHIC IAIN 'IC SHEUMAIS

'S a Mhic Iain 'ic Sheumais,

    Tha do sgeul air m'aire,

    Air fair ó al e ó,
    Air fair ó al e ó,

Latha Blàr na Féithe,

    Bha feum air mo leannabh,

    I hó I rì ó,
    I éileadh é hó,
    I rì 's na ho ro ho hao ó,
    Chall éileadh ó hi ri ó ho, ì ó.

Translation

O son of John son of James,
    Your story is on my mind,

The day of the Battle of the Bog,
    There was need for my child.

Recorded by J. L. Campbell at Beaver Cove on 1/10/37. Tune and words (all sung) transcribed by Séamus Ennis. The singer only remembered the first two couplets and the divided refrain.

SE 103; Mode, G, Hexatonic, no 7.

For full (conflated) text and translation, see *Hebridean Folksongs* III, no. CIV, pp. 94–9; for the full story of the circumstances that gave rise to the song, based on the traditions collected by the late Rev. John McDonald (1830–68), a native of Benbecula, see the notes to the same text, *ibid.* pp. 250–6. The song is about the famous battle of Carinish, fought in North Uist in 1601 between a band of MacLeod raiders, who were taken off their guard while feasting by a much smaller party of MacDonalds led by Donald MacDonald. 'Domhnall mac Iain 'ic Sheumais', tacksman of Eriskay, whose brilliant leadership and tactics resulted in a total defeat of the MacLeods. In the battle Domhnall mac Iain 'ic Sheumais was himself wounded.

ARCHIBALD JAMES MACKENZIE
Christmas Island, Barra tradition

Archibald James MacKenzie, known as 'Eairdsidh Sheumais' was born at Rear Christmas Island, Cape Breton, on 12 May 1861, and died there on 30 May 1939. He was the son of James MacKenzie, 'Seumas Dhomhnaill 'ic Eachainn' (James son of Donald son of Hector), and Catherine MacDougall, 'Catriana Eachainn Ruaidh 'ic Calum Muilleir' (Catherine daughter of red-haired Hector, daughter of Calum the Miller). The Hector MacKenzie who was Archibald James's great-grandfather was Hector MacKenzie of the Glen, near Castlebay, Barra, who was mentioned approvingly by Col. Roderick MacNeil of Barra in a letter to the Rev. Angus MacDonald, parish priest of Barra dated 8 August 1816.

In his time Archibald James MacKenzie was one of the outstanding personalities in the Gaelic world of Nova Scotia. He was very well known as a teacher, scholar, Gaelic poet, genealogist, and farmer. His *History of Christmas Island Parish*, 1926, with Introduction by the Rev. Patrick J. Nicholson, is a mine of information on local traditions and local families going back to the time of the settlement of the district (the east side of the Bras d'Or Lake from Benacadie to Beaver Cove) mostly by emigrants from South Uist and Barra in Scotland.

Besides this information, the book contains eighteen topical Gaelic songs by twelve different persons, nine men (one himself) and three women. MacKenzie was most sympathetic to our recording work; he himself recorded nine traditional songs for us, as well as three of his own compositions, his songs on the 'Hunters', on 'Old Age' and his song 'In Praise of the Old Lady'. One of the traditional Barra songs which he sang was 'A Mhic a' Mhaoir' (The Son of the Steward), which is discussed here in Mrs Neil MacInnis's section (see page 166), and in *Hebridean Folksongs* II, 150–3, 244–6 and 338–40. he also recorded a story he wrote, 'Driod-fhortain Ruairidh', 'Rory's Misfortunes', which he told us had been printed in the magazine *Teachdaire nan Gaidheal*, published at Sydney (vol. IV, no. 12, p. 5).

MacKenzie also contributed many articles on historical subjects to the Cape Breton Press, and was a noted violinist. He was greatly missed. After his decease, his son Hugh carried on the tradition, becoming a prominent figure in Cape Breton Gaelic circles, and hosted the Canadian Broadcasting Corporation's programme, 'MacTalla an Eilein' (The Echo of the Island). He died in 1971.

16.   A. J. MacKenzie, Christmas Island, Cape Breton

9 GURA MISE THA FO MHULAD, 'S MI AIR UILINN NA STÙIC

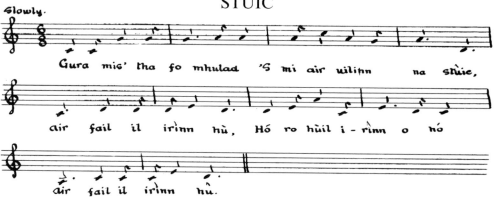

Fonn: Air fail i rinn hù,
Hó ro hùil i rìnn o hó,
Air fail i rìnn hu.

1. Gura mise that fo mhulad
   'S mi air uilinn na stùic

2. 'S mi coimhead Caol Muile,
   'S cha ghrunnaich mi null,

3. Far na dh'fhàg mi mo mhàthair
   Air a càradh 'san ùir.

4. Far na dh'fhàg mi mo leannan.
   Caol mhala is rosg ciùin.

5. Chì mi bàta caol daraich
   A' dol seachad ri smùid.

6. Mura deachaidh mi am mearachd,
   Tha mo leannan air an stiùir.

7. I air bharr nan tonn uaine,
   Is muir a' suaineadh na siùil.

8. I air bharr nan tonn glasa,
   Is muir a' slachdraich m'a bùird.

9. A' dol seachad air Eige,
   Tìr chreagach nan stùc.

10. A' dol seachad air Ile,
    Leam is ìseal a cùrs'.

11. A' dol seachad air Éirinn,
    Chaidh m'eudail do'n ghrùnn.

12. Chaidh m'eudail do'n fheamain,
    A' dol fairis a null.

13. 'S daor a cheannaich mi an t-eòrna,
    Cha mhór a dh'òl mi dha 'n liùnn.

14. 'S daor a cheannaich mi 'n sgadan,
    Chaidh a phacadh as ùr.

Translation

1. I am sorrowful on the shoulder
   of the peak.

2. Looking at the Sound of Mull,
   unable to wade across.

3. Where I left my mother, who had been
   put into the ground.

4. Where I met my sweetheart
   of thin eyebrows and calm eyes.

5. I saw a slender oaken ship
   going past at speed.

6. Unless I am wrong, my lover
   was at the helm.

7. On the top of the green waves,
   with the sea twisting the sails.

8. On the top of the grey waves,
   with the sea breaking on her planks.

103

9. Going past Eigg, the rocky land
   of peaks.

10. Going past Islay, I thought her
    course was off-shore.

11. Going past Ireland, my
    love went to the bottom.

12. My love went to the
    seaweed going over across.

13. Dearly I paid for the barley,
    little I drank of the beer.

14. Dearly I paid for the herring,
    which had been packed fresh.

Recorded from A. J. MacKenzie at Christmas Island, Cape Breton, on 29/9/37; text communicated by the singer.

Gaelic Songs in Nova Scotia, p. 20, 17 verses, from Angus MacLellan, Grand Mira South.

SE 144; Mode, C pentatonic, 4:7.

10 O, GUR MISE THA FO MHÌGHEAN

Fonn: O, gur mise that fo mhìghean,
         'S iad 'gam dhìteadh 's mi 'nam ònar;
         O, gur mise tha fo mhìghean.

1. Iad 'gam dhìteadh moch is feasgar,
       Chionn gun dug mi greis air gòraich;
   Iad 'gam dhìteadh air son gruagaich;
       Chionn gun gheall mi uair a pòsadh.

2. Iasd 'gam dhiteadh air son gruagaich,
       Chionn gun gheall mi uair a pòsadh;
   Thug iad mise leo am prangal,
       Agus sreang ac' air mo dhòrnan.

3. Thug iad mise &c
   Nuair a ruigeas iad Dùn Éideann,
       Chì iad fhéin gu bheil iad gòrach.

4. Nuair a ruigeas iad &c
   Coirneil Iain is Caiptein Caimbeul,
       Anns gach cainnt gu bheil iad eòlach.

5. Coirneil Iain &c.
   Ruigidh sinn an Coirneil Grannda,
    'S bheir e 'n t-sreang-sa far mo dhòrnan.

6. Ruigidh sinn &c.
   'S gum bi mise an uair sin sgaoilte
    Feadh an t-saoghail, mar bu chòir dhomh.

7. 'S gum bi mise &c
   Tillidh mi dhachaidh gu m' mhàthair,
    Bho 's i fhéin a dh'àraich òg mi.

8. Tillidh mi dhachaidh &c.
   Far am biodh na gillean sùgach,
    Leam bu shunndach dol 'nan còmhdhail.

9. Far am biodh &c.
   B'aotrom a rachainn 'nan coinnibh
    Air mo bhonnaibh gun na brògan.

10. B'aotrom a rachainn &c
    Ged a bhiodh an reothadh cruaidh ann,
     'S sneachda 'ga chur suas air mhòintich.

11. Ged a bhiodh &c
    'S truagh nach robh mise is mo ghruagach
     'N lagan uaigneach buain an eòrna.

12. 'S truagh nach robh &c
    Mo làmh air do chuailein rìomhach,
     'S an sìoda 'ga chur an òrdan.

THE SINGERS AND THEIR SONGS

Translation

Refrain: O, I am in ill humour,
Condemned and alone;
O, I am in ill humour.

1. They condemn me late and early
   Because for a while I was foolish,
   They condemn me because of a maiden
   Because once I promised we would marry.

2. They condemned me for a maiden,
   Because once I promised we would marry;
   They put me in the stocks,
   With a rope upon my wrists,

3. They put me in the stocks, *etc.*
   When Edinburgh they reach,
   They will see that they were foolish.

4. When Edinburgh they reach, *etc.*
   Colonel Ian and Captain Campbell,
   In every talk that they are knowing.

5. Colonel John and Captain Campbell, *etc.*
   We will reach Colonel Grant,
   He'll take the rope off my wrists.

6. We will reach Colonel Grant, *etc.*
   I will then be let free
   Through the world, as I ought to.

7. I will then be let free, *etc.*
   I will go home to my mother,
   Since 'twas she who reared me young.

8. I will go home to my mother, *etc.*
   Where there were merry lads,
   I'll be happy in their company.

9. Where there were merry lads, *etc.*
   Lightly I'd go to meet them
   On my bare feet, without shoes on.

10.   Lightly I'd go to meet them, *etc.*
       though there were hard frost,
       And snow falling on the moorland.

11.   Though there were hard frost, *etc.*
       Pity my girlfriend and I were not
       In a lonely valley reaping barley.

12.   Pity my girlfriend and I were not, *etc.*
       with my hand on your pretty tresses,
       With silk put in order.

Recorded at Christmas Island on 29/9/37. Tune transcribed by Séamus Ennis; text communicated by the singer.

See *Bàrdachd a Albainn Nuaidh*, pp. 87–8, 16 lines and refrain, from A. A. Quinn, Coxheath.

SE 145; Mode, A 2 and # 6 once each, weak.

11 CÙL RI M' LEANNAN 'S E THUG MI AN DIU

Fonn: Cùl ri m' leannan 's e thug mi an diu,
        'S ùr an cailin tha mi an deídh oirr';
        Cùl ri m' leannan 's e thug mi an diu.

1.   Cùl ri m' leannan briathrach, bòidheach,
     Beul nan òran 's nan deagh-bheusan,
     Cùl ri m' leannan 's e thug mi an diu &c.

2.   Cùl ri m' leannan ciallach, banail,
     B'òg dhuinn dealachadh ri chéile.
     Cùl ri m' leannan 's e thug mi an diu &c.

3.   Gur tric a bha mi 's tu mireadh
     Timchioll air innis na spréidhe.
     Cùl ri m' leannan &c.

4.   Gur tric a bha mi 's tu sùgradh
     Muigh air chùl nam beanntan sléibhe,
     Cùl ri m' leannan &c.

5.   Giùlain mo shoraidh g'a h-ionnsaigh,
     I phùsadh a rogha céile.
     Cùl ri m' leannan &c.

109

THE SINGERS AND THEIR SONGS

Translation

Refrain: I left my sweetheart behind today,
young is the lass whom I'm fond of;
I left my sweetheart behind today.

1.   I left behind my pretty, talkative sweetheart,
of tuneful lips and good manners;
Today my sweetheart and I parted.

2.   I left behind my sensible, womanly sweetheart,
we were young parting from each other.

3.   Often you and I were playing
On the meadow of the cattle.

4.   Often you and I were flirting
outside behind the mountain slope.

5.   Take to her my best wishes,
may she marry a choice husband.

Recorded at Christmas Island, 29/9/37; tune transcribed by Séamus Ennis; words communicated by the singer.

There are two more verses on the ediphone cylinder, which cannot be played now.

SE 146; Mode A, Dorian.

12 GURA MISE THA GU CIANAIL

Gura mise tha gu cianail 'S e seo bhliadhna a cràidh mi, Ó horó na hùg hó, Seinn ó horó nàil-ibh, Ó horó na hùg hó.

Fonn: O ho ró na hùg ó,
Seinn ó ho ró nàilibh,
O ho ró na hùg ó.

1. Gura mise tha gu cianail,
    'S e seo bhliadhna a chràidh mi.

2. 'S mi ri coimhead nan stuaghan
    Thug bhuam mo thriùir bhràithrean.

3. 'S mi ri faicinn nan gillean
    'S iad 'san linne 'gam bhàthadh.

4. Dh'fhalbh mo chompanach gasda,
    Fàth mo chreach *thu 'gad bhàthadh.*

5. Gura mise th'air mo sgaradh
    Tilleadh dhachaidh gu *m'fhàrdach.*

6. 'S mi gun mhac, gun *fhear-taighe,*
    Gun athair, gun bhràithrean.

111

Translation

1. 'Tis I who am sorrowful, this is the year
   which has hurt me.

2. Watching the waves, which took my three
   brothers from me.

3. Waiting for the lads, who were drowned in
   the firth.

4. My fine husband has gone, I am bereft by
   his drowning.

5. I am distraught coming home to my dwelling.

6. I am without a son, without a husband,
   without a father, without brothers.

Recorded from Archibald J. MacKenzie at Christmas Island on 29/9/37. Tune transcribed by Séamus Ennis; words taken down by J. L. Campbell. The words in italics are supplied to fill blanks in my transcription.

See *Folksongs and Folklore of South Uist,* p. 262, and the *MacDonald Collection*, p. 351. One of the Hebridean songs that lament deaths by drowning, a tragedy too frequent in the old days.

SE 147; Mode, 6-note compass—A.

Mrs DAVID PATTERSON (née MacNeil)
Benacadie, Barra Tradition

Mrs David Patterson, the gifted traditional singer living at Benacadie, Cape Breton, in 1937, was a daughter of Allan MacNeil and Mary MacInnis. Allan was the son of Malcolm MacNeil and Catherine MacDonald, who was a daughter of Major MacDonald of the Isle of Moray (*sic*), who was in charge of the garrison at Chatham, New Brunswick. This Malcolm in early life was working in the lumber woods of Miramichi, New Brunswick; he afterwards settled at Benacadie in Cape Breton.

Malcolm was the son of Rory MacNeil and Ann MacKinnon; Ann MacKinnon was a daughter of Donald Ban MacKinnon who came to Pictou in Nova Scotia in 1802 from the Isle of Barra in Scotland, and settled at Coopers Pond, Grand Narrows, in Cape Breton. (Grand Narrows, where the railway bridge crosses the Bras d'Or Lake, was originally called in Gaelic 'Caolas nam Barrach', from the number of emigrants from the Isle of Barra who settled on each side.)

Rory MacNeil came to Pictou in 1802, and from there to Piper's Cove, Cape Breton, in 1805, settling there; he was a son of John MacNeil, son of Rory MacNeil, who was piper to the Laird of Barra (this was probably Roderick MacNeil of Barra, 1693–1763). Rory MacNeil was the great-great-grandfather of Mrs Patterson on her father's side.

Mrs Patterson's mother Mary MacInnis was a daughter of John MacInnis and Catherine MacKinnon; Catherine MacKinnon was the daughter of John MacKinnon at Big Pond, Cape Breton.

John MacInnis settled in Castle Bay, Cape Breton (called after Castlebay on the Isle of Barra, and near to Benacadie); he was the son of Michael MacInnis and Catherine Galbraith; he came from Barra in the year 1817, and settled at Castle Bay. He was the son of Rory MacInnis from Barra. This Rory MacInnis on Barra was the great-great-grandfather of Mrs Patterson on her mother's side of the family.

The marriage of Mrs Patterson's paternal grandparents involved an elopement which was famous in Cape Breton. The story was communicated to me by the late Rt Rev. Monsignor P. J. Nicolson, President of St Francis Xavier University, who himself obtained it from his friend Rod Farrell, the postmaster at Benacadie, and sent it to me in a letter dated 7 October 1948.

17. Mrs Patterson, Benacadie, and JLC, who had lost his voice

The story of Malcolm MacNeil's escapade in the Miramichi woods is a Cape Breton legend. At the time, which was around the middle of the last century, one of the very few ways in which Cape Breton farmers could earn a little money with which to pay taxes, priest's dues and such things, was to work in the lumber woods of Miramichi district, which is still famous for its woods, and this is a small miracle in view of the millions of tons that have been removed since the pioneer days. Malcolm MacNeil walked to a lumber camp and it seems that the Major's daughter took a fancy to him. He was not tall, but he was well set up, active, and exceedingly strong. Anyhow, according to the story she eloped with him and walked through the woods to Benacadie where she was received into the Church and an old-time wedding was held in a log hut. The women of the district came in to prepare the wedding feast, and the bride's lack of sophistication is illustrated by her inquiry as to why the silverware was not being put on the table. I do not know how much luxury there was in Major MacDonald's home but it is reasonable to suppose that the standard of living was much higher than that of the Benacadie woods. The tradition is that she got down to doing the farm work and to raising a family and that no one ever heard her complain about her lot.

One of her grandsons, James MacNeil, is a coal mine manager.... One of his boys studied medicine in Scotland, practised his profession in England during the early war years, entered the Canadian army and is now located in Montreal.

13   TROD NAN CAILLEACH

I

Mrs Patterson

Cha déid Mór a Bharraidh bhrònaich, Hó ró, hùg a bhì.

Mode: Hexatonic ?E. No. 2. Variable. 6

II

Mrs N. MacInnis

Cha déid mór a Bharraidh bhrònaich, Hó ró, hùg a bhì.

Mode: Pentatonic ? E. 2:6.

Cha déid Mór a Bharraidh bhrònaich,
Hó, ro, hùg a bhì,[1]
Cha déid Caitriana 'ga deòin ann,
No Anna bheag ma's i as òige,
Far am bi na sgait a' fleòdradh,
5. Muirsgein 'gan tarruing a lònaibh,
Bheireadh strùbain 'sa bhiadh lòin dhaibh!

'S marbhaisg air bleideig na Ròdha!
C'uim' nach do dh'fhoighneachd thu 'm bheò mi?
Gheobhadh tu comain do chòmhraidh!
10. 'S truagh nach robh thu seal air m'òrdan
'S da shac diag gu teine mòna,
'S do theanga a bhith air bior ròsda,
Slaodadh ris an Tùr air ròpa,
'S na coin mhóra bhith 'gad shròiceadh,
15. Na mucan ag iche t'fheòla!
C'a' na shuidh i air a còta
Nighean Tighearna no Tòisich,
Ged a bhiodh i air a h-òradh
O mhullach a cinn gu a brògan
20. Nach b'airidh Gill' Eóghanan Òg oirr'?
'S ann bha e shliochd nam fear móra
Thogadh creach 's a thilleadh tòrachd!
Cha b'e mo thìr an tir bhrònach,

[1] An déidh a h-uile streath.

116

Tir a' choirce, tir an eòrna,
25. Tir uisge bheatha agus beòire,
Dh'fhàsadh peasair, dh'fhàsadh pònair,
Dh'fhàsadh biolair air a lòintean,
Gheobhadh Eireannaich an leòr ann,
Nam fòghnadh muc, ìm, is feòil dhaibh!

Cha do ghabh Anna Nill Ruaidh an Casadh idir, ach ghabh Bean Dhàibhidh Patterson e, an déidh dhith na ceathramhnan 1, 2, 3, 4, 23, 24 28 an seo a ghabhail:

An Casadh

Chailleach chrubach, ó hùg o, Lùgach, iollagach, ó hùg o.

An Casadh

30. Chailleach shùgach,   lùgach, iollagach,
      ó hùg o,   ó hùg o,
    Bheireadh tu, na,   long fo a seòlain,
    'M barraibh nam beann   mór Di-Dòmhnaich,
    B'fheàrr a bhith muigh   'na mo bhreacan—
    Chailleach shùgach   *bu tu a' bhradag,*
35. Shluigeadh tu   a' mhuc le gaoiseid,
    Shluigeadh tu na   searraich mhaola.

Translation

THE OLD WIVES' FLYTING

The South Uist bardess begins:
Mór will not go to miserable Barra
Nor will Catriana of her free will,
Nor little Anna, the youngest,
Where skates are being marinated,
5. Razor fish are pulled from puddles,
Cockles are the food that's eaten.

The Barra bardess replies:
Curses on the Uist blether
Why didn't you ask if I were living?
You'd get a return for your language!
10. Pity you weren't a while at my order
With twelve sacks of peat for a bonfire,

With your tongue on a spit for roasting
Hanging from the tower of the castle
With big dogs tearing at you
15.   And swine feeding on your flesh!

Where did there sit in her mantle
A laird's or a thane's daughter,
Though from head to foot she were gilded,
Of whom young Gilleonan was unworthy?
20.   For he was of the race of great men
Who'd lift a spoil, repulse pursuers?

My land is not a wretched country,
A land of oats, a land of barley,
A land of beer and of whisky.
25.   Peas and beans would grow there
Upon its ponds grow water cresses,
Irishmen would find their plenty
If pork, butter and beef sufficed them!

The Accelerated Part
30.   O you drunken   creeping, giddy, hag,
You would set   a ship on its courses,
On the top of the great   hills on Sunday
I'd sooner be outside   in my plaid!
Drunken Cailleach   you were the thief,
You'd eat the pig   with its bristles
You would eat   the hairless foals.

The first part of the song recorded from Mrs MacInnis at Glace Bay on 8/10 37; Seven lines of the first part, and the *Casadh* or accelerated second part was recorded from Mrs David Patterson at Benacadie on 30/9/37.

Tunes transcribed by Séamus Ennis; words transcribed by J. L. Campbell. SE gives the *Casadh* the same key signature as the main tune, but with C written in the first bar. It seems rather to be C sharp slightly flattened. AMF ascribes the same mode.

See *Hebridean Folksongs* II, pp.112–21, for a full version based on the versions preserved by Calum and Annie Johnston on Barra. This was the first time the song had been printed. The Cape Breton singers only sung the first line of the refrain of the first part, as they had no supporting singers to complete the refrain, which in full as sung on Barra is:

> Hó ró, hùgaibh ì,
> Hùgaibh íse, 'n dùgaibh éileadh,
> Hó ró, hùgaibh ì.

The first line is sung by the soloist, the second and third lines by the chorus. In Cape Breton, no chorus was present.

The song concerns the occasion of the bardic contest at the waulking board between Nic Iain Fhinn, 'the daughter of white haired John ', MacNeil of Barra's bardess, and Nic a' Mhanaich, 'the Monk's daughter', Clanranald's bardess. The two chiefs had bet each other that their protégée would win. The contest was held at the waulking board, at Ormaclate Castle, Clanranald's residence in South Uist, with Nic 'a Mhanaich beginning, as above. She was soon cut off by Nic Iain Fhinn (who is said to have acquired the art of composing poems from a fairy lover) who attacked her so bitterly with biting satire, that she fell dead at the waulking board. The Uistmen rose up to attack Nic Iain Fhinn, but she escaped with the Barra crew who brought her, triumphant.

I was told in Cape Breton that this song was not allowed to be sung at concerts or céilidhs where Uistmen and Barramen were present, as it could provoke a fight.

Notes

Lines 1, 2, 3. The historicity of this song is shown by the fact that Mór, Catriana and Anna were the actual daughters of Iain Mùideartach of Clanranald, living in the middle of the seventeenth century, and Catriana actually did marry Gilleonan MacNeil of Barra, the wedding contract, which exists in the Clanranald papers, being dated 28 April 1653. Mór (now usually used in the diminutive 'Mórag', or anglicised 'Sarah') married MacLean of Coll, and Anna married Macdonald of Benbecula.

Line 4. *Fleòdradh* means 'washing', see Fr Allan McDonald's *Gaelic Words from South Uist*. Skates have to be washed in salt water before being cured or eaten, to get rid of the urea in their flesh. Skate, razor fish (a long bivalve shellfish living in the sand) and cockles, were held in contempt as sea food in the old Highlands, where only salmon and trout amongst fish were respected.

Line 7. The Ròdha is a promontory of the west side of South Uist; I have translated it 'Uist' here, as it is used figuratively for the island.

Line 12. *Ròsda* is the genitive of *ròsdadh,* compare *pòsda* genitive of *pòsadh*.

Line 13. An Tùr—The tower of Kishmul Castle, residence of the MacNeils of Barra. The *Casadh* as sung by Mrs Patterson is very incomplete. On Barra the refrain *O hùg o* preceded the half lines; in Cape Breton it followed them.

Line 30. Translating *sùgach* in the Irish sense of 'joyful after drink'.

Lines 31, 32, imply that Nic a' Mhanaich was a witch.

Line 34. Second half of line supplied from Barra version.

SE 49, 50.

14 BHA MISE 'N RAOIR AIR AN ÀIRIGH

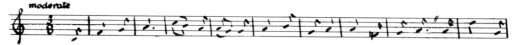

Bha mise 'n raoir air an àirigh, Hù hoirionn ó, hù hòi rionn ó ; Cha b'ann ri

aighear a bha mi, Hò ro éileadh, ó hoirionn ó.

Hù hoireann ó, hù hoireann ó,
Bha mise 'n raoir air an àirigh.
Hù hoireann ó, hù hoireann ó,
Cha b'ann ri aighear a bhà mi,
Ho ro èileadh, ó hoireann o.
Cha b'ann ri aighear a bhá mi,
Hù hoireann ó, hù hoireann ó,
Ach a' smaointinn ort, a ghràidhein,
Ho ro èileadh, ó hoireann ó.
Ach a' smaointinn ort, a ghràidhein,
Hù hoireann ó, hù hoireann ó,
'S mi 'n dùil nach cumadh muir làn thu,
Ho ro èileadh, ó hoireann ó.
'S mi 'n dùil, *etc.*
  5. 'S nach cumadh lìonadh no tràghadh,
'S nach cumadh athair no mhàthair,
'S nach cumadh piuthar no bràthair,
'S nach mutha chumadh an té bhàn thu,
A dh'aindheoin a cuid cruidh no gràisich.

 10. Bha mi'n raoir air àirigh luachrach,
Dh'fhairich mi crith 's cha bu chrith fuachd i;
Dh'fhairich mi fear làimhe fuaire
Sgaoileadh nan arm 'n taobh shuas dhomh,
Sgaoileadh nan criosan mu'n cuairt dhomh,
 15. Bhuail mi sad air 's leag mi bhuam e,
Thug cùl a chinn lag 'san luathaidh.

Fhleasgaich a shiubhlas am fireach,
Gabh mo chomhairle 's dean tilleadh,
Na taobh ri banchaig a' ghlinne,
 20. O, ged a ruigeadh a falt a slinnein.
'S e nach dona an tochradh fir e
'S e na's fheàrr na tochradh gille.

120

Fhleasgaich, ma théid thu 'n taigh òsda,
Na bi ri ceannach an stòpa,
25. Masa math leat mise phòsadh,
Gabh an togsaid mhór 's gu leòr innt'.

Translation

LAST NIGHT I WAS AT THE SHEILING

Divided refrain: 1. Hù hoireann ó, hù hoireann ó
2. Hó ro éileadh, ó hoireann ó.

Last night I was at the sheiling,
I was not joyful,
But thinking of you, my beloved,
Expecting that high tide would not keep you,
5. That full tide nor ebb would keep you,
That father nor mother would keep you,
That sister nor brother would keep you,
That neither would the fair girl keep you,
In spite of her granary or her cattle.

10. Last night I was in a rushy sheiling,
I felt shivering, but not from sickness,
I felt a cold-handed fellow
Spreading his weapons on the far side of me,
Spreading belts around me;
15. I struck him a quick blow and thrust him from me,
The back of his head made a hollow in the ashes.

Young man who walks on the moorland,
Take my advice, turn back now,
Don't take up with the dairymaid in the glen,
20. Even if her hair reaches her shoulders,
And is no poor dowry for a man,
And is better than a lad's dowry.

Young man, if the inn you enter,
Do not stoups be buying;
25. If you want to marry me,
Take the big hogshead, it holds plenty.

121

Recorded from Mrs Patterson at Benacadie on 6/10/37. Tune transcribed by Séamus Ennis; words transcribed by J. L. Campbell.

See *Gaelic Songs in Nova Scotia* 130 (six lines), recorded from Hugh F. MacKenzie, Grand Narrows; HF II, 54–9, two versions, 31 and 30 lines; KCC 24, 44 lines (these three versions including a purely formulaic passage of 8 or 9 lines that occurs in several different songs); Calum Johnston, Barra, notebook p. 10, 26 lines, very close to Mrs Patterson's version.

It would be very interesting to know the story behind this song. Sheilings were huts used by the women who tended and milked the cattle put on the mountain grazings during the summer. A *banchag* was a woman in charge of a dairy, more important than a *banarach* 'milkmaid'. The point of lines 20–2 is that though the beauty of the dairymaid might be sufficient dowry for an established man, it was not enough to endow a young man's marriage.

SE 109; Mode, D, Dorian 2:6.

15   COISICH, A RÙIN

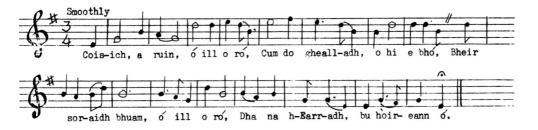

Cois-ich, a ruin, ó ill o ró, Cum do gheall-adh, o hi e bhó, Bheir

sor-aidh bhuam, ó ill o ró, Dha na h-Earr-adh, bu hoir-eann ó.

Coisich, a rùin, ó ill oró,   cum do ghealladh, o hì e bhó,
Bheir soraidh bhuam, ó ill oró,   dha na h-Earradh, bu hòireann ó.
Bheir soraidh bhuam, ó ill oró,   dha na h-Earradh, o hì e bhó,
Gu Iain Caimbeul, ó ill oró,   donn mo leannan, bu hòireann ó.
Sealgair geòidh thu,   ròin is eala,
5 Bric a nì leum,   'n fhéidh nì langan.

S fliuch an oidchche   nochd 's gur fuar i,
Ma thug Clann Nìll   druim a' chuain orr'
Luchd nan seòl geal,   's nan long luatha,
'S nam brataichean   dearg is uaine,
10. Cha n-fhear cearraig   bheireadh bhuat i,
No fear deaslaimh   ma's i as cruaidhe;
Beannachd 'n sin dha   'n t-saor a dh'fhuaghail i,
Dh'fhàg e dìonach   laidir luath i.
Aigeannach gu   siubhail cuain i.

15. 'S gur tric a laigh   mi fo d'earradh,
Ma laigh, cha b'ann   aig a' bhaile,
Duilleach nan craobh   bhith 'gar falach,
Deatach a' cheò   bhith 'gar dalladh,
Uiste (sic) fìorghlan   fuarghlan fallain.

20. Gura mise   th'air mo sgaradh!
Réiteach a nochd   bhith 'nad bhaile,
Ma thà, 's cha n-ann   gus do bhanais,
Ach gus do chur   an ùir am falach,
'N ciste chinn-chaoil,   saoir 'ga barradh.

Translation

Walk my beloved,   keep your promise,
Take greetings from me   to the isle of Harris,
To John Campbell   my brown-haired lover,
Hunter of geese   of seals and swans,
5. Of leaping trout   and of bellowing deer.

Wet is the night   tonight, and cold
If Clann MacNeil   took to the high sea,
Folk of white sails   and of swift ships
And of banners   red and green
10. It was no left-hander   would take it (the helm) from you
Nor a right-hander   even if stronger,
A blessing then   to the wright who seamed her,
Who left her watertight,   strong and speedy,
Seaworthy to   sail the ocean.

15. Often I lay   beneath your habit,
If I did, 'twas   not at home
The foliage of the trees   did conceal us,
The misty fog   made us unsighted,
In clean cold rain,   pure and healthy.

20. It is I   who am distraught,
A betrothal party   tonight in your townland!
If there is, it's not   for your wedding,
But to bury you   in concealment,
In a slender coffin   closed by joiners.

Recorded at Benacadie on 4/10/37. Tune transcribed by Séamus Ennis; words transcribed by J. L. Campbell. Disc copies were made of this recording; one was presented to St Francis Xavier University, Antigonish, another to the National Library of Scotland.

See particularly *HF*, II, 149 (to compare with Miss Annie Johnston's version, from Barra), where the translation of line 1344 *Nan cluinninn té eil' bhith luaidh ort* should be 'If I heard another woman named in connection with you.'

Line 15. His 'habit' would have been the Highland plaid.
Line 19. The singer (Mrs Patterson) had the pronunciation *Uiste* for *Uisge*, 'water'. I have not heard this elsewhere, but it occurs in Manx Gaelic, *Usht* or *Ushtee*.

The song is of the type in which an eight-syllable line is divided into halves, and the halves sung in pairs with alternating refrains, as is indicated here at the beginning of the Gaelic text.

SE 105; Mode, E, Hexatonic, no 6 (2:6). the key signature is given by SE as two sharps, but C# does not occur in the tune.

Nuair a leugh mi do dh'Anna Neil Ruaidh an t-òran seo mar a ghabh Bean Dhaibhidh Patterson e, chuir i na ceathramhnan a leanas ris:

    Gura mise   th'air mo chuarradh,
    Réiteach anochd   'sa bhail' uachdrach,
    Sùilean gobhair   an ceann gruagaich,
    Cha léir dhaibh péin gu dé buannachd.
  5. Cha b'ionnan 's a bha mo luaidh-sa,
    Iain òg mac Dhubhghaill Iarla Chluainidh,
    Nan cluinninn té   eile 's tuar dhut,
    Spìonainn bun is   bàrr mo chuailein,
    'S leumadh mo shròn àird na stuaighe,
 10. 'S dh'fhalbhadh m'anail 'na ceò uaine.

Translation

When I read to Mrs MacInnis the song as Mrs Patterson sung it, she added the following lines to it:

    Tonight 'tis I   who am tormented,
    A betrothal tonight in the upper townland,
    Eyes of a goat   in the head of a maiden,
    They do not see   what is the profit.
  5. It's not like this that was my lover,
    John son of Dougall the Earl of Clunie;
    If I heard   another foretold for you,
    I would pluck out my hair entirely,
    My nose would leap the height of the gable,
 10. My breath would go in a green mist.

Notes

Line 3. Compare the Gaelic proverb *Bidh sùilean ghobhar aig na mnathan a' gléidheadh am fear dhaibh fhéin,* 'women have goats' eyes in keeping their husbands to themselves'. Nicolson, *Gaelic Proverbs*, p. 66. And their lovers, if it comes to that. Nicolson adds that 'goats are very sharp-sighted'.
Line 6. Not identified.

16 AILEIN DUINN AN TILL THU 'N TÙBH-SA?

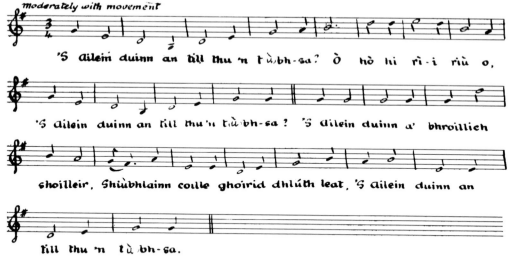

Fonn: 'S Ailein duinn, an till thu 'n tùbh-sa?
O ho hi ri i riu o,
'S Ailein duinn, an till thu 'n tùbh-sa?
'S Ailein duinn a' bhroillich shoilleir,
Shiùbhlainn coille ghoirid dhlùth leat,
'S Ailein duinn, a ghaoil is eudail,
Dh'fhàg thu mi gu deurach tùrsach,
'S Ailein duinn, a ghaoil 's a thasgaidh,
'S trom an sac a tha mi giùlain.

Translation

Brown-haired Allan, will you return here?
Brown-haired Allan.
I would walk the close wood with you
Brown-haired Allan, my love, my darling,
You have left me sad and tearful,
Brown-haired Allan, my love, my treasure,
Heavy's my burden of melancholy.

Recorded at Benacadie on 14/10/37. Tune transcribed by Séamus Ennis; words transcribed by J. L. Campbell.

See *Gesto Collection*, Appendix, p. 16.

SE 108; Mode, G Hexatonic, no 4.

17 CARSON A MHOL THU MÓIRTHIR MOSACH?

Fonn: Heitirean à rinn ù rinn ó ro,
Heitirean à rinn, ó ró

C'arson a mhol thu Móirthir mhosach
Airson stoban calltuinn?

Móirthir mhosach, doirbh ri coiseachd,
'S iomadh sloc is allt innt'.

5. Cailin buidhe crathadh muidhe,
'S i 'na suidh' air plangaid.

Fir 'gan ruigheachd le cion bithidh,
Dh'icheadh cridhe a's t-samhradh.

'S iomadh fear gun bhiadh gun aodach,
10.   Gach taobh do Loch Aoillte.

Daoine bochd dol bàs le gorta,
'S beag an sog ri dannsadh.

Tràth air snothach 's tràth air ola,
'S tràth air cnothan calltuinn.

15. 'S a' choill' uile fo cuid duilleach,
'S i 'na culaidh bainse.

Thig a Uidhist fear caol buidhe,
'S gum b'e struth a dh'eòlas.

Thig a Mùideart fear mór mùgach,
20.   Strùbagan 'na phòca.

127

THE SINGERS AND THEIR SONGS

'S thig a Eige fear beag ceigeach,
Breabain air a bhrògan.

Thig a Éirinn mac Rìgh Seumas,
Le dhéideagan airgid.

25. Thig a Barraidh fear chùil chlannaich,
Blàthshuil mheallach bhòidheach.

Translation

WHY DID YOU PRAISE THE HORRID MAINLAND?[1]

Refrain: Heitirean à rinn ù rinn ò ro,
Heitirean à rinn ó ró.

1. Why did you praise the horrid Mainland
for hazel stobs?

2. The horrid Mainland, difficult to walk on,
There's many a pit and stream there.

3. A yellow-haired lass shaking a churn,
Sitting on a blanket.

4. A man stretched out with want of food,
Who'd eat a heart in the summer.

5. Many a man without food or clothes,
On each side of Loch Aoillte.

6. Poor people dying of hunger,
Little their pleasure for dancing.

7. Living a while on sap, a while on fish-oil,
A while on hazel nuts.

8. The whole wood under its leaves
Like a wedding garment.

---

[1] i.e. Clanranald's mainland estates, Morar, Arisaig, and Moidart, as compared with his island ones, Canna, Eigg, Benbecula, and most of South Uist.

9. There comes from Uist a thin yellow-haired man,
   who was a fund of knowledge.

10. There comes from Moidart a big churlish fellow,
    with cockles in his pocket.

11. There comes a man from Eigg a small thick-set person,
    whose shoes will be a-kicking.

12. King James's son will come over from Ireland,
    with his jewels of silver.

13. There comes from Barra a man with curling black hair,
    and warm, seductive eye.

This is a version of John MacCodrum's song composed around 1755 in reply to Alexander MacDonald's poem *Fàilte na Mòrthir* 'Welcome to Morar', see the Rev. William Matheson's edition of MacCodrum's poems, p. 50. The version printed there has only seven verses. Of these, one was quoted in the introduction to *Uist Bards* by the Rev. A. MacDonald, and three are from *The Maclean Bards*, i, 251, by A. MacLean Sinclair. MacDonald's *Fàilte* was first printed in Ranald MacDonald's collection (usually called the Eigg Collection) in 1776, having 39 verses. It appears in the 1835 edition of MacDonald's poems with 33 verses, similarly in the 1892 edition. The 1924 edition, contains a long meandering conflated version of 58 verses. The editors do not say where the additional verses were obtained.

The *Fàilte* contains references to Loch Sheil and Loch Ailort, which are not considered as being part of Morar now; MacDonald appears to be using the name, which in the Hebrides is the same as the word for Mainland *Mòr-thìr* to cover most of the district known as the *Garbh-Chrìochan* or 'Rough Bounds' of which Morar, Arisaig and Moidart, MacDonald's home country, were important parts. The name 'Morar' really comes from *Mór-Dhobhar*, 'Great Water', and is pronounced by the local native speakers Moro'ar. It might be better written in English *'Moror'*.

Versions of the tune have been printed by K. N. MacDonald in the *Gesto Collection*, p. 43, and by Lucy Broadwood in Vol. VIII of the *Journal of the English Folksong Society*, p. 300.

Recorded from Mrs Patterson at Benacadie on 30/10/37. Holograph text communicated by A. J. MacKenzie. Tune transcribed by Séamus Ennis. The last six verses clearly do not belong to this song, certainly not No. 8, which comes from Alexander MacDonald's song in praise of the Morar district. On the other hand, MacLean Sinclair quotes a verse which is not included in this version, *Mnathan binneach air bheag grinneas, | 'S iad ri inisg chainnteach,* 'Crazy women, unpleasant, given to reviling language'.

Mrs Patterson thought the song was made by Nic Iain Fhinn (see No. 13) but that is impossible, if it was a reply to Alexander MacDonald's.

In December 1897 Fr Allan McDonald of Eriskay took down 131 songs and stories from Marion MacLennan, a well-known traditional singer, some of whose songs were printed in the *Macdonald Collection*, sister of Ewen MacLennan who had the shop on Eriskay from 1890 to 1900, and John MacKinnon 'Iain mac an Tàilleir' Daliburgh, South Uist, a well-known storyteller. Among the songs was a version of some verses belonging to this one. Fr Allan wrote 'I wonder if the following is part of the production that awakened Alasdair mac Mhaighstir Alasdair's one. It seems a parody on his *Fàilt ort a Mhòrthir bhòidheach.*'

1. Carson a mhol thu Mhòrthir mhosach
    Airson stoban calltainn?

2. Is iomadh fear gun bhiadh gun aodach
    Mu dhà thaobh Loch Ainneart   (*sic*)

3. Is iad 'gan ruighe le cion bidhe
    'S iche chruidh a's t-samhradh

Fonn: Heitigin ìrinn àrinn o ho ro
          Heitigin o ro Mhàiri.

He continued, 'The following seem to be additions:

4. Thig a Cola fear bheoil bhioraich
    'Gam bi an coire slabhcain

5. Thig a Eige fear beag ceigeach
    Ceageannan fo bhrògan   *or* shàiltean

6. Thig a Muile (*some say* Uibhist)
    Fear chùil bhuidhe . . .'

He says nothing about the song being ascribed to John MacCodrum.

Translation

1. Why did you praise the horrid Mainland for hazel stakes?
2. There is many a man without clothing or food around the two sides of Loch Aileort.
3. And they stretched out (on their deathbeds) from want of food, eating their cattle in the summer.

130

4. There will come from Coll a sharp-spoken man, who has a cauldron of sloke (a kind of edible seaweed).
5. A small unkempt man will come from Eigg, with lumps under his shoes (or heels).
6. A man will come from Mull (or Uist) with yellow back hair . . .

Notes

Line 2. Implying that the wild hazels growing there were all that the Clanranald lands on the mainland were good for.

Line 7. R(u)igh means 'to stretch out on a death-bed', see Fr Dieckhoff's Glengarry dictionary. To kill and eat cattle in the old days in the Highlands before the autumn, would have been an act of desperation.

Lines 8, 10. The Uist reciters have confused their Loch Eynort with Loch Ailort in the above lands.

SE 101. Mode, A Ionian, weak 4.

18 Ó HÙ HAO 'S MI FO MHÌGHEAN

Fonn: Ó hù hao, 's mi fo mhìghean,
Òganaich, cha mhi do leannan,
Ó hù hao, 's mi fo mhìghean.

Gura muladach 'san amm mi,
Air faiche nam beann air m'aineoil.

Mi buain air iomairean air m'ònrachd,
Mi cumail còmhraig ri balach

5. 'S bhithinn cinnteach a bhith làimh ris,
Mur gearrainn mo làmh le mearachd.

132

Translation

O HÙ HAO, I AM DISPLEASED

Refrain: O hù hao, I am displeased
          Young man, I am not your sweetheart;
          O hù hao, I am displeased.

          I am sorrowful at this time
             On sward of hillsides unfamiliar.

          Reaping on riggs alone,
             Competing with a young fellow.

5. I would be sure to be up with him
             Had I not cut my hand in error.

Recorded at Benacadie on 4/10/37. Tune transcribed by Séamus Ennis; words transcribed by J. L. Campbell.

This was all Mrs Patterson remembered of the song, but on 18 March 1949, Mgr Nicholson communicated to me a letter from Mr J. H. MacNeil, Sydney, N.S., containing a copy of a version of the text which had been communicated to him by Mr Joseph MacKinnon, also of Sydney, whose great-grandmothers had brought it from the Isle of Barra around 1825. I reproduce this in full:

My Dear J.H:
    She, in bardic soliloquy, thinks back, to another nice summer, out in the wood places, gathering nuts. Now, working for a non-Scotch farmer,[1] in a reaping competition, with the servant boy, feeling that she was a better reaper; and, that, had she not cut her hand—likely touched it to the sickle, she would be up to, and past him, in the race. As to the 'fellow' who used to be around, and quit—well, O.K. too bad; but, what can she do?

[1] Rather 'for a Lowland farmer'. In the old days many from the Highlands and Islands used to go to help with the harvest in the Lothians.

SE 106. Mode, E Aeolian (2:6).

Gura muladach mi am bliadhna.
'S fhada leam dà thrian an earraich.

Fonn: Hù o, o hù, 's mi fo mhìghean,
Òganaich, cha mhì do leannan,
Hù o, o hù, 's mi fo mhìghean.

'S tric mi cuimhneachadh a' chòmhlain
10.   An coille nan cnò, 'gan gearradh.

Gura muladach 'san amm mi
Air achadh nan Gall air m'aineoil.

A' buain air iomaire am ònar,
Cumail còmhdhail ris a' bhalach.

15. Bhithinn cinnteach a bhith làimh ris,
Mur gearrainn mo làmh le mearachd.

Mur gearrainn mo làmh le dearmad,
Bhithinn earbsach as a' bharrachd.

Òganaich bhuidh' a' chuil dualaich,
20.   'S ann orm fhìn nach fuath do ghealladh.

Ach a nis, ma thug thu cùl rium,
'S coma leam, co dhiù, do leanachd.

Di-Sathuirne rinn sinn gluasad
Gu dol an taobh-tuath air marachd.

25. Bha sinn 'ga ruith troimh na caoiltean,
An amm cur a h-aodaich ri crannaibh.

Dol seachad air Rubh' an Dùná[in],
Bha 'n ceò dùmhail mu na meallaibh.

Dol seachad air ceann Loch *Aoineort*,
30.   Fhuair sinn boisgeadh air a' ghealaich.

Thog sinn Maighdeanan Mhic Leòid
Am beul Loch Ròdhaig, 's i 'na deannaibh.

Thilg sinn acair air gach taobh dhi,
'S thug sgiobair mo ghaoil dhuinn drama.

35. 'S tric mi smaointinn air a' chòmhlan
An coille nan cnò 'gan gearradh.

Translation

Sorrowful am I this year,
    Long I feel two thirds of spring time.

Of the company I recall,
10.   Gathering nuts in the (hazel) forest.

Unhappy am I now
    In the unfamiliar Lowlands.

Reaping on a rigg alone
    In the company of a stripling.

15. I'd be certain to keep up,
    But that I cut my hand in error.

Carelessly I cut my hand,
    But for that I would excel him.

Youth of curling yellow back-hair,
20.   To me your promise is not hateful.

Now, if you've turned your back on me,
    To follow you I am indifferent.

He, after landing in a distant sea port, following a rough voyage, likely had struck a chance to earn some little money, and had to go quick. Now his thoughts also, go back to 'Coille nan cno' (the hazel wood).

On Saturday we went away,
    Sailing to the northward.

25. We were running through the narrows
    When we hoisted up her canvas.

Going past Rubha an Dùnain,
    The mist was heavy on the mountains.

Going past the head of Loch Eynort,
30.   We got light from the moonshine.

We made the Maidens of Macleod
    At full speed, off Loch Roag.

We dropped anchor on each beam,
    And got drams from our dear skipper.

35. Often the company I recall,
    Picking nuts in the hazel forest.

THE SINGERS AND THEIR SONGS

The transcriber added the comment,

> If he thought he heard her singing, and she thought she heard him, perhaps things came O.K. for them later, anyway. Even as one of the lighter lyrics, the song is kind of nice, with a delicious plaintiveness. It has been kept up at Rear Big Pond, and at Glen Garry, Cape Breton, since my two great-grandmothers brought it over from Barra, some century and a quarter back.

This was written in 1949.

See *Hebridean Folksongs* III, 142–9, 272–5, and 386–7; Calum I. MacLeod, *Bàrdachd a Albainn Nuaidh*, p. 92 (30 lines) from A. A. Quinn, Coxheath, between 1952 and 1956.

Notes

Line 10. Hazel nuts and apples were very popular items in Gaeldom, and are often mentioned in old songs and stories. Allusions to 'nuts', *cnothan*, always mean hazel nuts.

Line 27. The MS has *Rutha 'N Duna*, but other versions of the song from Scotland show that this must be *Rubha an Dùnain*, 'the promontory of the little fort' on the south west of the Isle of Skye, along which the boat was sailing. There is a chambered cairn there.

Line 29. The MS has *Loch-Oidhehe* with a question-mark. Other versions show it was *Loch Aoineort* (Loch Eynort).

Line 31. Macleod's Maidens are two prominent rocks off Idrigill Point at the mouth of Loch Roag in Skye. In the MS Loch Roag is corrupted to *Loch Odha*. It is the western inlet of Loch Bracadale.

Line 34. Other versions show that *Sgiobair mo ghaoil*, the 'dear skipper', was Colonel Alasdair Maclean of Coll, nicknamed *Am Fear Ruadh*, the auburn-haired man.

19   TAPADH LEIS NA GÀIDHEIL GHASDA

Tune transcribed by Margaret Fay Shaw.

Fonn: Hì hó hó, tha mì fo lionn-dubh,
Hoireann ó, 's trom gun dìreadh,
Hì hó hó, tha mì fo lionn-dubh.

1.   Tapadh leis na Gàidheil ghasda
Thug am breacan daithte a Struibhle.

2.   Nuair sheallas mi air mo chasan,
Tha 'n t-urram air na gartain shìoda.

3.   Nuair sheallas mi air mo bhrògan
Miad mo bhròin cha n-fhaod mi innse.

4.   'N oidhche bha mi 'n taigh a' Mhuilinn,
Chruinnich iad uiliag mu m' thimchioll.

5. Chuir iad an t-airgiod 'nam phòca,
   Fàth mo leòin cha n-fhaod mi innse.

6. 'S chuir iad an ite ud 'nam bhonaid,
   'S bha siod dorannach le m' mhuinntir.

7. 'S ma bha, ged nach robh mi deònach,
   Chàirich iad an cleòc an rìgh mi.

8. 'S bidh *recruits* a' falbh a màireach,
   Bidh sinn a' *marchadh* gu Lìte.

9. Dìreadh ris na beanntan àrda,
   'S Donnchadh Bàn 's a chùl ri Ìle.

10. Dìreadh ris na beanntan Diùrach,
    'S mór mo shùil an déidh na h-ighneig.

11. Bheir soraidh bhuamsa gu Màiri,
    Gur h-i as cràitich' dh'fhàg mi 's tìr-sa.

12. 'S truagh nach robh mi leat an Éirinn,
    Bàta réidh 's an t-airgiod rìgh leat.

13. Soirbheas gaoth a deas 'nar deoghaidh,
    'S gheobhainn gu seo'ach Caol Ìle.

14. Nuair thog sinn ar siùil ri crannaibh,
    A Rìgh! bu shalach an oidhche.

15. Bha sinn 'ga ruith le cruinn rùis'te,
    Cha ghiùlaineadh i siùil chinn dhuinn.

Recorded at Benacadie, on 30/9/37. Tune transcribed by Margaret Fay Shaw; words transcribed by J. L. Campbell.

See *Tocher* no 42, School of Scottish Studies 1990, p. 380, where a version of six couplets recorded by Margaret Bennett in 1970 from Allan MacArthur of Canna descent is given.

Two songs run together, the second beginning at verse 9?

THE SINGERS AND THEIR SONGS

Translation

Refrain: Hi ho ho, I'm in deep depression,
Hoireann ó, I'm sad and weary;
Hi ho ho, I'm in deep depression.

1. Good luck with the splendid Gaels, who took the coloured (tartan) plaid to Stirling.

2. When I look at my legs, there is honour for the silken garters.

3. When I look at my shoes, I cannot tell the amount of my sorrow.

4. The night I was in the Mill house, they all gathered around me.

5. They put money into my pocket, the cause of my wound I could not tell of.

6. They put a feather in my bonnet, which was painful to my people.

7. If it was, I was unwilling; they put on me the king's cloak (i.e. uniform).

8. Recruits will be leaving tomorrow, we'll be marching to Leith.

9. Climbing to the high hills, and Duncan Bàn with his back to Islay.

10. Climbing the hills of Jura, great was my longing for the young woman.

11. Give a farewell from me to Mary, (parting from her) in this land was most painful.

12. Pity I was not with you in Ireland, a calm boat and the King's money, with you.

13. A southerly breeze behind us, I would fetch easily the Sound of Islay.

14. When we raised the sails, my God! the night was dirty.

15. We were running her with bare masts, she would not carry top sails for us.

139

20   A CHUACHAG NAM BEANN

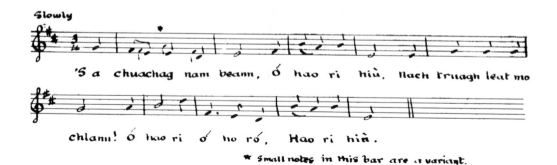

'S a chuachag nam beann, ó hao ri hiù. Nach truagh leat mo chlann! ó hao ri ó ho ró, Hao ri hiù.

* Small notes in this bar are a variant.

'S a chuachag nam beann, ó hao ri hiù,
Nach truagh leat mo chlann,
Ó hao ri ó ho ró, hao ri hiù.

Nach truagh leat mo chlann, ó hao ri hiù,
Té eile 'nan ceann,
Ó hao ri ó ho ró, hao ri hiù.

Té eile 'nan ceann, ó hao ri hiù,
Bidh buillean mu'n ceann,
Ó hao ri ó ho ró, hao ri hiù.

5. Buille eile mu'n làimh,
    'S an cridheachan fann;
    Cha dug mi sin riamh,
    Do dhuin' air son Dia,
    Ach buiseagan dha'n t-sìol,
10. Ceann carrach an lìn,
    Chuid bu taine dha'n mhiad;
    Nan diginn-sa beò,
    Gun riaghlainn gu leòr
    Do dh'airgiod 's do dh'or,
15. Do bhainne nam bó.

140

Translation

> O Cuckoo of the hills,
> Do you not pity my children?
> With another woman over them,
> Their heads will get cuffed,
> 5.   Other blows on their hands,
> While their hearts are weak;
> I never gave that
> To anyone, for God's sake!
> Only small handfuls of grain,
> 10.   The rough tops of lint,
> The thinnest part of the amount.
> If I revived,
> I would distribute in plenty
> Silver and gold,
> 15.   And of milk from cows.

Recorded at Benacadie from Mrs Patterson on 4/10/37. Tune transcribed by Séamus Ennis; words transcribed by J. L. Campbell. The song was recorded again on wire from Mrs Patterson by J.L.C. on 24/5/53, and by Annie Johnston on tape on 2/8/59. See *Gaelic Songs in Nova Scotia*, p. 156, from the same singer.

The theme is the dead mother deploring the treatment of her children by her successor.

SE 107. Mode E hexatonic, no 6.

21 'S MOCH AN DIU GUN D'RINN MI GLUASAD

Fonn: Fail iù, ill eó, ho ro éileadh,
Fail iù, ill eó, hi rinn is ó,
Fail iu, ill eo, ho ro éileadh.

'S moch an diu gun d'rinn mi gluasad,
Ràna mi lag an fhraoich uaine.

Chìr mi mo cheann 's dh'fhàg mi gruaig ann,
'S thug mi sealladh far mo ghualainn,

5. 'S chunna mi tighinn na h-uaislean,
Air choltas Raghnaill agus Ruairi.

'S ged a bha, cha robh mo luaidh-s' ann,
Och cha robh, a ghaoil, b'fhada bhuam thu.

Chunna mi an dé seachad suas thu,
10.   Dol a shealg na h-éilde ruaidhe,

'S gunna bheulchaol air do ghualainn,
'S claidheamh chinnghil air do chruachann.

'S an ròin léith o bheul na stuaighe,
'S aithne dhomh fhìn de chum bhuam thu,

142

15. Miad mo ghaoil ort 's lughad m'fhuath ort,
    Tainead mo chrodh-laoigh air buailidh,

    'S gun gin dhubh ann, no gin ruadh ann,
      No gin air an rachadh buarach.

    Ochón, a Dhia, 's minig thug bhuam thu,
20.   'S e mi fhìn bu mhutha luaidh ort!

    Na chunna, no chì, no chuala,
      No chuireas saoghal air uachdar.

    Ghabh thu banarach na buaile,
      Bidh a cuinneag air a gualainn.

25. Bidh a cuinneag air a gualainn,
    'S giùlainidh tu fhéin a' bhuarach.

Translation

Early today I went away,
I reached the valley of the green heather.

I combed my head, and left hair there,
And I gave a glance over my shoulder

5. I saw gentry coming
The likeness of Ronald and Rory.

Though they were there my love was absent,
Alas, my dear, you were far from me.

I saw you going past yesterday,
10. Going to hunt the red hind.

With narrow-bore gun upon your shoulder,
And a bright-hilted sword at your side.

Going to hunt the grey seal from the mouth of the wave.
I know myself what kept you from me,

15. The amount of love for you, the smallness of my hate for you,
The fewness of my milk cows at the cattlefold.

143

Without one black or one red one there,
Or one on which there would go a spancel.

Alas, o God, pity for her who took you from me,
20. And my love for you was greater,

Than the world has seen, or sees, or heard,
Or will establish.

You have taken the dairymaid of the cattlefold,
With her churn upon her shoulder.

Her churn will be upon her shoulder,
25. While you carry the cow-fetter.

Recorded at Benacadie on 30/9/37. Tune transcribed by Séamus Ennis; words taken down by J. L. Campbell. The singer only sang the first line of the refrain (the 'Solo Refrain') after each couplet, as often occurs when such songs are sung without a chorus to take up the refrain.

The transcription has been revised to give a complete refrain, for the sake of learners, by including a second line from a very similar version sung by a good Barra singer (see *Hebridean Folksongs* I, pp. 82 and 278). It is an attractive song, that was popular in Barra and South Uist. Seven versions of the tune are printed in *Hebridean Folksongs*.

In rewriting Ennis's transcription, the pitch has been raised by the interval of a third.

Notes

Reversal of the fifth and sixth couplets gives a better order.

Lines 9–14 and *15–25* are formulaic. See *Hebridean Folksongs* III, pp. 20 and 24 ('successful hunter' and 'tocherless lass').

SE 100; Mode, B hexatonic, no 2.

22   'S TU MO NIGHEAN DUBH

Fail ill e bhó, hao rì ri hó,
'S tu mo nighean dubh, o hó hù a,
Fail ill e bhó, hao rì ri hó.

Mo laogh 's mo lur, o ho hù a,
Faill ill e bhó, hao rì ri hó.
Chaidil thu muigh
An dé 's an diu,
Mo gheòidh air gur,
'S mo choirce tiugh.

Translation

You are my black-haired girl.
My darling, my delight.
You slept outside
Yesterday and today
While my geese brood
And my oats grow thick.

Recorded at Benacadie on 6/10/37. Tune transcribed by A. Martin Freeman; words transcribed by J. L. Campbell.

Mode Pentatonic, no C, no F.

23 FLIUCH A BHA MI 'N COIRE BHREACAIN

```
Fire, fàire, hó ro hó,
1. Fliuch a bha mi, ó ro hó,
   Fire, fàire, hó ro hó,
   'N Coire Bhreacain, o hì o hó,
   Fire, fàire, hó ro hó.
   'N Coire Bhreacain, o hì ro hó,
   Fire, fàire, hó ro hó.
2. Bha struth mór ann, o hì o hó,
   Fire, fàire, hó ro hó,
   Bha struth mór ann, hó ro  hó,
   Fire, fàire, hó ro hó,
   Bha struth mór ann, o hì o hó,
   Fire, fàire, hó ro hó,
   Bha struth bras ann, hó ro hó,
   Fire, fàire, hó ro hó,
3. B'fheudar dhuinn na        siùil a phasgadh.
4. Gura h-iad mo        ghaol na bràithrean
5. Dh'fhalbh o sheachdain        gus am màireach.
```

Translation

1. Wet was I in Coire Bhreacain
2. There was a big, a strong tide there,
3. We had to furl the sails.
4. My brothers are my beloveds,
5. They went away a week ago tomorrow.

Recorded on 15/10/37 from Mrs Patterson. Tune transcribed by Séamus Ennis; words transcribed by J. L. Campbell. a fragment. Each half line, except the first, is repeated with a different phrase of the refrain. The first two lines are set out to show this. We have substituted G♮ for G# in the third bar from the end, G# does not accord with the mode.

Notes

Line 1. Coire Bhreacain is the famous tidal whirlpool between the islands of Jura and Scarba in the southern inner Hebrides.

SE 124; Mode not assigned.

24 DH'ÉIRICH MI MOCH MADUINN CHÉITEIN

Dh'éirich mi moch maduinn Chéitein
Hì ri rìnn 's a hùg a bhó,
Chunnaic mi bhuam baidein spréidheadh,
Hiù nàilibh hao ri o hù,
Hi rì o hó lebh ó hi ó,
Hùg a bhó.

Chunnaic mi bhuam baidein spréidheadh
Hì ri rìnn 's a hùg a bhó,
Air tulaich ghuirm 's iad ag éirigh,
Hiù nàilibh hao ri o hù,
Hi ri o hó lebh ó hi ó
Hùg a bhó.

Air tulaich ghuirm 's iad ag éirigh, &c

Ghreas mi chas 's gun chas mi 'n ceum ann, &c

Translation

Early I rose on a May morning,
I saw a small herd of cattle
On a green mound arising,
I hastened my footsteps and approached there.

Recorded at Benacadie on 6/10/37. Tune transcribed by Séamus Ennis; words transcribed by J. L. Campbell.

See *Hebridean Folksongs* II, pp. 66–71, and note the similarity of this version of the attractive tune to that sung by the late Miss Annie Johnston, expressed there in 2/4 (6/8) time.

SE 110; Mode, ? A. Dorian, 2:6.

25 CÓ AN TÉ ÒG A TH'AGAM MAR CHÉILE?

PAIRING-OFF SONGS

Were sung in jesting at the end of the waulkings.

(a) *What young woman am I getting as a wife?*

The young man speaks:

Let me say, *ho éile bho hó*, let me say, *éileadh*.
What young woman am I getting as a mate? *Chall o éile*,
let me say!

Various names would then be suggested, often to cause the maximum embarrassment.

Recorded from Mrs David Patterson at Benacadie on 4/10/37. Tune transcribed by Margaret Fay Shaw; words transcribed by J. L. Campbell.

Note

Labhram is pronounced *lauram*, 'Let me say' from *labhair*, speak.

26 CÓ BHEIR THU DHOMHSA?

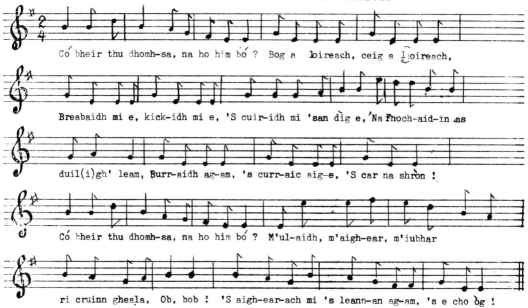

Có bheir thu dhomh-sa, na ho him bó ? Bog a boireach, ceig a loireach,

Breabaidh mi e, kick-idh mi e, 'S cuir-idh mi 'san dig e, 'Na Fhoch-aid-in as

duil(i)gh' leam, Burr-aidh ag-am, 's curr-aic aig-e, 'S car na shròn !

Có bheir thu dhomh-sa, na ho him bó ? M'ul-aidh, m'aigh-ear, m'iubhar

ri cruinn gheala, Ob, bob ! 'S aigh-ear-ach mi 's leann-an ag-am, 's e cho òg !

(b) *Whom will you give me?*

The young woman speaks:

> Whom will you give me, *na ho him bó*?

An unsuitable name is suggested by someone. The young woman replies:

> Dunk the muddy bedraggled fellow, kick him,
> I'll kick him, I'll kick him,
> I'll put him in the ditch!
> I think him the sorriest object of mockery;
> 5. I have a fool, with a woman's cap on,
> And a bent nose!

Someone then suggests a suitable partner:

> Whom will you give me, *na ho him bó*?
> My treasure, my joy, my yew-tree,
> My . . . with tall masts

> 10. Ob, bob! I'm joyful,
> I have a sweetheart, and he so young!

Recorded from Mrs David Patterson at Benacadie on 4/10/37. Tunes transcribed by Margaret Fay Shaw; words transcribed by J. L. Campbell.

The word at the beginning of line 9 could not be made out from the recording.

DANIEL JOSEPH MACDOUGALL
Christmas Island, Barra tradition

Daniel Joseph ('D.J.') MacDougall was born in Christmas Island, Nova Scotia, in 1870, the son of Catherine Macdonald, Castle Bay, Nova Scotia and Michael MacDougall of Christmas Island.

As a young man he went to Boston where he opened up a business with a partner. This venture was short-lived, as he was called home to care for his ageing parents. And so he was forced to abandon the business in Boston and to return to Christmas Island, where he worked for a lifetime. He opened a general store in Christmas Island, a business which he managed until his death in 1945. He married Mary Ann Gillis, daughter of Isabel MacDonald and Donald Gillis, of Arisaig, Antigonish County. They had ten children, seven sons and three daughters. One son, Norman, died as an infant, and another son, Colin, was killed while serving with the R.C.A.F. in Europe.

Mr MacDougall served as general assessor for Cape Breton County for more than ten years. He was a well-known figure in municipal and provincial politics for over 30 years. His logical mind and his unerring judgment made him an invaluable citizen of the community which he was always ready to serve, and drew many to him from other parts of the municipality for counsel. He was a great lover of all things Scottish and was especially interested in Scottish history. He spoke Gaelic fluently and wrote it with equal ease. During his time as chief of the Scottish Catholic Society he was called upon to lecture on aspects of Scottish history at various gatherings and conventions. Mary Ann Gillis shared her husband's passion for music. She served as choir director and organist at St Barra's church for almost 40 years. Two legacies which they can be said to have bequeathed to their children were love of learning and love of music.

Daniel J. MacDougall died at his home in Christmas Island on 19 October 1945. His wife, Mary Ann, died on 16 October 1969.

18.   D. J. MacDougall, Christmas Island, in his earlier days

CROM AN FHÀSAICH

'N uair a bha mi òg is a bha sin a' dol dha'n sgoil, ga b'e na cluichean eile a bhiodh againn, bhitheadh na gillean a' cluich fear ris an canadh iad 'Toirst a mach an Fhàsaich' agas bha iad 'ga chluich car mar seo: Bha ne gillean uile a' dol a mach 's a' streath mar siod, agas bha a' fear bu mhutha is bu làidire aig an darna ceann dhith. Bha fear eile dhe na gillean bu tapaidhe a bh' ann, dh' fheumadh e fal^{a}bh agas 'walkadh' m'an cuairst 'ga mallaichadh agas thigeadh e air bialu chàich dìreach mar gun tigeadh e as an fhàsach agas chanadh e:

'Diogada, diogada, Dia a seo.'

Fhreagradh a' fear a bha air ceann na streith:

'Dia dhut fhéin, a Chrom an Fhàsaich; có as an dànaig thu an diugh?'

Fhreagradh a' fear eile:

'Thàna mi bho m' fhearann, bho m' fhonn is bho m' fhàsaich fhéin.'

'Gu dé chuir fearann is fonn is fàsach agat-sa, is mise gun fhearann, gun fhonn, gun fhàsach?'

'Chuir mo chruas agas mo luas agas mo làidireachd fhéin.'

'An dà, tha gille beag caol, glas agam-s' ann a seo a bheir do chluas is do cheann is do chaitheamh beatha dhiot.'

'A mach 'n seo a's a' mhineid e, ma thà', dh'éigheadh a' fear eile.

Bha a' chiad fhear a bhiodh aig ceann na streith' a' gabhail a mach a sin agas bha e fhéin agas Crom an Fhàsaich a' gabhail gu gleachd an uair sin. Nan cuireadh Crom an Fhàsaich druim an fhir sin ri talamh, bha esan a' seasamh an darna taobh, agas bha an ath-fhear a' tighinn a mach. Bha iad a' leantail mar sin gus a rachadh Crom an Fhàsaich, a dhruim a chur ri talamh, agas an uair sin bha esan a' seasamh an darna taobh, agas a' fear a leag e bha esan 'na Chrom an Fhàsaich an uair sin. Agas bha iad a' toiseachadh air a' chluich a rithist as ùr suas mar sin. Agas bha i 'na cluich a's a robh na feadhainn òga a faighinn fuathas de thoileachadh is de thoil-intinn, a bharrach air a bhith a' fàs eòlach air gleachd agas a' fiachainn có fear bu làidire dhiubh.

Translation

CROM OF THE WILDERNESS

When I was young and we were going to school, whatever other games we might have, the boys used to be playing one they called 'Taking out the Wilderness'. They were playing it somewhat like this: the boys were going out in a line like this, and the biggest and strongest one was at the end of it. Another of the boys who was ablest, had to go walking around cursing them. He would come in front of the rest just as if he had come out of the pasture and he'd say:

'Diogada, diogada, Dia here.'

The one who was at the end of the line would answer:

'Dia to yourself, Crom of the Wilderness; Where did you come from today?'
The other would reply:
'I came from my soil, from my land, and from my own Wilderness.'
'What gave you soil, land, and wilderness, when I'm without soil, land, or wilderness?'
'My hardiness and my speed and my own strength.'
'Well, I have a little thin, pale lad here here, who will take your ear and your head and your livelihood from you!'
'Out here at once with him, then!' The other would cry.

The first one who was at the end of the line would go out then, and 'Crom an Fhàsaich' would go to wrestle him. If 'Crom an Fhàsaich' put the other's back on the ground, he stood aside, and the next lad came out. They kept on like that until 'Crom an Fhàsaich's' back was put on the ground, and then he stood aside, and the one who had put him down became 'Crom an Fhàsaich' then.

It was a game from which young people got a lot of pleasure and entertainment, as well as getting to know how to wrestle and to find out which of them was strongest.

'Crom an Fhàsaich', compare 'Crom na Cairrge', 'Crouch of the Rock', *Heroic Poetry from the Book of the Dean of Lismore*, p. 80. See also the Lay of Beinn Ghualann, verse 68, *Duanaire Finn* II 380. 'Crom na Cairrge' was a fearful giant, who met the Ossianic hero Goll mac Morna in mortal combat. 'No two in the world ever fought so good a fight'. Goll killed him.

Recorded from D. J. MacDougall at Christmas Island on 6/10/37. Transcribed by Dr Calum MacLean. I have kept his orthography.

Mrs NEIL McINNIS (née MacDonald)
MacKay's Corner, South Uist and Barra tradition

Mrs Neil McInnis, *née* Ann MacDonald, was born in 1860. She lived at MacKay's Corner, near Glace Bay, in Cape Breton. Her father was Neil Macdonald, son of Iain Ruadh MacDonald, a native of South Uist, of the Clanranald MacDonalds, who came to Cape Breton in 1822 and settled in the highlands, Rear Christmas Island. He was married to Christie MacLean, daughter of Alexander MacLean (Cairistiana nighean Alasdair Gobha nic 'ille Sheathain). Mrs McInnis's father Neil Macdonald was born in Cape Breton after three sisters and two sons were born in Barra, being the youngest of the family. He was noted as a composer of humorous songs, a gift inherited by two of his daughters. See A. J. MacKenzie, *History of Christmas Island Parish*, page 28.

Mrs McInnis's mother was Ann MacDonald, daughter of Neil MacDonald and Christie MacNeil, the daughter of Rory MacNeil, son of Donald Og MacNeil. Neil MacDonald and his wife Christie came to Cape Breton from Barra in the year 1822, and settled at Barra Glen, in Victoria County. Mrs McInnis was therefore descended from scions of three distinguished Hebridean clans, MacDonalds, MacLeans, and MacNeils. She learnt some of the traditional songs she sang, from her maternal grandmother, Christie or Cairistiana MacNeil. Of all the singers we have met in Cape Breton Mrs McInnis had the best memory for the words of the old waulking songs; five of her texts are reproduced in *Hebridean Folksongs*:

Vol. II, No. L*b*. Tha caolas eadar mi is Iain.

LXXXVIII. Latha bha mi'n lic Dùn bheagain.

Vol. III XCVIII. Lìon mulad, lìon mulad (all the words except the first couplet).

CVII*b*. Dh'fhalbh mo rùn o chionn bliadhna.

CXXV. Cha déid mi chìobair nam fuarbheann.

She was indeed a great tradition bearer, worthy to be classed with her best contemporaries in South Uist and Barra. She died in 1947, aged 87.

19.   Mrs Neil McInnis, and friends, MacKay's Corner

27 BIODH AN DEOCH SO 'N LÀIMH MO RÙIN

Fonn: Biodh an deoch seo an làimh mo rùin,
Deoch slàinte le Fear an Tùir;
Biodh an deoch seo an làimh mo rùin.

1. Òladh no an òladh càch i,
   Biodh i làn air ceann a' bhùird.

2. Dh'òlainn-sa deochslàint' mo thighearn',
   'S e tighinn mar bu mhath liùm.

3. Sùil gun dug mi far mo ghualainn,
   'S rinn mi cuairteach' air a chuan.

4. Chunnacas bàta air an fhairge,
   'S làmh dhearg air an stiùir.

5. Chunnaic mi dol seachad na caoil i,
   'S badan fraoich 'san t-slat-shiùil.

6. Fhir a chunnaic air an t-sàil' i,
   Beannaich an long bhàn 's a criù.

7. Beannaich a croinn àrd 's a h-acfhuinn,
   A cuid acraichean 's a siùil.

8. Ged a tha mi 'n seo an Colla,
   B'e mo thoil a dhol a Rùm.

157

9. Agus as a sin do dh'Uidhist,
    Nan d'fhuair mi mo ghuidhe liùm.

10. Is mairg a shamhladh Colla Creagach
    Ri Dunbheagain no Duntuilm.

11. Mo rùn air muime nam macaomh,
    A bhiodh 'gan altrum aig a' ghlùin.

12. 'S gura ladarna labhair am balach
    Ri Mac Ailein an Tùir.

13. Mura h-e gur tu mo bhràthair,
    'S mi nach àicheadh idir thù.

14. 'S e 'm mac a b'fheàrr na an t-athair
    An cliù, an aighear, 's an sunnd.

15. 'S truagh nach fhaicinn Caisteal Dùbhairt
    Dol na sprùdhan anns a' ghrùnnd.

16. Dh'òlainn deoch-slàinte Rìgh Seumais
    Bhith 'ga éibheach air a' chrùn.

17. Bidh mi nis a' sgur dha m' sheisreach,
    Bho'n tha 'm feasgar leagail driùchd.

Seo an sgeul a th'aig *MacTalla* air an òran seo:

Bha pàisde aig nighean Mhic 'ic Ailein ris a' ghille aig a h-athair. Chaidh an gille a shracadh as a chéile eadar dà each. Thugadh an leanabh do thé ann an Uibhist gus an aire a thoirt air. Theich an nighean do Cholla. Bha i cóig bliadhna an sin. Bha i 'na searbhanta an caisteal Thighearna Cholla. B'e a h-obair a bhith freasdal aig a' bhòrd. Cha d'innis i riamh có i.

Bha dùil aig Tighearna Cholla ri Mac 'ic Ailein air là àraid. Bha Mac 'ic Ailein fada gun tighinn. Thubhairt Tighearna Cholla, 's e fàs sgìth a' feitheamh ris, 'Cha dig na balaich an diu.' Nuair thànaig Mac 'ic Ailein, chunnaic e gu robh an té a bha freasdal aig a' bhòrd anabarrach coltach ri a piuthair. Thuit e ann an gaol oirre. Nuair a bha e deas gu falbh, sheinn a phiuthar an t-òran an lathair na bha 'san chaistel. Thug Mac 'ic Ailein leis dhachaigh i.'

'Sin an eachdraidh a thugadh dhuinne mu'n òran' ars am fear-dheasachaidh, 'dh'fhaoidte nach eil facal de dh'fhìrinn innte.'

THE SINGERS AND THEIR SONGS

Translation

Refrain: May this drink be in my love's hand,
A health to the Laird of the Tower;
May this drink be in my love's hand.

1. Whether or not everyone drinks it,
   Let it be at the head of the table, full.

2. I would drink the health of my chief,
   And to his coming as we would wish.

3. When I looked over my shoulder,
   I took a look around at the sea.

4. I saw a ship on the sea,
   With a red hand on the helm.

5. I saw it go past the narrows
   With a sprig of heather at the yard.

6. He who saw it on the ocean,
   Let him bless the white ship and her crew.

7. May he bless her high masts and her tackle,
   Her anchors, and her sails.

8. Though I am here on Coll,
   I would like to go to Rum.

9. And from there to Uist
   If I got my prayer's wish.

10. Pity him who'd compare rocky Coll
    To Dunvegan or Duntuilm.

11. My love to the foster-mother of the youths,
    Who was nursing them at the knee.

12. Boldly the young fellow spoke
    To Clanranald of the castle.

13. If you were not my brother,
    I would not acknowledge you.

14. The son was better than the father,
    In fame, in joy, and happiness.

15. Pity I would not see Castle Duart
    Falling in ruins to the ground.

16. I would drink a toast to King James
    Being proclaimed for the crown.

17. I will now untie my oxen
    Since the evening dew falls.

Recorded at MacKay's Corner on 20/10/37. Tune transcribed by Séamus Ennis. Mrs McInnis only sang the refrain and the first couplet. This song was first printed in Sinclair's *Oranaiche* in 1873; an identical version was printed in Sydney *Post Record* at about the time of our visit, with the addition of the second couplet here. Other versions of the song appeared in *Mac Talla*, vol. II, 5 August 1893 (20 couplets) and in the transaction of the *Gaelic Society of Inverness*, Vol. XXVI, p. 236, in a paper on Gaelic poems read by the Rev. A. MacLean Sinclair on 23 November 1905, also 20 couplets, but not identical with the the *Mac Talla* version. Music as sung by Malcolm Angus MacLeod, Birch Plains, N.S. The text in the *Oranaiche* is printed here, with the additional second verse from the *Post Record* version. (The MacDonald Collection version was from the MS Collection made by Rev. J. N. MacDonald in Benbecula, Scotland.)

The *Mac Talla* version adds the following note in Gaelic:

Clanranald's daughter had a child by her father's man-servant. The man-servant was torn to pieces between two horses. The baby was given to a woman in Uist to look after. The daughter fled to the Isle of Coll and was there for five years. She was a servant in the castle of the Laird of Coll (MacLean of Coll). Her work was waiting at the table. She never told who she was. One particular day the Laird of Coll was expecting Clanranald. Clanranald was late coming; MacLean growing tired of waiting, said, 'The fellow won't come today.'

When Clanranald arrived, he noticed that the girl who was serving at the table was extremely like his sister. He fell in love with her. When he was ready to go, his sister sang the song before everyone in the castle. Clanranald took her home with him.

This is the story about the song that was given to us; perhaps there isn't a word of truth in it, adds the editor (Jonathan MacKinnon).

MacLean Sinclair, who says he got the song from 'Jane MacLeod', Sìne Mhór nan Òran', gives the same account, omitting the episode of the horses.

Séamus Ennis found the song known in Morar.

The song of the same refrain on p. 340 of the MacDonald Collection of Gaelic Poetry, and in the Killearnan MS, p. 32, is a song in praise of Donald Gorm MacDonald of Sleat, and has nothing to do with Clanranald, or with the story of the song in *Mac Talla*.

Rev. Angus MacDonald who compiled the Killearnan MS said this was one of the songs collected on Benbecula by the Rev. J. N. MacDonald (1830–68), and communicated to him in 1855.

The 10-verse version in *Gaelic Songs in Nova Scotia*, p. 208 is a mixture of couplets from the two songs.

As regards the last two couplets in the *Oranaiche–Post Record* version; the first of them, about a health to King James, is obviously an interpolation; the second, about loosing the plough team, belongs rightly to the song about Donald Gorm MacDonald.

Notes

Refrain, & in verse 12. An tùr, 'The Tower', a kenning for the Chief's castle.
Verse 5. Heather was the badge of MacDonalds.
Verse 10. Dunvegan Castle was the seat of the Chiefs of the Macleods; Duntuilm that of the MacDonalds of Sleat. Both are on the Isle of Skye.
Verse 15. Castle Duart is the seat of the Chiefs of the MacLeans of Duart, on the Isle of Mull.

SE 129; Mode, ? E. Aeolian.

28 BEINN A' CHEATHAICH

I

Mar a ghabh Anna Nill Ruaidh e

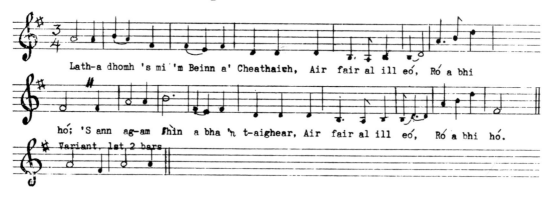

SE 65; Hexatonic, D, no 4.

II

Mar a ghabh Cairistiana nighean Eachainn am fonn

SE 64; Pentatonic. In the MS, the last three notes of the second bar were written C, B, B, but this was a tone too high.

> *Fonn:* Air fair al ill eó, ro a bha hó,
> Hoireann is ho, na hó hi oho, i,
> Hi rì ho ro ho bha, hó hug ho.

162

    Latha dhomh 's mi 'm Beinn a' Cheathaich,
    Ruagail nan caorach, is ' gam faighinn,
    Cha b'e caigeann an dà pheathar,
    No caigeann beag ceann an rathaid!
5.   'S ann agam fhìn a bha an t-aighear
    Faicinn do bhàta bhith 'ga gabhail,
    A' bhiurlainn dubh, 's i seòladh aighearach,
    Toirt a cinn o'n seana-chuan domhain
    Mach a dùthaich Mhic 'ill' Eathain,
10. *Steach gu dùthaich Mhic 'ic Ailein,*
    Steach gu Ciosamul am Barraidh
    Far am faicte cuirm 'ga gabhail,
    Fìon 'ga òl o oidhch' gu latha,
    Sìoda fionn 'ga chur air mnathan,
15. Pìobaireachd nam feadan laghach;
    Thug i 'n latha an diu gu frasan,
    Ma chaidh bàta Cloinn Nill seachad,
    'S i gun stiùir, gun stagh, gun bheairt rith',
    Gun cheann-cumail air a h-astar,
20. *Bhrist i 'n cabul 's dh'fhàg i 'n acair',*
    Bhrist i gach nì a b'fheàrr a bh'aice—
    B'aithne dhomh fhìn fir do bhaile,
    Niall Gruamach mac Ruairi an Tartair,
    Gill' Eóghanain mór an gaisgeach,
25. Dà mhac Iain 'ic a' Phearsain,
    Domhnall Donn o Ghleann nan Dearcag,
    Murchadh Ruadh a ceann a' chlachain,
    Murchadh Beag, céile Ni Lachlainn,
    Ruairi òg an t-oighre maiseach,
30. Fearchar air stiùir 's a làmh ri tapadh.

    An Casadh: a bhith 'ga ghabhail na's luaithe

    Nam bithinn 'nam nighinn fo lighe mo ghruaige,
    Cha rachainn dham' thaobhadh ri taobh bhalach suarach,
    B'annsa liom agam fear geal nach biodh gruaim air,
    Fear buidhe donn àluinn gun àrdan, gun uabhar,
35. A dhìreadh am mullach 's a ghunn' air a ghualainn,
    A dh'fhàgadh a' mhaoiseach air a taobh air a' chruadhlach,
    Sealgair dhamh chabrach 'san lag am bi luachair,
    Sealgair a' choillich 's na h-eilide ruaidhe,
    'S na circeige duinne dheanadh gur anns an fhuarniod
40. *'S nach gabhadh mar mhasladh an deachamh thoirt uaiche.*

163

THE SINGERS AND THEIR SONGS

Translation

      One day on the Misty Mountain,
      Rounding up the sheep, gathering them,
      Not the pair of the two sisters,
      Nor the small pair at the end of the road!
5.   It was I who felt joyful,
      Seeing your ship her way making,
      The black Galley, sailing joyfully,
      Turning her bow from the deep old ocean,
      Away from the MacLean country,
10. Towards the country of Clanranald,
      Towards Kismul Castle at Barra
      Where there could be seen feasting,
      Wine being drunk from night to day break,
      White silk being worn by women,
15. Bagpipes played, with pleasant chanters;
      The day today has turned squally,
      If the Clan MacNeil's ship has gone by
      Without helm or stay or tackle.
      Without head way on her passage,
20. She's broken her cable and lost her anchor,
      She's broken every best thing about her.
      I know myself the men of your township,
      Gloomy Neil son of Rory the Noisy
      Gilleonan the great hero,
25. The two sons of Ian, son of the Parson,
      Brown-haired Donald from the glen of berries,
      Red-haired Murdo from the end of the village,
      Little Murdo, spouse of Lachlan's daughter,
      Young Rory, the handsome heir,
30. Farquhar the clever active steersman.

With accelerated tempo
      Were I a girl with beautiful tresses,
      I would not go in the company of trivial striplings,
      I would much sooner have a fair man who's not gloomy,
      A handsome dark yellow-haired man, without touchiness,
35. Who'd climb to the summit with his gun on his shoulder,
      Who'd leave the roe lying on its side on the hard ground,
      A hunter of antlered stag in the dell of the rushes,
      A hunter of red hind and of blackcock,
      And of the brown grouse which breeds in a cold nest
40. And feels it no shame if her tenth egg is taken.

Recorded at MacKay's Corner on 8/10/37. Tune transcribed by Séamus Ennis; words taken down by J. L. Campbell. See *Hebridean Folksongs* I, 151–3, 191–2, and 335–6. Said to have been made by the Barra poetess Nic Iain Fhinn (Daughter of Fair-haired John) who lived in the seventeenth century, and won the famous flyting with the South Uist poetess Nic a' Mhanaich, which begins *Cha déid Mór a Bharraidh bhrònaich,* 'Marion will not go to miserable Barra.'

This fine song (the origin of Mrs Kennedy-Fraser's Kishmul's Galley, *Songs of the Hebrides* I, 80, which those who are acquainted with the traditional version do not feel an improvement on it), is or was well known on the Isle of Barra, Scotland. It is a considerable strain for an elderly person as Mrs McInnis then was, to sing in full; she lightened the burden by omitting certain lines, reproduced in italics here from Miss Annie Johnston's version, and omitting the last two lines of the refrain except at the very end of the song, where Séamus Ennis did not hear it when transcribing. It is included in Mrs MacLean's version of the air, printed above.

Notes

Lines 4, 5. Imply that the flock of sheep she was gathering was not an insignificant one.

Line 9. MacLean's country—the islands of Mull and Coll.

Line 11. Kishmul Castle was the ancestral stronghold of the Chiefs of the MacNeils of Barra; Castlebay is called for it; it is on a small island there, and has recently been restored.

Line 23. Ruairi an Tartair, Rory the Noisy, or the Turbulent, was chief at the end of the sixteenth and beginning of the seventeenth centuries. He was eventually confined in the castle by the eldest son of his second marriage until he died, whereupon this son usurped the succession, as is described by Fr Ward the Irish Franciscan missionary who visited Barra in 1625. Niall Gruamach 'Gloomy Neil' or 'Surly Neil', was probably Niall Og, the usurper, who remained in possession of the island. See J. L. Campbell, 'The MacNeils of Barra and the Irish Franciscans', *Innes Review*, v, 33.

Line 24. Gilleonan Mór was chief of the Barra MacNeils from about 1655 until about 1670.

Line 25. Ruairi Og, 'Young Rory' was the son and heir of Gilleonan Mór. He and his brother James were tried in Edinburgh in 1679 for deforcing a King's Messenger sent to collect a debt owed to Macleod of Dunvegan.

Line 31. The tune quickens here, having to accommodate lines of 12 instead of 8 syllables. See *Hebridean Folksongs* I, 335. The poetess changes to another subject, the formulaic one of the successful hunter preferred as a lover.

fo lighe mo ghruaige, literally 'under (the) lustre of my hair'. *Lí*, 'beauty, glory, brightness, splendour'. See *Contributions to a Dictionary of the Irish Language*, which also gives *fo lí* as 'well complexioned' in another context.

Line 40. *Deachamh* = tenth, literally. Cf Fr Allan McDonald, *Gaelic Words from South Uist*, 'When eggs are set for hatching, it is always an odd number that is set. It is said that there is always one egg that fails to be hatched. This egg is said to go into the *deachamh* (tithe?).' The suggestion is that the expression refers to the habit of putting the worst animal, etc, into the tithe or teind paid to the local clergyman.

29   A MHIC A' MHAOIR

I

Mar a ghabh Anna Nill Ruaidh e

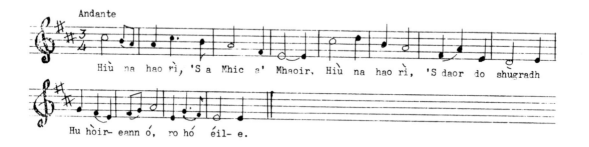

SE 72; A, Mixolydian.

II

Mar a ghabh Eairdsidh Sheumais e

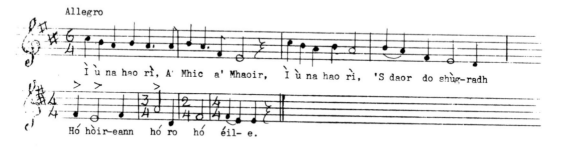

SE 71; A, Hexatonic, no 7 (4:7).

THE SINGERS AND THEIR SONGS

A MHIC A' MHAOIR

Hiù na hao ri,
  'S a Mhic a' Mhaoir,   's daor do shùgradh,
Hiù na hao rì,   Hu hoireann o, ro hó eile.
                Hu na hao ri,
                  's daor do shùgradh,
                Hu na hao ri,

Mharbh thu grugach   uallach, dhualdhonn,[1]
Gur h-ann 'sa choill   rinn thu 'n diùbhail,
Piostal do thaoibh   *rinn mo chiùrradh,*
5. 'S e t'fhùdar ghorm   las mo shùilean,
    Chuir thu luaidhe   ghlas 'nam ghlùinean!
    A bhràithribh gaoil   bithibh ciùin ris,
    S cha do thog e   *riamh r'a shùil e;*
    Caidil thu raoir   air mo chùlaibh,
10. Ghaoil, ma chaidil   cha b'ann brùideil,
    Cha bu bhruaillein   leam do shùgradh.
      Ghaoil, ma théid thu   as an dùthaich
    Na taobh Diùraidh,   *na taobh Lùngaidh,*
    No Colbhasaigh   nan struth siùbhlach,
15. No bidh m'athair   riut a' cùnntais,
    Bidh mo phiuthar   an droch-rùn dhut,
    Bidh mo mhàthair   as a ciùnn dhut,
    Thig mo bhràithrean   òg dha m' iùnnsaigh,
    'S bheir iad mise   leo air ghiùlain,
20. Air each garga   le strian dùbailt,

    'S a Mhic a' Mhaoir   's gur tu as docha
    Shiubhail sliabha   fiar no fochann,
    Laigh air a thaobh   deas no tosgail,
    No chuir bròg air   stròn a choiseadh.

25. B'fhearr gun cluinninn   siod 's gu faiceadh
    Farum do luaidh,   fuaim do bhrataich,
    Air luing, air bàt',   no air barca,
    'S ge nach beò mi   *gus siod fhaicinn*
    Gum bu mhath liom   sin a thachairt.

---

[1] The rhyme suggests strongly that the last word of this line should be *dubhdhonn*, 'dark brown'.

167

Translation

O, son of the Steward,   your love-making was costly,
You have killed a proud   curling haired maiden,
You did the injury   in the forest,
Your side pistol   did my wounding,
5. I was blinded   by your powder,
With your bullet   in my knees you shot me—
Beloved brethren   treat him kindly,
He never raised it   to take aim at me.

Last night you slept   close beside me,
10. My love, if you slept   it was not roughly,
Your love-making   was no vexation.
My love, if you go   from the district,
Avoid Jura,   avoid Lunga,
Avoid Colonsay   of the tidal currents,
15. Or my father will have   an account to settle,
My sister will be   hostile to you,
My mother will be   of them the foremost,
My young brothers   will come for me,
They will take me   on my funeral
20. With an unbroken horse   with doubled reins.

O Son of the Steward,   you are the dearest,
Who trod hillside   braird, or grassland,
Who lay on his right   or on his left side,
Or put a shoe   on his forefoot.

25. I'd sooner hear   that and see it,
The noise of your lead,   the sound of your banner,
On ship, on boat,   or on galley;
Though to see it   I shall live not,
That is what I would   like to happen.

Recorded from A. J. MacKenzie at Christmas Island on 6/10/37, and from Mrs Neil McInnis at MacKay's Corner two days later. Her text being the longer, is used here; passages in italics are taken from Mr MacKenzie's version.

Previously recorded from Roderick MacKinnon 'Ruairi Iain Bhàin' on the Isle of Barra, on 26/5/37, and again on Presto disc in March 1938; another version was taken down from Elizabeth Sinclair on Vatersay in June 1949.

See *Gaelic Folksongs from the Isle of Barra*, p. 30, the first time the full text appeared in print; and *Hebridean Folksongs* II, 150, from Canon Duncan MacLean's MS collection, reciter uncertain. The only previous printing so far known occurs in Finlay Dun's *Orain na'h Albain*, *c.*1860, in which the songs are arranged as art songs. In this the text given (in normal spelling) begins *Dheagh Mhic ant-Saoir. Mharbh thu'n cailin, 's b'fheàrr a pùsadh,* 'Good MacIntyre, you killed the girl, it were better to marry her.'

As the song is obviously connected with Argyll, in which all the islands mentioned, Jura, Lunga, and Colonsay are, and with which county the MacIntyres are connected, it is quite likely that the name *Mac an t-Saoir* 'Son of the carpenter; MacIntyre' was corrupted into *Mac a' Mhaoir* 'Son of the Steward' in Barra, where the song was preserved after it had been forgotten in Argyll. *Maor* = a ground officer, under-factor, on a Highland estate.

The song appears to be a ballad adapted as a milling or waulking song; it tells a perfectly straightforward story of an accidental shooting of a girl by her lover, and the consequences, without the introduction of passages on other subjects, or formulaic padding, which occur so often in the older waulking songs. Two lines from Elizabeth Sinclair's and Canon Maclean's version which add to the sense can be quoted here; they would follow line 11:

> *Cha phàigh an Donn dhut an t-ùnnlagh,*
> *No Dubhbheag, no Chiar, no 'n t-Siùbhlach.*
> The Brown would not pay the fine for you
> Nor the Small Black nor the Dun, nor the Wanderer

Names of cows the value of which would not pay the fine that would be imposed on the girl's lover for manslaughter. These lines were misunderstood when Elizabeth Sinclair's version was taken down, and the passage as it stands on pp. 32 and 33 of *Gaelic Folksongs from the Isle of Barra* should be corrected.

169

30 MHIC 'IC AILEIN, THA MI'N DÉIDH ORT

Fonn: Hó ró, ho là ill e hó,
Ho hì, o ho nàilibh,
Hó ró, ho là ill e hó.

Mhic 'ic Ailein, tha mi an déidh ort,
    Hó ró, hó là ill e hó.
Tha mi 'n troma-ghaol ort mar chéile,
Tha mi teisteal, as a dhéidh sin,
Rachainn leat air Chuan na h-Éireann
5. Far am bi muir àrd ag éirigh,
'S muca mara 'san t-sruth ag éibheach,
Luingeas ri gualainn a chéile,
Iarann fuar 'gan cur 'na chéile.

Nàile! chuirinn mo gheall 's gun cumadh,
10. 'S ann anall a thig an curaidh
Leis an òlte fìon an tunna,
Leis an éireadh na fir uile.

Nan éireadh gach eun le a fhine,
Dh'éireadh na Camshronaich linne,
15. Domhnallaich o Ràid a' Ghlinne,
Stiubhartaich o'n àit' ro-thioram,
Clann 'ic Leòid nan ròisgeul binne,
Caimbeulaich cha n-fhiachainn fhìn iad—
Bidh Clann Nill air tùs gach fine,
20. Leathanaich cha leubh iad giorrag.

170

'S rachainn leat dha'n Chaisteal dùinte,
Far am faighinn modh is mùirne,
Daoin' uaisle mu bhòrda dùmhail,
Ruidhle mu seach air an ùrlar,
25. Fidhleireachd bu ragha ciùil dhaibh.

Translation

1. Clanranald, I am fond of you,
   I am deeply in love with you,
   I am of good fame, after all;
   I would go with you on the Irish Sea,
5. Where high seas are rising,
   Whales in the current crying
   Ships beside each other lying,
   Cold steel putting them together.

   Indeed! I'd make my bet and keep it,
10. That over will come the hero
    By whom wine would be drunk in hogsheads,
    With whom all the men would rise up.

    If every chief rose with his clansmen,
    The Camerons would rise up with us,
15. Macdonalds from the Glens of Antrim.
    Stewarts from a very dry country,
    Clan MacLeod of sweet . . . ,
    Campbells I myself don't value,
    Clan MacNeil before each clan,
20. MacLeans who never show panic.

    I would go with you to the closed castle,
    Where I'd find joy and manners,
    Numerous gentry round the table,
    Reels in turn on the floor dancing,
25. Fiddling was their favourite music.

Recorded from Mrs Neil McInnis at McKay's Corner on 5/10/37. Tune transcribed by Séamus Ennis; words taken down by J. L. Campbell. See *HF* I, 66; *FFSU*, 250; *KCC*, 94.

Notes

Refrain. In this type of refrain, the first line is normally sung by the soloist, and is called the solo refrain; the following two lines are sung by the chorus. When recorded at home without the presence of a chorus, traditional singers often omit the chorus refrain, or only sing it at the very end of the song. This is what happened here. Mrs McInnis did not sing the chorus refrain at all, but the full refrain is well known from other versions, and is restored here.

Line 7. Other versions have *Luingeas a' losgadh air a chéile,* 'Ships firing at each other', or *a' cogadh ri chéile,* 'warring with each other'. Line 8. May refer to grappling irons.

Line 15. Ràid a' ghlinne may refer to the Route in Antrim, Northern Ireland, MacDonald territory.

Line 17. Ròisgeul means 'romance; boasting', but there may be a confusion here with the word ròiseol, a word of uncertain meaning found in such texts. See *HF* I, lines 416, 1058, and the glossary in *Carmina Gadelica,* vol. VI.

Line 18. Some other versions have *Bhiodh na Caimbeulaich 'san linnidh,* 'the Campbells would be in the linn', possibly a reference to Loch Linnhe at the time of the battle of Inverlochy, AD 1644, see song no. 57 here.

Line 21. *HF ro' chùl-taigh dùinte; FFSU gu cùl Taigh 'n Dùnain.* Mrs McInnis's version seems best, but there may be an underlying corruption.

SE 112; Mode, G, Pentatonic, 4:7.

31 'S MI 'M SHUIDHE AM MUIGH AN GLEANN NA GÉIGE

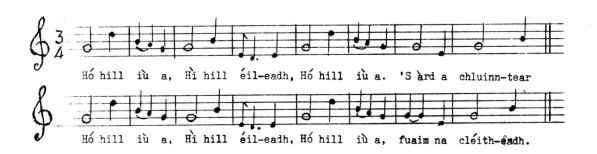

Fonn: Hó hill iù á,
Hì hill éileadh,
Hó hill iù a.

'S mi 'm shuidhe amuigh   an gleann na Géige
'S àrd a chluinntear   fuaim na cléitheadh,
'S binn guth nighinn ann   's binn guth moighdin,
'S binn guth cinn   mo leannain fhéin ann,
5.   Ma's binn a guth   's fheàrr a feum ann.

'S muladach mi   am Braighe Liantaidh,
'S fhad' an sealladh   bhuam a chì mi,
Chi mi Rùm is   Eige 's Ìle,
Colbhasaigh bheag   . . . . . .
10.   Far na rinn Mac   Colla 'n dìobhail,
Far na ghabh Mac   Leoid a dhìnneir,
Dh'ol e deoch ann,   chaisg e a ìotadh,
Cha b'ann dha'n bhùrn   dubh na dìge,
Uisge beatha   feadan fìorghlan.

15.   'S mur b'e eagal   a dhà phàrant
'S mi 'n eilean dubh   air an t-sàile,
Dh'iomairinn, dh'éibhinn,   dh'òlainn, phàighinn,
Chuirinn mo chluich   air an tàileasg,
Air na dìsnean   geala cnàmha,
20.   'S air na cairtean   breaca, bàna.

173

Translation

	Sitting outside in	the Glen of Branches
	Loud I hear the	sound of the waulking (milling frolic)
	Sweet the song of	girl and maiden,
	Sweet the voice there	of my own lover,
5.	If sweet her voice,	her help is better.

	Sorrowful am I	on the Brae of Liantaidh,
	Far from me	the view I'm seeing,
	I see Rum and	Eigg and Islay,
	Little Colonsay	....
10.	Where Mac Colla	wrought the ill deed,
	Where MacLeod	took his dinner,
	He drank a drink	and quenched his thirst there,
	Not of black water	from the ditches,
	But of whisky	of clean distilling.

15.	But for fear of	my two parents ? her two
	And I in a black isle	on salt water,
	I would play, I would shout,	I'd drink, I'd pay,
	I would make my play	at backgammon,
	With the dice	of bright bone,
	With the cards	white and speckled.

Recorded from Mrs Neil McInnis at Glace Bay on 8/10/37. Tune transcribed by Séamus Ennis; words transcribed by J. L. Campbell.

Notes

Line 1. 'The Glen of Branches' occurs in some other songs, see *Hebridean Folksongs* I, 634 and III, 365. I have not yet located it.

Line 2. *Fuaim na cléitheadh*, the sound of cloth being thumped on a board while the waulking or milling was going on. For the opening lines of this song, compare lines 1107 to 1111 of *Hebridean Folksongs*, Vol. I.

'S àrd a chluinntear fuaim na cléithe
Aig mnài Uibhist, 's aig mnài Shléibhte,
'S binn guth cinn mo leannain fhéin ann,
Ma's binn a guth, 's fheàrr a beusan
Air chùl corrain 's air chùl cléithe.

Many such passages are found in more than one of the old waulking (milling) songs.

Lines 6–9. Wherever the Brae of Liantaidh is, the only places from which it might be possible to see all the islands mentioned are Morenish or Treshnish in the Isle of Mull.

Line 9. The rhyme shows the second half of this line is missing. It probably would have been some epithet of Colonsay.

174

THE SINGERS AND THEIR SONGS

Line 10. This must refer to the violent dispossession of the MacPhees or MacFies of Colonsay by Coll Ciotach MacDonald in 1623. I can find no historical event that explains the allusion to MacLeod in the next line.

Lines 17–20. Formulaic lines, see *Hebridean Folksongs* I, 1036–9 and II, 1256–8.

SE 115; Mode, G, Pentatonic, 4:7.

32 DÒMHNALLAN DUBH, DÒMHNALLAN

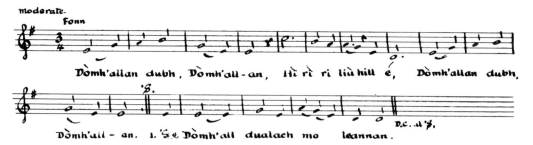

Fonn: Dòmhnallan dubh, Dòmhnallan,
Hi rì ri liù hill é
Dòmhnallan dubh, Dòmhnallan.

'S e Dòmhnall dualach mo leannan,
Gaol nan gruagach's luaidh nan caileag,
'S toil leam thu bhith 'n làimh 'sa charraig,
Iarann air do bhasan geala;

5. 'S e dh'fhàg mo rùn gun bhith glégheal,
Seasamh fada air cuan na h-Éireann,
Cumail coinneamh ri Rìgh Seumas.
Sgoltadh gort a' bhradain fhìoruisg'
Air an té thug bhuam mo leannan,

10. Mi fhìn seachd bliadhna 'ga àlach
Air uisge nan lòn 's air aran.
A Dhòmhnaill, nan dig thu do m'iarraidh,
Cha b'e an t-aran tur bu bhiadh leat,
Biolair òg is ubhlan fiadhaich,
15. Bainne bruich nan aighean ciallach.

Translation

Refrain: Little dark Donald, little Donald,
Hì rì rì Hill é
Little dark Donald, little Donald.

1. Curling haired Donald is my sweetheart
Love of the maidens, darling of the lasses,
I'm pleased that you are imprisoned on the rock
With irons on your white hands.

176

5. What caused my love to lose his fairness
   Was staying long on the Irish Sea.
   Waiting to meet with King James.
   May the girl who stole my lover
   Be split like a freshwater salmon,

10. I had spent seven years nursing him
    On pond water and in bread.
    Donald, if you came to seek me,
    Your food would not be dry bread.
    But young cress and wild apples,
    And warm milk of tame heifers.

Recorded from Mrs Neil McInnis, MacKay's Corner, Cape Breton on 8/10/37; tune transcribed by Séamus Ennis; words transcribed by J. L. Campbell.

Notes

Line 3. 'the rock'. Possibly a kenning for some castle, such as Dunvegan, or Duntuilm.

Line 5. The Gaelic nobles, who did not have to work in the fields, were usually distinguished by their fair skins.

Line 8. Compare J. F. Campbell, *Leabhar na Féinne,* p. 212:

    Ach a nighean ud 'san dorus,
    Gu faicinn triùir air do bhanais,
    A nì sgoltadh a' bhradain fhìoruisg'
    Eadar do dhà chìch 's do bhroilleach.

'But yon girl in the doorway, may I see three at your wedding who will split you like a freshwater salmon between your two breasts and your sternum.'

This verse comes in a song, sung to a beautiful melody, made by a girl who reproaches her sister bitterly for having betrayed to their parents that she had a fairy lover, after having promised to keep it a faithful secret. In consequence, the heroine was kept a prisoner by their parents, while her three brothers killed the fairy lover.

The reference is to the atrocious method of killing sometimes used by the Vikings, called 'spread-eagling'.

See also the Inverness collection (*Co-chruinneacha Dhan, Orain* &c.), p. 68.

Alexander Carmichael refers to the imprecations *Sgoltadh beithreach ort! Sgoltadh bradain ort!* 'The bursting of the serpent on thee! The bursting of the salmon on thee!' saying that they referred to the idea that the serpent and the salmon burst their bellies in bringing forth their young; but salmon are not viviparous. Elsewhere he gives *fara-bhradan* for 'a spent salmon' (*Carmina Gadelica* II, 230, 289).

SE 111; Mode, Hexatonic E, no 2.

33   AN COIRE RIABHACH

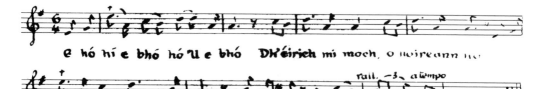

e hó hì e bhó hó 'll e bhó   Dh'éirich mì moch, o hòireann hó

hì e bhó   hó 'll e bhó,   Dh'éirich mì suas, ó   hug oró

E ho hì e, bhó hó ill e bhó,
Dh'éirich mi moch, ó hòireann ó,
E ho hì e bhó, hó ill e bhó,
[maduinn ghrianach,] ó hug o ró,
E ho hì e bhó, hó ill e bhó,

     Dhìrich mi suas   [an Coire Riabhach,]
     Thiarainn mi nuas   an gleann air fhiaradh,
     Cha d'fhuair mi ann   na bha mi 'g iarraidh,
  5. Banchag a' chruidh   dhruimfhinn, chiardhuibh,
     Sùil 'gan sireadh   cas 'gan iarraidh,
     'Gan toirt as na   beannan fiadhain
     Ris na lagain   ìseil ghrianach.

     Gura h-e mo   rùn an t-uasal,
 10. Chunnaic mi an dé   seachad suas thu,
     Éileadh ort, *na*   a bhreacan uaine,
     Claidheamh chinnghil   or 'o chruachan,
     Do ghunna sneap   or 'o ghualainn,
     Dol a shealg na   h-éilde ruaidhe,
 15. 'N eala cha dig   slàn o d' luaidhe.

     Mo thriall, mo thriall,   mo thriall dhachaigh,
     Far an d'fhuair mi   gu h-òg m'altrum
     Air bainne chioch   's air fìon frasach,
     Air plaideachan   mìne geala;

 20. Gura h-e mo   rùn mo mhuime,
     Cha dug i riamh   dhomh droch-urram,
     Mo chur dha'n tràigh   bhuain an duilisg,
     'S ann a bhithinn   àrd an uraidh,
     Fuaghal feurlaidh   [leughadh dhuilleag,]
 25. Sìor-chur ghleus air   léin' a' churaidh.

Translation

	Early I rose	on a sunny morning,
	I climbed up	the Brindled Corrie,
	I came down	the glen in zig-zags
	I found not there	what I was seeking
5.	The dairymaid of	the white-backed black cattle,
	Eye seeking them,	foot looking for them,
	Bringing them from	the wild mountains
	To the low-lying	sunny valleys.
	My loved one is	the noble person
10.	I saw passing	yesterday,
	Wearing a plaid	of green tartan
	At your side	a sword bright-hilted,
	Your triggered gun	at your shoulder
	Going to hunt	the red deer hind,
15.	The swan won't go	by your lead unwounded.
	My path, my path	my path homewards,
	To where I got	my childhood rearing,
	On breast milk	and wine in plenty
	On fine, white,	blankets.
20.	My love is for	my foster-mother,
	Who never gave me	any ill treatment,
	Or sent me to shore	to gather seaweed;
	Last year I'd be	in upper story
	Sewing	reading pages
	Embroidering	the hero's shirt.

Recorded at MacKay's Corner on 15/10/37. Tune transcribed by Séamus Ennis; words transcribed by J. L. Campbell. See *HF* II, 172–5. The words in brackets restore the proper form of the first two lines. On the Isle of Barra this was considered one of the most beautiful waulking songs.

Notes

Lines 1–5. describe bringing the cattle down from the summer hill grazings to the winter pasture.

Line 4. Banchag means the woman in charge of the dairy, a very important person on farms in the Highlands.

Lines 9–15. Are formulae, compare *HF* I, 466–75, 'My lover is a successful hunter'; likewise, *lines 16–25.* 'I was reared in happier circumstances not doing servile work'. Cf. *HF* II, 679–83 and *HF* II, 1545–51, for instance.

Lines 12, 13. or'o is the colloquial form of *air do*, 'on thy'.

Line 25. The second half is supplied from another version of this passage.

SE 3; Mode, Hexatonic A, no 6.

34 'S MISE 'N BHEAN BHOCHD AIR MO SGARADH

'S mise bhean bhochd air mo sgaradh,
Air fair al al é ho,
O hòireann ó ho.

Air mo chuaradh 's air mo ghearradh,
Air fair al al e o ho
Ho ró ó hi hò ri gealladh éileadh,
Ó hòireann o hó.

Air mo chuaradh 's air mo ghearradh,
Air fair al al é ho,
Ó hóireann o hó.

Chuir mi dàreug fo'n talamh,
Eadar fear is mhac is leanabh;
5.   Cóigear ann an cnoc na seanach,
'S a' chuid eile a thaigh mór nan aingeal,
'S b'fhaide na sin líom bàs Anna,
Bean a' chuailein chuachaich chlannaich,
'S guirme sùil na driùchd na maidne,
10.   'S deirge gruaidh na chuach air chrannaibh,
'S gile taobh na 'n fhaoileann mhara.

180

Translation

I am a poor, distraught woman,
I am hurt, I am wounded,
I have put twelve beneath the soil,
Between husband and son and baby
5. Five in the knoll of the foxes,
And another part to the great house of the angels;
I felt worst the death of Anna,
The woman of curling ringleted hair,
Her eyes more blue than morning dew,
10. Her cheek more red than flowers on trees,
Her flank more white than the seagull.

Recorded at MacKay's Corner on 20/10/37. The song like many others of the old waulking songs, was sung with each line after first sung twice, followed by a different phrase of the refrain. Tune transcribed by Séamus Ennis. Words taken down by J. L. Campbell. A fragment. The section preserved here is formulaic, compare *HF* I, lines 101–10.

Notes

Line 1. *Bochd* means 'ill' as well as 'poor' in Uist and Barra.
Line 5. This is reading *sean(n)ach* as an alternative form of *sionnach*, see Dinneen's Irish Dictionary.
Line 6. 'The great house of the angels', presumably a kenning for an important church, but I have not seen this elsewhere.
Line 10. It is uncertain what blossoms were meant in the expression *cuach air chrannaibh*. Probably bunches of rowan berries are meant; a version of the same passage in a song in K. C. Craig's collection has *'S deirge gruaidh na a' chaor air mheangan*, 'Redder her cheek than rowan berry on branch'. Fr Dieckhoff's Dictionary gives rowan as the meaning of *caor*.

SE 128; Mode, D, Ionian.

35 THA SNEACHD AIR NA BEANNAIBH DIÙRACH

Fonn: O hì u, bhì hó,
          I iùrabh ó ro, hùg éileadh,
          O hì u, bhì hó.

Tha sneachd air na beannaibh Diùrach,
Cha doir uisge no ceò dhiù e—
A Righ! ma thà, gu dé sin dhùinne!
Cha truimid iad fhéin a ghiùlain;
5. Tha féidh air leacraich an dùine,
   'S truagh nach mise bh'air an cùlaibh
   Le m' ghunna 's le m'adhraic fhùdair,
   Dh'fhàgainn an damh ruadh 'na chrùban,
   Com na fala sileadh siùbhlach,
10. 'S an eala bhàn as binne tùchan.

Tha port aig gillean Mhic Eachainn,
'S cha phort a th'orra, ach cion aisig,
'S truagh nach robh mo dhùrachd aca,
Bhiodh port orra gu cionn seachdain,
15. Cuideachd branndaidh 's ragha thom-baca,
    Togsaidean fhìon air an cearcladh.

Nighean chruinn donn, na bi 'n gruaim rium,
Cha n-iarrainn bó dhubh no ruadh leat,
No bó bhreac an iomall buaile
20. Tha do thochradh leam 'nad ghruaidhean.

182

Translation

Snow is on the hills of Jura
Rain nor mist will not remove it,
My God! If so, what does it matter?
Carrying it they are no heavier.
5. There are deer upon the hillside,
'Tis a pity I'm not after them
With my gun and my powder horn
I would leave the brown stag crouching,
With his heart shedding blood freely,
10. And the white swan which sweetest utters.

MacEachen's lads have got a tune (*port*),
It's not a 'port', they have, but no ferry;
It's a pity they don't have my wish,
They would have a tune till the week's end.
15. Also brandy, and choice tobacco,
Hogsheads of wine with hoops around them.

Neat brown maiden, don't be annoyed with me,
That I don't ask a black or red cow with you,
Nor a piebald cow at the edge of the cattlefold,
20. For me your dowry is in your cheeks!

Recorded at MacKay's Corner on 8/10/37. Tune transcribed by Séamus Ennis; words transcribed by J. L. Campbell. *HF* II, 110, KCC, 74; Dornie MS, *TGSI* xli, 350, poems from (ed. Angus Matheson); *Gesto Collection*, Appendix, p. 15.

Notes

Line 10. The reference is to the old Gaelic idea that the swan, not normally a tuneful bird, calls sweetly when at the point of death. See *Carmina Gadelica* II, p. 278.

Mar eala bhàn an déigh a reubadh,
Guileag bàis air lochan feurach.
'Like to the white swan after she is wounded
singing her death dirge on a ready lake.'

Lines 11–14. There is a play on words on *port* = tune and *port* = port, harbour. *A bhith ri port* = To be in a port held up waiting for a ferry. The Dornie MS shows that the waiting was for the ferry to Pabbay in the sound of Harris.

Line 15. The Dornie MS has *Togsaid branndaidh*. In my transcript the *-eachd* of *cuideachd* is clearly indicated by the conventional MS abbreviation. *Rogha* might be *robha,* 'roll'.

SE 114; Mode, D, Hexatonic, no 7; variant Pent: 3:7.

36   CHA DÌRICH MI 'M BRUTHACH

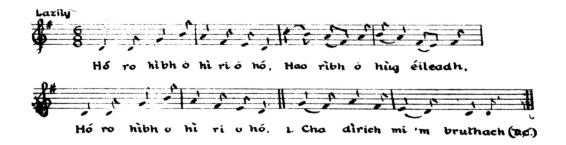

Fonn: Hó ro hìbh o hì ri o hó,
Hao rìbh o hùg éileadh;
Hó ro hìbh o hì ri o hó.

Cha dìrich mi 'm bruthach,
    Cha siubhal mi eutrom;
Nàile! goirtead mo choise,
    Cha dochann i feur dhomh;
5. Chiad leannan a bh' agam,
    Tha i bagradh mo thréigsinn
Ma thà, tha cead aice,
    Cha bhith fadachd 'na déidh orm;
Ma th'agad sgeul rùin orm,
10.   Cum gu dlùth agad fhéin i,
    Na doir idir do chàch i,
      Iad cho bànranach, breugach;
    Siod mo chomhairle, 's gabh i,
      Na gabh cailin mar chéile,
15. No té uasal 's i falamh,
    'S don' an t-earras le chéil' iad;
B'fhearr dhut searbhana cumant
    Le baidein beag spréidhe,
A rachadh na bhuailidh
20.   'S a dh'fhuaighleadh do léine
'S nì 'n todhar 'sa chladach,
    'S nì an fheannag, ma's fheudar.

Translation

I will not climb the hillside,
I cannot walk lightly,
With the pain in my foot,
It will not crush the grass.
5. The first lover I've had
Now threatens to leave me,
If she does, she has leave to,
I won't be missing her.
If you have a secret story about me,
10. Keep it close to yourself,
Don't tell it to any others,
They are gossipy and untruthful;
That's my advice, take it,
Don't take a lassie as your wife,
15. Nor an indigent gentlewoman,
They are both a bad bargain.
Better for you an ordinary farm-girl,
With a small herd of cattle,
Who'd go to the cattlefold,
20. Who'd sew your linen,
Who'd get from the shore seaweed,
And make the lazybed if need be.

Recorded at MacKay's Corner on 12/10/37. Tune transcribed by Séamus Ennis; words transcribed by J. L. Campbell.

See *HF* III, 68. Mrs McInnis was the sole source of the words here; only an initial couplet (not here) and the tune was remembered on the Isle of Barra by July 1975.

Notes

Line 8. Has *dhéidh* in my original transcription, but elsewhere the subject is feminine.

Line 15. Impecunious gentry were not well thought of in the Highlands, hence the saying, *Uaislean gun chuid, maragan gun gheir,* 'Gentry without wealth, sausages without fat'. A gentlewoman would not be likely to be of much use as a farm wife. Nor would be a 'maid from a mansion', *cailín tighe mhóir* (Dinneen's Dictionary).

Line 17. Searbhana, a woman servant on a farm.

Line 21. The seaweed was used for manuring the land. Lazybeds (*line 22*) were made for planting potatoes. The seaweed was laid on the grass in strips, and the sods on each side turned over the seaweed. The potatoes were planted with a dibble, *pleadhag* in Gaelic. See *FFSU*.

SE 118. Mode, D, Dorian.

37 'S MOCH AN DIU GUN D'RINN MI ÉIRIGH

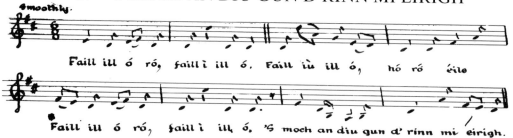

Fonn: Faill ill ó ró, faill ì ill ó,
Faill iù ill ó, hó ro éile,
Faill ill ó ró, faill ì ill o.

'S moch an diu gun d'rinn mi éirigh,
Ma's moch an diu, 's moch an dé e;
Dhìrich mi suas guala an t-sléibhe,
Fhuair mi gruagach dhonn gun éirigh,
5. 'S thug mi 'n lùib mo bhreacain fhéin i,
Shaoil mi nach robh tuilleadh déidh oirr'.

"'S bòidheach dualach mo thriùir leannan,
'S fear dhiu 'n Ìle, 's fear 'm Manainn,
Fear eile 'n tìrmor na h-Earradh."

Translation

It was early today that I arose,
If early today, earlier yesterday,
I climbed up the shoulder of the hill,
I found the brown-haired lass still lying,
5. I took her within my own plaid,
I thought there was no more she wanted.

'My three lovers are curly-haired and handsome
One on Man and one on Islay,
Another on the land of Harris.'

Recorded at MacKay's Corner on 20/10/37. Tune transcribed by Séamus Ennis; words transcribed by J. L. Campbell.

A fragment. There is a version of 13 lines in *FFSU*, p. 226. There is also one of 17 lines in KCC, p. 47. The last three lines are not found in either of these. See also the first ten lines of No. XXXI in *HF* I, 134. There are similarities in the tunes.

SE 130. Mode, Pentatonic, no 4.

186

38   A MHÀIRI BHÀN AS ÀILLE SEALLADH

Hi rì hó, Mhàiri bhuidh', Hó ró hao hó, Hi rì hó, Mhàiri bhuidh'.

Mhàir-i bhàn as àill-e seall-adh, Hi rì hó, Mhàiri bhuidh'.

Fonn: Hi rì hó, Mhàiri bhuidh',
       Hó ró hao hó,
       Hi rì hó, Mhàiri bhuidh'.

       A Mhàiri bhàn as àille sealladh,
       C'à' 'n a dh'fhàg thu na fir gheala?
       'Dh'fhàg mi an dé 'san Eilein mhara
       Beul ri beul ag òl an leanna.'
  5. 'Éisd a Mhàiri, sguir dhe d' fhanaid,
       Tha iad an diu marbh gun anam
       Cùl ri cùl a' call na fala';

       'S chì mi long a' falbh gu siùbhlach
       'S i dol timchioll Rudh' an Dùna[in]
 10. 'S mo leannan fhéin làmh 'ga stiùireadh
       Fhad 's a mhaireadh ball no lùb dhith
       Na buill chainbe ri cruinn rùis'te
       No giuthas os cionn a h-ùrlair.

       Chì mi, chì mi, chì mi, thall ud,
 15. Chì mi na h-eòin chruinne gheala,
       'S iad 'a falbh ri cois na mara,
       Mo ghiamanaiche féin 'gan leantail;
       'S nam bithinn-sa an riochd na h-eala
       Shnàmhainn an caol, rachainn fairis,
 20. O, ruiginn an t-àite far bheil mo leannan,
       Air do làimh, gu faighinn cadal.

SONGS REMEMBERED IN EXILE

Translation

Refrain: Hi rì hò, golden-haired Mary,
Hó ró, hao hó.

1. 'Fair-haired Mary, loveliest sight,
Where did you leave the fine men?'
'I left them yesterday on the sea island,
Mouth to mouth drinking beer.'
5. 'Listen Mary, stop your mocking, .
They are today dead and lifeless
Back to back losing blood.'

I see a ship travelling swiftly,
Going around Rubh' an Dùnain,
10. My own lover's hand is steering her,
As long as rope or tackle lasts for her,
Or canvas ropes to the bare masts,
Or fir above her deck.

I see, I see, I see yonder,
15. I see the round white birds,
Going at the edge of the sea,
The hunter himself following,
And if I were in the shape of the swan
I would swim the narrows, I would go over,
20. I would reach the place where is my lover,
By thy hand, I would get sleep.

Recorded from Mrs McInnis, McKay's Corner, on 19/10/37. Tune transcribed by Séamus Ennis, written a fourth lower, and including an F sharp sign in the signature, not needed as the note does not occur. Words taken down by J. L. Campbell.

Notes

Line 9. *Rubha an Dùnain*, probably the promontory on the Isle of Skye, west of Soay and NW of Canna.

Line 21. Swearing 'by thy hand' was a common asseveration in the Highlands. *Làmh th'athar, a Dheòrsa, Gum faigh sinne buaidh ort*, 'By thy father's hand, King George, we'll get the victory over you', Alexander MacDonald wrote in a poem written after 1746.

SE 126; Mode G, Hexatonic, no 7.

39 SEINN O HO RÓ, SEINN

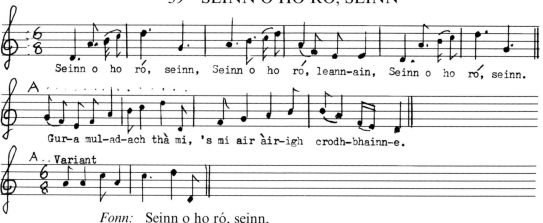

Seinn o ho ró, seinn, Seinn o ho ró, leann-ain, Seinn o ho ró, seinn.

A........

Gur-a mul-ad-ach thà mi, 's mi air àir-igh crodh-bhainn-e.

A...Variant

Fonn: Seinn o ho ró, seinn,
Seinn o ho ró, leannain,
Seinn o ho ró, seinn.

Gura muladach thà mi,
    'S mi air àirigh crodh-bhainne.

Gura muladach sgìth mi,
    Leam fhìn an tìr aineoil.

5. Cha b'ionann mar bhà mi,
    Mu dh'fhàg mi Bràighe Rainich,

Le m' phiuthar 's le m' bhràthair,
    Cead bhith bànran ri m' leannan.

'S tric a bha mi's tu sùgradh,
10. Cha b'fhiù leinn ach ceanal.

Ann am bothag an t-sùgraidh,
    'S e bu dùnadh dhith barrach.

Thormaid fear nan gorm-shùilean meallach,
    Ruairi bidh daoin' uaisle air do bhanais.

15. Làmh a stiùireadh a' bhàta,
    Muir garbhlach m'a bhallaibh.

Làmh a stiùireadh i dìreach,
    Ro' Chaol Ile 'na deannaibh.

'S tu a stiùreadh i tioram,
20. Muir a' mire ri darach.

189

SONGS REMEMBERED IN EXILE

Translation

Refrain: Sing o ho ro, sing
Sing o ho ro, darling
Sing o ho ro, sing.

1. Sorrowful am I at the sheiling of the milking cattle.

2. Sorrowful and tired by myself in a strange country.

3. Not so was I ere I left the Brae of Rannoch.

4. With my sister and my brother, and leave to talk with my lover.

5. Often were you and I flirting, we only thought fondness worthy.

6. In the hut of love-making, closed by birch branches.

7. Norman of blue smiling eyes, Rory, gentry will be at your wedding.

8. Hand that would steer the boat, with a rough sea around her ropes.

9. Hand that would steer her straight through the Sound of Islay swiftly.

10. You would not let a drop come aboard her, while the sea played around her oak.

Recorded from Mrs Neil McInnis, MacKay's Corner, on 8/10/37. Tune transcribed by Séamus Ennis; words transcribed by J. L. Campbell.
See *FFSU* 238, where other sources are given.

Notes

SE 116; Mode D, variable 7 (3:7).

Ennis transcribed this song with two sharps, and wrote C♮ in the Variant. But F# does not occur at all, and the singer's C might be described as indeterminate in pitch. The very similar version in *FFSU* is written in the key of C.

40 GUR TU MO CHRUINNEAG BHÒIDHEACH

Fonn: I ù òr a hù ó,
Gur tu mo chruinneag bhòidheach,
I ù òr a hù ó.

1. A nighean donn bhòidheach mheall-shuileach,
   Tha fir a' bhaile an tòir ort

2. A nighean donn bhòidheach bheadarrach,
   Cha bheag orm do chòmhradh.

3. 'S mise tha gu muladach
   Air m'uilinn anns an t-seòmar.

4. Ag éisdeachd ris na tighearnan
   A' bruidhinn air do bhòichead.

5. Ag éisdeachd ris na caiptinean
   Ag iarraidh ceart is còir ort.

6. A Mhàiri thug mi gaol dhut,
   Nuair bha mi aotrom gòrach.

7. Shiùbhlainn leat an saoghal,
   A ghaoil, nam biodh tu deònach.

8. Rachainn leat a dh'Éirinn,
   Nam b'fheudar, dha'n Òlaind.

9. Rachainn leat a dh'Uidhist
   Far am buidhicheadh an t-eòrna.

10. Rachainn leat a dh'Ìle,
    Cinn Tìre a' bharraich bhòidhich.

191

11. Rachainn an ear 's an iar leat,
    Gun each gun strian gun bhòtain.

12. Rachainn fada fada leat,
    Na b'fhaide na bha m'eòlas.

13. Turus Raghnaill Ruaidh a Bhorghraidh
    Dh'fhàg gun fhoirm ri m' bheò mi.

14. Nuair a thug e bhuam mo leannan,
    Bean nam meallan lòghmor.

15. Nan saoilinn gun cumte bhuam thu,
    Bhuannaich mi as m'òig' thu.

16. 'S truagh nach robh mi 's m'eudail,
    'N Gleann Éit' a' bharraich bhòidhich.

17. 'S truagh nach robh mi còmhla riut
    An seòmar dlùth nam bòrdan.

18. 'S mise tha gu muladach
    Air m'uilinn, 's mi air m'ònar.

19. Cuimhneachadh do shùgradh,
    Lùb ùr a' bhroillich bhòidhich.

20. Cuimhneachadh do bheadraidh,
    Cha bheag a fhuair mi òg dheth.

21. Mun robh mi dusan bliadhna
    Gum b'e mo mhiann bhith còmh' riut.

22. 'S cha b'ann air sgàth nam bruachan,
    A luaidh, a fhuair mi t'eòlas.

23. Marbhaisg air a' ghaol sin
    Nach faodte chur air fògradh.

24. Cha robh ann ach faoineis
    Bha an aorabh nan clann òga.

25. 'S thug an gille fireach air
    A shireadh nan damh cròiceach.

26. 'S thug am bàta 'n caol air,
    'S cha robh mo ghaol 'ga sheòladh.

27. 'S thug am bàta 'n cuan air,
    'S cha bhuannaich e gun dòrainn.

28. 'S tha do mhàthair deurach,
    'S gu bheil mi fhéin glé bhrònach.

29. 'S cinnteach mi nach toilicht' i
    Ad fhortan, ged a phòs thu.

Translation

Refrain: I ù ò ro hù ò,
    You are my pretty maiden.
    I ù ò ro hù ò.

1.   Pretty girl of smiling eyes,
    the township lads are pursuing you.

2.   Pretty flirtatious girl, I like your
    conversation.

3.   Tis I who am sorrowful, on my elbow
    in my chamber.

4.   Listening to the lairds talking
    about your beauty.

5.   Listening to the captains seeking to have
    a right to you.

6.   Oh Mary, I fell in love with you when
    I was light and foolish.

7.   I would travel the world with you
    my love, if you are willing.

8.   I would go with you to Ireland, and if
    I might, to Holland.

193

9.   I would go with you to Uist, where the barley
ripens.

10.   I would go with you to Islay, to Kintyre
of the pretty birchwoods.

11.   I would go east and west with you,
Without horse, without rein, without bootings.

12.   I would go so far, far with you, further than I knew
of.

13.   The journey of auburn Ranald to Boreray
left me out of form for my life.

14.   When he took my sweetheart from me,
the woman of bright beguiling eyes.

15.   If I were to think you would be kept from me—
I won you in my youth.

16.   Pity I and my darling were not in Glen Etive
of the pretty birchwoods.

17.   Pity I was not with you, in a tight
room made of boards.

18.   Tis I who am sorrowful, on my elbow
all alone.

19.   Remembering your lovemaking, o youth of
handsome form.

20.   Remembering your flirting, I got plenty of it
when I was young.

21.   Before I was twelve, it was my desire to
be together with you.

22.   It was not under the shelter of river banks that
I got to know you, my love.

23.   Curses on that love, which cannot be banished
away.

24.   There was only in it the folly that is natural
to young folk.

25.   The lad took to the moor to seek the
antlered stags.

26.   He took to the slender boat,
and my love was not sailing in it.

27.   The boat took to the ocean, it did not win it
without trouble.

28.   Your mother was weeping, and I myself
was very sorrowful.

29.   I am sure she was not pleased at your fortune,
though you married.

Recorded from Mrs Neil McInnis, MacKay's Corner, on 15/10/37. Tune transcribed by Séamus Ennis; words taken down by J. L. Campbell.

The text of this song appears to be composed of the words of two very similar songs being taken together, the one after the other. The first twelve couplets have a good deal in common with the song *Gur tu mo nighean donn bhòidheach*, MacDonald Collection, p. 209 (16 couplets), and *Folksongs and Folklore of South Uist*, p. 222 (seven couplets); seven couplets of the first and three of the second are found here. The last fourteen couplets of the song are almost identical with those of the song *A fhleasgaich ghrinn, fhir chùil duinn*, printed in the *Oranaiche* (1879), p. 461.

I have no information on when or from whom Mrs Neil McInnis learnt the song as she sang it. Couplets in songs of this type easily get transported from one song to another in oral tradition. With regard to this, I have not yet found couplets 1, 2, 5, 6, 13, 14, 15 of Mrs McInnis's version anywhere else.

Notes

Verse 13. Boreray is an island in the Sound of Harris between Harris and North Uist, formerly held by a Maclean family.

Verse 14. My transcript in which the song is described by the singer as an *Òran deaslaimh*, song sung near the end of the waulking, has *leòmbar* and *lòghmhor* as alternative transcriptions of the last word of this couplet. *Meallan*, the preceding word, might just possibly be a mishearing of *meallshuil*.

Verse 16. Loch Etive is in Argyll, north of Oban. This is the *Oranaiche* reading, *Eite*. My transcription was *Eud*.

Verse 19. Oranaiche version *a' bhroillich* substituted for transcript *a' bhalaich*.

Verse 24. Aorabh = nature, constitution, what is inherent. So MacBain's *Etymological ·*

Dictionary, where the word is not explained. The singer explained it as *inntinn*, 'mind'. See *Carmina Gadelica* II, 58, 60, where it is translated 'constitution', and IV, 172, 184, 266, 'inherent in'. See also Rev. A. Stewart, *Nether Lochaber*, p. 202 where the word occurs in a charm from North Uist communicated by Alexander Carmichael. Stewart thought it meant 'reins' i.e. kidneys; Fr Allan MacDonald thought it might mean 'bodily parts or members', see under *Adhraibh*, in *Gaelic Words from South Uist*, quoting the expression *Tha 'n greim-loin* (sciatica) *'nam aorabh*. Cf. English 'kidney' with the meaning 'temperament', 'nature'.

Verse 27. Oranaiche, 's cha bhuanaichd i 'n doirlinn, 'she did not win the isthmus'.

Verse 28. O. chairdean, 'relations'.

Verse 29. O. toilicht' thu; phòs thu.

41 SORAIDH LEIS A' GHILLE DHONN

Fonn: Soraidh leis a' ghille dhonn,
        'S fhada leam o dh'fhàg thu 'm fonn,
        Soraidh leis a' ghille dhonn,
           Tha m'inntinn trom o'n sheòl thu.

1. An cuala sibh mu'n ghille bhàn
   A lig a leannan le càch?
   Gura mise nach eil slàn
      Fad o. . . .

2. 'S bruadalach a nì mi cadal
   Thu fhéin, a ghaoil, a bhith agam,
   Nuair a dh'éireas mi 'sa mhaduinn,
      Fada bhuam do chòmhradh.

3. Nam bithinn-s' aig Port an Aisig
   Peann is pàipeir a bhith agam,
   Sgrìobhainn-sa leth dusan facal
      Chuireadh stad 'nad chòrdadh.

4. Gillean carach fada thall,
   'S lìonmhor té dha'n dug iad geall;
   Coma leam a bhith 'nan cainnt,
      Gun bhith 'nan taing bu chòir dhith.

197

5. Gura mise a bha faoin
   Nuair a thug mi dhut mo ghaol,
   Aigne [agad] mar a' ghaoith
      A ch-uile taobh dha'n seòl i.

6. Ged a bhiodh tu miosg treud,
   Bidh tu briodal ris gach té;
   Nist o dh'aithnich mi do bheus,
      Bidh mi réidh 's do chòmhradh.

7. Nuair a bheir thu rium do chùl,
   Bidh do ghealladh aig té ùr;
   'N saoil sibh pféin nach olc an cliù
      Triùir chur an dòchas?

8. Bha bhu modhail, bha thu sìobhalt
   Dh'aithnghinn fhìn thu measg nam mìltean
   Cas as deise théid 'san ruighle,
      Beul o'm binn an t-òran.

9. 'N oidhche a bha mi 'n taighe a' bhàigh
   Thug mi an aire uair no dhà
   Bha té ùr agad 'nam àit'
      Treis mu'n dh'fhàg mi 'n seòmbar.

10. 'S gur h-e m'athair 's mo ghaol
    Ghabh an t-aiseag thar a' chaol,
    Tha mo dhùrachd dhut, a ghaoil
       A ch-uile taobh dha'n seòl thu.

11. Mo cheist an Caimbeulach ùr
    'S fhada bhuam a dh'aithnghinn thù;
    Shiùbhlainn Muile leat, a rùin,
       A null gu Tìr an Eórna.

12. Nam cluinntinn thu féin an tìr,
    Thu bhith timchioll brugh an Rìgh,
    'S aotrom a dh'fhairghinn mi fhìn,
       Nam faighinn brìodal còmh' riut.

SONGS REMEMBERED IN EXILE

Translation

Refrain: Farewell to the brown-haired lad,
    I feel it long since you left the land;
    Farewell to the brown-haired lad,
        Since you sailed I'm feeling sad.

1. Did you hear about the fair headed lad,
    who left his sweetheart with the rest,
    'tis I who am not well, far from . . .

2. My sleep is full of dreams of having you,
    love, with me; when I get up in the morning,
    your conversation is far from me.

3. If I were at Port an Aisig, having pen and paper,
    I would write half a dozen words, which would
    put a stop to your engagement.

4. Tricky lads far away over there, there's many a girl to whom they
    gave a promise: I don't care to be talking with them;
    not to be under obligation to them would be right for her.

5. Truly I was foolish when I gave you my love,
    your mind is like the wind, which blows in every direction.

6. Though you were amongst many, you will be flattering
    every girl; now that I know your way, I shall be clear
    of your converse.

7. When you turn your back on me, a new girl will have
    your promise; don't you think it is a bad reputation,
    to put three in hope?

8. You were well mannered and civil, I would recognise you
    amongst thousands; neatest foot that goes in the reel,
    sweetest mouth for singing songs.

9. The night I was the house of the bay, I noticed
    once or twice that you had a new girl in my place,
    a while before I left the room.

10. It was my father and my love who took the ferry
     across the sound; my best wishes to you, my love,
     every where you sail to.

11. My love is the young Campbell, I would recognise you
     far from me, I would travel Mull with you,
     my love, over to the land of barley (Uist).

12. If I heard you were in the land, that you were
     around the King's palace, I would feel happy
     if I were to have converse with you.

Recorded from Mrs Neil McInnis, MacKay's Corner, 19/10/37. Tune transcribed by Séamus Ennis; words transcribed by J. L. Campbell.

Notes

Verse 1, last line. This line in my hurried transcript made while Mrs McInnis was singing, reads *Fad on cairdeas zósa.* The last word is uncertain; it could be my abbreviation for *dhòmsa.* The girl is clearly far from her friends.

Verse 5, line 3. My transcript has *Aigneadh mar a' ghaoith,* but the addition of *agad* is necessary both for the sense and the metre.

Verse 6, last line. *Réidh 's do chòmhradh,* 'free from your conversation'. *Réidh is,* cf. *saor is i,* 'free from her', Fr Allan McDonald, *Gaelic Words from South Uist.*

Verse 11, line 4. *Tìr an Eòrna,* 'land of barley', is a kenning for the Island of South Uist.

The last three verses appear to belong to another song.

SE 125; Mode D, Ionian.

42 A GHILLE DHUINN GUR TU BU TOIGH LEAM

Fonn: 'Ille dhuinn, gur tu bu toigh leam,
    Co dhiù theireadh càch e;
    'Ille dhuinn, gur tu bu toigh leam.

1. Gura mise tha fo mhulad,
    M'uilinn air a' chàrnan.

2. Mi ri smaointinn air mo leannan,
    Fear nam meall-shùil blàtha.

3. 'Ille dhuinn an leadain dualaich,
    Dheanainn suas ri d' nàdur.

4. 'Ille dhuinn a' chòmhraidh mhilis,
    'S e do mhire chràidh mi.

5. 'Ille dhuinn, ma dh'fhàg thu 'n dùthaich,
    'Gad chumha an so a thà mi.

6. Gus an déid thu dha na h-Innsibh
    Bidh mi strìth gu bràch riut.

7. Ged a rachadh tu dha'n Òlaind,
    Dh'òlainn do dheoch-slàinte.

8. 'S truagh nach robh mi's tu pòsda
    Òrdan an fhir bhàin linn.

201

9. Gheobhamaid pòsadh gun éibheach,
   O nach eil sinn càirdeach.

10. Gheobhainn cadal leat gun chluasag,
    Leaba chruaidh na h-àireadh.

11. Rachainn fo dhubhar nan creag leat
    Gun eagal no sgàthadh.

12. Rachainn 's cha n-fhoighneachdainn piuthar,
    Gun umhail do bhràthar.

13. 'S mi gu rachadh 'n sin 's gu faodadh,
    Mur chaochail thu 'nad nàdur.

14. 'S Iseabal Bhuidhe Nic Neacail,
    Rìgh! gu faicinn slàn thu!

15. 'N còmhradh a bh'againn 'san fhraoch,
    Cha chluinn clann daoin' an dràsd e.

Translation

Refrain: Brown-haired lad, 'tis you I liked,
What ever others might say;
Brown haired lad, 'tis you I liked.

1. I am sorrowful, with my elbow
   on the little cairn.

2. Thinking of my lover, the man with warm
   smiling eyes.

3. Brown-haired lad of curling locks,
   I would correspond to thy mood.

4. Brown-haired lad of sweet conversation,
   it is your play that hurt me.

5. Brown-haired lad, if you've left the country,
   'tis missing you here that I am.

202

6. Until you go to the Indies, I shall be always
   striving for you.

7. Though you went to Holland, I would drink your
   health.

8. It's a pity we weren't formally married
   by the fair-headed [clergy] man.

9. We might have been married without proclamation
   (of banns), since we aren't related.

10. I would sleep with you without pillow,
    on the hard bed of the sheiling.

11. I would go beneath the shade of the crags
    with you, without fear or danger.

12. I would go with you without asking a sister,
    without paying attention to a brother.

13. I would go there, (well) I might, before your
    mood had changed.

14. Yellow-haired Isabel Nicholson
    O God! May I see you well.

15. The converse we had in the heather, mankind will
    never hear.

Recorded from Mrs Neil McInnis, MacKay's Corner, on 15/10/37. Tune transcribed by Séamus Ennis; words taken down by J. L. Campbell.
Compare KCC 51, 36 lines. Couplets nos. 1, 10, 11, 13 here are found there.

Notes

Verse 10. àireadh is the genitive of àirigh, 'sheiling'.
Verse 14. Seems out of place in this song.

43 CHA TAOBH MI CLANN

* We feel strongly that these notes should be written as D and not C#; the latter is not in the mode. The D was probably slightly flattened. M.F.S.

Fonn: Hug hòireann ó, cha taobh mi clann,
O nach saoilinn thu bhith ann;
Hug hòireann ó, cha taobh mi clann.

1. Cha taobh mi fhìn a chloinn nighinn,
Cha n-eil gaol mo chridh' ach gann.

2. Cha taobh mi àl a Luain na Dòmhnach
Cha n-eil fàth mo shòlais ann.

3. 'S o'n a thug mo leannan cùl rium
'S truagh nach robh 'n ùir air mo cheann.

4. Nuair a bha do bhàta seòladh,
Bha mi aig òrdan a bhith ann.

5. Nuair a thog sibh rithe a h-aodach
Bhuail do ghaol mi 's cha b'e'n t-amm.

204

6. 'S ann théid mi dh'ionnsaigh na Móirthir,
   Nì mi còmhdail ruit 'san amm.

7. C'àit an robh e anns an dùthaich
   H-aon air an robh triùir an geall?

8. Gur h-e fear dhiu sin am fìdhleir,
   Sheinneadh gu binn an cèol danns'.

9. Fear eile, saor a' bhàta,
   Sgiobair théid air bhàrr nan crann.

10. Bha mise 'n raoir air a' bhanais,
    Chunna mi an cailin ud ann.

11. 'S grinn a dhannsadh i air ùrlar
    Modhail mùirneach gun bhith mall.

Translation

Refrain: Hug hoireann ó, I'll not frequent young folk,
Since I think you won't be there,
Hug hoireann ó, I'll not frequent young folk.

1. I'll not go with young girls, the love of my
   heart is but scarce [for them].

2. I'll not go with the young from Monday or
   Sunday, the cause of my joy does not lie there.

3. Since my sweetheart turned her back on me,
   its a pity that earth isn't over my head.

4. When your boat was sailing, I was ordered
   to be there.

5. When you hoisted her sails, I fell in love
   with you, it was not the right time.

6. When I go towards the mainland, I will meet
   you at the time.

205

7. Where was there in the country one who was
    promised to three?
8. One of them was the fiddler, who'd play sweetly
    at the dance.

9. Another was the ship's carpenter, (another) a
    skipper who'll go to the mast-tops.

10. At the wedding feast last night,
    I saw yon lass there.

11. She would dance prettily on the floor,
    well-mannered, joyful, and quick.

Recorded from Mrs Neil McInnis at MacKay's Corner, on 15/10/37. Tune transcribed by Séamus Ennis; words taken down by J. L. Campbell.
See KCC, p. 15, refrain and four lines; *Gesto Collection*, p. 50, eight lines.

44 FONN AIR MO MHÀIRI LAGHAICH

Fonn: Fonn oirre, féill oirre,
Fonn air mo Mhàiri laghaich,
Fonn oirre, féill oirre.

1. Fonn oirre nuair thig an oidhche,
   Féill oirre nuair thig an là.

2. Comhairle dh'fhear a nì an t-suirghe,
   E bhith cuimhneach air an latha.

3. Mun crath an coileach a sgiathan
   E bhith 'g ialaidh ris na fraighibh.

4. Air eagal 's gun dig an tòir ort,
   Fàg do bhrògan air an rathad.

5. Cum an triùir ud far an rathaid—
   An coire, an drola, 's am bula.

6. Ged a bhristeadh tu do luirgnean,
   As na fuirm, na bi 'ga labhairt.

7. Bruidhinn beag is coiseachd fàilidh,
   Mun cluinn mo mhàthair thu, 's m'athair.

207

Translation

Refrain: Happy, cheerful Mary,
My happy, pretty Mary,
Happy, cheerful Mary.

1. Happy when the night comes, cheerful when
comes the day.

2. Advice for one who is love-making,
he should be thinking of the day.

3. Before the cockerel shakes his wings,
he should be creeping close to the walls.

4. For fear the pursuit may catch up with you,
leave your shoes on the road.

5. Keep these three out of the way, the kettle
the pot-chain and the bowl.

6. Though you bark your shins against the benches,
don't say anything.

7. Talk little and move quietly, in case
my mother and father hear you.

Recorded by Mrs Neil McInnis, MacKay's Corner, on 20/10/37. Tune transcribed by Séamus Ennis; words transcribed by J. L. Campbell.

There is another song on this subject in K. C. Craig's *Orain Luaidh Màiri nighean Alasdair*, p. 33, with a refrain beginning *Mo nighean chruinn dhonn air bharraibh nan tonn, 'S tu thogadh am fonn air m'inntinn-sa*, 'My neat brown-haired girl on the tops of the waves, you would raise the disposition of my mind'.

Notes

Refrain. Fonn could be translated 'good disposition' and *féill* 'festival disposition'.
Verse 4. Reading *Fàg do bhrògan* for *tha do bhrògan* of the transcription.

SE 131. Mode, D, Hexatonic, no 6, 3 only once, weak.

45   CHA DÉID MI DO DH'FHEAR GUN BHÀTA

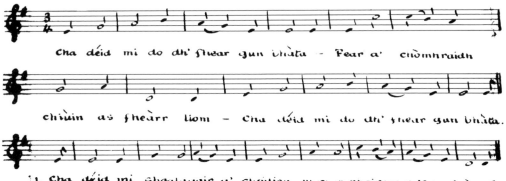

Cha déid mi do dh'fhear gun bhàta,
Fear a' chòmhraidh chiùin as fheàrr leam;
Cha déid mi do dh'fhear gun bhàta.

1. Cha déid mi chìobair nam fuarbheann,
    Cha taobh mi buachaille an fhàsaich.

2. Cha déid mi shealgair a' choilich,
    Moch a ghoireas e 'san fhàsach.

3. Cha déid mi dh'iasgair na h-abhuinn,
    Chunnaic mi fear dhiù 'ga bhàthadh.

4. Cha déid mi do shaor nan cuman,
    Cha taobh mi truimeir na clàrsaich,

5. Cha déid mi do shaor na locrach,
    Gur neoshocair nì e m'fhàgail.

6. Cha déid mi a ghille na fidhle,
    Feumaidh e 'n teud bhinn a chàradh.

7. Cha déid mi idir dha'n phìobair',
    Bidh e cur a bhrìgh 'sa mhàla.

8. Cha déid mi thàilleir nan cleasan,
    'S bochd an teisteach leam an t-snàthad.

209

9. Cha déid mi idir dha'n ghriasaich'
    Bidh na briagan a' comh-fhàs ris.

10. Cha déid mi idir dha'n t-soighdeir,
    Bidh e dol le mhusgaid 's gach àite.

11. Cha déid mi mhuilleir an t-sadaich,
    Cha lig e leam cadal sàmhach.

12. Cha déid mi do dh'fhear am bliadhna
    Bhios 'gam iarraidh comh' ri mhàthair.

13. 'S mór gum b'annsa leam ri m' ghualainn
    Tuathanach, 's e 's buaine laithean.

Translation

I'll not go to a man who hasn't a boat,
I prefer the man of quiet converse;
I'll not go to a man who hasn't a boat.

1. I'll not go to the shepherd of the cold hills,
    I'll not approach the cowherd of the pasture.

2. I'll not go to the hunter of the blackcock,
    early it calls in the wild land.

3. I'll not go to the man who fishes the river,
    I saw one of them drown.

4. I'll not go to the carpenter who makes wooden dishes,
    I'll not approach the strumming harper.

5. I'll not go to the carpenter with his plane,
    he will leave me feeling uneasy .

6. I'll not go to the lad who plays the fiddle,
    he has to tune his sweet string.

7. I'll not go at all to the piper, he'll be putting
    his strength into blowing.

8. I'll not to the tricky tailor, I think the needle's
   a poor recommendation.

9. I'll not go at all to the shoemaker, he
   will turn into a liar.

10. I'll not go at all to the soldier, he'll be going
    everywhere with his musket.

11. I'll not go to the dusty miller, he won't let me
    sleep quietly.

12. I'll not go this year to anyone who asks for
    me along with his mother.

13. I'd far sooner have a farmer beside me, his
    days last longest.

Recorded from Mrs Neil McInnis at MacKay's Corner, on 15/10/37. Tune transcribed by Séamus Ennis.
See *Hebridean Folksongs* III, No. CXXV.

Notes

Verse 2. It is unlikely that *fàsach* would have occurred twice in consecutive verses, perhaps the actual word was forgotten. But the word can be construed 'wilderness' and 'pasture', as if it were two words, one derived from *fàs*, 'empty', and the other from *fàs*, 'grow'.

Verse 4. Dishes and such utensils used to be made out of wood in the old days.

Verse 8. Tailoring was an indoor occupation often followed by less hardy persons.

Verse 9. Shoemakers in the Highlands had a reputation for being untruthful, as the shoes they repaired were never ready on the day they promised.

SE 120.

46 LÀ SIUBHAL BEINNE DHOMH

Small notes denote variant

Ìll ó bhòidheach,
Na hi ill ó ro bha hó,
Là siubhal beinne dhomh,
Na hi ill ó ro bha hó,
Ill ó bhòidheach,
Na hi ill ó ro bha hó.

Là siubhal mòintich
Thachair orm gruagach
Dhualach bhòidheach,
5. Sgian bheag 'na làimh,
'S gearra-chas òir innt',
'S i buain biolaire,
'S i buain eòintean,
An cois gach lòinein;
10. O, theann mi anull rithe,
O, dh'iarr mi pòg oirr';
'Èisd a ghiullain,
Sguir dhe d' ghòraich'!
'S ann an taigh m'athar fhéin
15. A gheobhte choisridh
Cruinn mu bhòrdan,
Fichead fear ada,
'S ciad fear chleòcan!'

212

Translation

One day as I walked the hill
One day as I walked the moor,
There met me a maiden,
A little knife in her hand,
5. With a short golden handle,
She was cutting cresses,
She was picking flowers,
At the foot of every pond.
I went over to her,
10. And asked her for a kiss;
'Listen, laddie,
Cease your fooling,
In my father's house
Footmen will be found
15. Around tables,
Twenty men with hats,
A hundred wearing cloaks!'

Recorded from Mrs Neil McInnis at MacKay's Corner, on 15/10/37. Tune transcribed by Séamus Ennis; words transcribed by J. L. Campbell.

A 'clapping song'. Compare *Gaelic Folksongs from the Isle of Barra*, p. 46.

SE 123.

MICHAEL S. MACNEIL
Benacadie Pond, Barra tradition

Michael S. MacNeil was a successful farmer of Benacadie Pond, Cape Breton County, who also owned and operated a sawmill, and was a mail contractor; his mail route was from Christmas Island to East Bay, a distance of thirty-one miles which was covered daily. He had a large family, and three of his sons were at home with him, helping in his various undertakings. His wife was Margaret, daughter of Donald Farrell of Benacadie, C.B.

He was the son of Alexander MacNeil ('Sandaidh Dhòmhnuill a' Chùil') who was also a farmer and owned and operated the farm on which his son Michael lived; he composed some songs worthy of note, and was a talented violin player, he was a son of Donald MacNeil (Dòmhnull Iain Ruairidh) also known locally as 'Dòmhnull a' Chùil' because he settled at the rear of Castle Bay, N.S.

This man was a son of John MacNeil (Iain Ruairidh) who came to Benacadie Pond from Antigonish with his wife and family and a cow in their Barra boat. It is related that on his taking up residence at Benacadie Pond, on several occasions their cow was missing, and that on these occasions the cow would be found at a certain place in Castle Bay after crossing the wooded hillside from Benacadie Pond. Iain Mac Ruairidh decided to move his wife and family to that spot, and take a plot of land there, which he did. The wisdom of this move is evident today, as it is one of the most productive and one of the best equipped farms in the district; it is owned and occupied by Dan A. and Joseph W. MacNeil.

Iain Ruairidh was a son of Rory MacNeil, who was a foster-brother of one of the chiefs of Barra, Scotland. Four of his sons and one daughter were among the first immigrants that came from Barra to Nova Scotia. He was the great-great-grandfather of our subject Michael S. MacNeil.

20. Mr and Mrs Michael S. MacNeil, Benacadie Pond

47 'S GURA MISE THA FO MHULAD, MI AN DIU BHITH FÀGAIL NA TÌRE

Fonn: Hug hòireann ó, 's mì fo mhìghean,
O ho o hao, luaidh nan nìghneag,
Hug hòireann ó, 's mi fo mhìghean.

1. 'S gura mise tha fo mhulad,
    Mi an diu bhith fàgail na tìre.

2. . . . .
    Gun dùil bhith tighinn gu dìleann.

3. Gun d'fhalbh mo chàirdean bho'n bhaile,
    Murchadh mo charaid dìleas,

4. 'S cha bhi òl no gaol no dannsa
    Gille Anndrais, gu'm bi sinn fhìn ann.

5. 'S dh'aithnichinn do long a' tighinn gu caladh,
    Le siùil geala 's le cruinn dìreach.

6. A mhic Dhòmhnaill 'ic Ruairi 'ic Dhubhghaill,
    Gur tu mo rùn seach na chì mi.

7. 'S mo cheist mac an duine uasail
    Chàradh mu m' ghualainn an sìoda.

8. 'S e mo cheist air Mac 'Ill' Onfhaidh,
    Sgiobair fairge, sealgair sìdhneadh.

216

Translation

Refrain: Hug hoireann o, I am displeased,
O ho o hao, my beloved of maidens,
Hug hoireann o, I am displeased.

1. 'Tis I who am sorrowful to be leaving the
country today.

2. .... without expectation of
ever coming.

3. My relations have left the township,
Murdo my faithful friend.

4. There will be no drinking, or love, or dancing,
Gillanndrais, until we ourselves are there.

5. I would recognise your ship coming into harbour,
with her white sails and her straight masts.

6. Son of Donald son of Rory son of Dugall,
you are my favourite beyond all I see.

7. My darling is the noble's son, who used to
put silk around my shoulders.

8. My darling is MacGilloney, skipper at sea,
hunter of venison.

Recorded from Michael S. MacNeil at Benacadie Pond, on 14/10/37. Tune reconstituted from A. Martin Freeman's notes; text transcribed by J. L. Campbell.

The tune shows that the song is in couplets, and the rhyme proves that the first line of the second couplet is missing. The song may be incomplete in other ways.

Notes

Verse 2. gu dìleann = literally 'until the Flood'.

Verse 4. Gillanndrais = 'servant of St Andrew', now anglicised as Gillanders or Andrew or Anderson, a name associated with the Rosses. See Alexander MacBain, 'Early Highland Personal Names', *Trans. Gael. Soc. Inverness* XXII, 163.

Verse 8. Mac 'ill' Onfhaidh = 'son of the servant of the Storm'. Anglicised as MacGilloney or Macillonie. This was a small, ancient clan living on the south side of Loch Arisaig in Lochaber.

See the Rev. Somerled MacMillan, *Bygone Lochaber* (1971), pp. 28–40. Mr MacMillan says that the earliest historical reference to the MacGillonies occurs in 1370, and that they were traditionally said to have been descended from a foundling cast up on the shore in a coffin at Corpach at the head of Loch Linnhe. hence the saying:

MacGhill' Onfhaidh
A chuir an onfhadh air an tràigh

'MacGilloney, whom the storm (*onfhadh*, pronounced *on-a-agh*) cast on the shore.'

The MacGillonies were eventually absorbed by the Camerons. Their ancient lands are now under the sitka spruces of the Forestry Commission.

It is curious to find this song of obvious Lochaber origin preserved by a singer of Barra descent in Cape Breton; but it is not unknown for songs composed on the mainland, and forgotten there, to have been preserved in the Outer Hebrides.

ANGUS MACISAAC
Antigonish, Moidart tradition

Born in 1875 at Giant's Lake, Guysborough County, Nova Scotia, the second youngest member of a family of seven brothers and four sisters, Angus was the son of Donald MacIsaac from Moidart, Scotland, and Catherine Gillis MacIsaac of Beech Hill, Antigonish County, Nova Scotia.

He was not one of the reciters we encountered in 1937, but I had the privilege of recording him when on a visit to St Francis Xavier University in 1953, when introduced by Monsignor P. J. Nicholson, then President of the University, and was able to make some wire recordings of him in the last days of May of that year.

Angus was then in his seventy-eighth year. He was a kindly, cheerful person, full of songs, some very amusing, and I regret that I did not have the opportunity to spend more time searching his memory.

The most remarkable item he produced was this portion of the Ossianic ballad *Teanntachd Mhór na Féinne*, 'The Greatest Difficulty of the Fiann', the semi-legendary band of heroes headed by the famed Fionn mac Cumhail.[1] Ballads on their exploits formed a very important part of the older oral literature of the Highlands, and were the basis—though not the literal originals, of the poems of Ossian fabricated by MacPherson in the days of Dr Johnson. So far as Scotland is concerned, the earliest recension of such ballads is contained in the sixteenth-century manuscript *The Book of Lismore*; a similar Irish Collection can be seen in the *Duanaire Finn*, 'Fionn's poetry book' written by an early seventeenth-century Irish scribe.

'The Greatest Difficulty of the Fionn' describes how in the course of a conversation on the relative merits of paganism and Christianity between St Patrick and Oisin, the last survivor of the Fiann, Patrick asks Oisin to tell him the story of the hardest battle the Fiann ever fought, which in the older versions of the ballad Oisin relates at considerable length.

I knew of the existence of this ballad, of course, before I met Angus, but he was the only person I ever met who knew any of it, and who sang it. As he sang every one of the eight quatrains he remembered, twice, in slow tempo, for him to have sung any longer version at his age would have been a considerable strain. He may well have known more verses and forgotten them. As it is, finding this relic of the ancient tradition in Nova Scotia, when no one had been able to sing it to me in Scotland, was a matter of great interest.

In 1745 the recitation of such ballads around the camp fires of the Highland army must have been enormously popular.

[1] See Derick Thomson, *The Gaelic Origins of MacPherson's Ossian*.

48 TEANNTACHD MHÓR NA FÉINNE

A Chléir-ich a chan-as na sail(i)m, Ar leam gur bàth do chiall; Nach éisd-eadh tu tam-ull ri m' sgeul Air an Fhéinn, nach cual' thu riamh ?

TEANNTACHD MHÓR NA FÉINNE

Seo agaibh òran a chaidh dheanamh dha na Fiantaichean, daoine móra foghainnteach a bha anns an t-Seann Dùthaich bho chionn dorlach linntean; agus an t-òran tha an seo, tha ceathramh no dha agam-sa dheth, agus tha mi creidsinn gu fiachainn ri a ghabhail cho math as urrainn dhomh, ach tha e dol:

1.   'San oidhche chaidh Pàdraig 'na mhùir,
        Bha sùrd air seirm is air òl,
    A' coimhead air Oisin na Féinn'
        O 's ann leis bu bhinne glòir.

Oisin:
2.   'A Chléirich a sheinneas na sailm,
        Ar liom fhéin gur bàth do chaill,
    Nach éisdeadh tu tamull ri m' sgeul
        Air an Fhéinn, nach cual' thu riamh?'

Pàdraig:
3.   'Cha n-éisd mi tamull ri d' sgeul
        Air an Fhéinn nach cuala mi riamh,
    Is blas nan salm air feadh mo bheòil—
        Gum b'fheàrr siod do cheòl dhomh fhìn.'

Oisin:
4.   'Ma's ann a' sanntachadh do shailm
        Ri Féinn Éirinn nan arm nochd—
    A Chléirich 's ro-thanadh liom
        Nach sgarainn do cheann bho d' chorp.'

Pàdraig:
5. ''S e do bheatha, mo thruaighe!
    Ugad air chuairt thànaig sinn—
    Dé 'n cath 's bu chruaidh' 'n robh an Fhéinn,
    O'n a ghein thu riamh 'nan lorg?'

Oisin:
6. 'Bha sinn latha 'sa bheinn t-seilg,
    'S cha dànaig an t-sealg 'nar car,
    'S gu faca sinn mile bàt'
    Air an tràigh air teachdaireachd.

7. 'Mac Rìgh Lochlainn bha 'n siod air cràdh—
    Gu dé fàth a bhith 'ga chleith—
    'S cha ghabh e cumail bho Fhionn
    Gu 'n ògbhean 's a chù thoirt leis.

8. ''S a Rìgh! cha dugainn-sa mo bhean
    Do dhuine a tha fo'n ghréin,
    'S cha doir mi Bran gu lath' bhràtha,
    Gus an dig am bàs orm fhéin!'

Translation

THE GREATEST DIFFICULTY OF THE FIANN

Here you have a song that was made to the Fingalians, big brave fellows who were in the Old Country a long time ago. I know a verse or two of this song, and I'll try to sing it as well as I can. It goes:

1. The night (Saint) Patrick went to his (i.e. Oisin's) dwelling,
    there was hilarity, singing and drinking—to see Oisin of the Fiann,
    since his speech was sweetest.

Oisin:
2. 'O Cleric who singest the psalms, methinks thy sense is simple;
    would you not listen awhile to my story about the Fiann,
    which you have never heard?'

Patrick:
3. 'I will not listen awhile to your tale about the Fiann,
    which I never heard, with the taste of the psalms on my lips—
    that is the music I myself would prefer.'

Oisin:

4.   'If you are prefering your psalms to the Fiann of Ireland of naked weapons,
    o Cleric, but for little I would sever your head from your body!'

Patrick:

5.   'You are welcome, alas! We came to visit you—[to ask]
    what was the hardest fight in which the Fiann were,
    since you were born of their race?'

Oisin:

6.   'One day we were on the hill for hunting,
    and the quarry did not come our way;
    we saw a thousand ships, come on an errand on the shore.

7.   'The son of the King of Norway was there, vexed—
    what reason is there to hide it?
    He cannot be restrained from Fionn, without taking
    Fionn's young wife and his dog with him.

8.   'My God! I will not give my wife to any man under the sun,
    and I will never give (my dog) Bran away,
    until death comes on me myself.'

Recorded from Angus MacIsaac, at Antigonish on 27/5/53, J.L.C. wire recording No. 1119. Tune transcribed by Margaret Fay Shaw.

See *Leabhar na Féinne*, pp. 96–103, and Angus MacLellan, *Stories from South Uist*, for stories about the Fiann or Fiantaichean and their leader, Fionn mac Cumhail, pp. 3–31. The ballad goes on to describe this famous battle at considerable length; possibly Angus MacIsaac knew, or had known and forgotten, more of it.

Some of the verses here are also associated with the ballad of Erragon and the Lay of Manus; see Reidar Th. Christiansen, *The Vikings and the Viking Wars in Irish and Gaelic Tradition*, pp. 249, 260, 283; J. F. Campbell, *Leabhar na Féinne*, pp. 74, 79; Calum I. MacLeod, *Bàrdachd a Albainn Nuaidh*, p. 15 (eight verses recorded from Duncan A. MacKay, Abhainn Mhór, Richmond County, in 1952).

ANGUS RIDGE MACDONALD

Upper South River, Antigonish County, Lochaber tradition

Angus the Ridge ('Aonghus a' Mhaim'), son of Alexander Ridge, son of Allan Ridge MacDonald, was born in the home of his father at Upper South River, Antigonish County, on 27 February 1866. His farm was across the river from his grandfather's homestead, which was also in his possession. Outside of ten years spent as a guard at the penitentiary at Dorchester, New Brunswick, Angus lived all his life at Upper South River, where we visited him in late October 1937.

A. MacLean Sinclair gives the following account of Angus's grandfather's family on page 216 of his *Glenbard Collection of Gaelic Poetry* (Charlottetown, P.E.I., 1888). The following is my translation:

> Angus Ridge's grandfather Allan MacDonald was born at Allt an t-Struthain in Lochaber in the year 1794. He was the son of Alasdair, son of Angus, son of Alasdair Ban son of Alasdair Mor, son of Angus of the Ghost, son of Angus Mor of Bohuntin, son of Alasdair, son of Ian Dubh, son of Ranald Mor of Keppoch.
>
> Allan was a cattle drover, who lived mostly at Achadh nan Coinnichean in Glen Spean. His mother was Mary Campbell, daughter of Donald, son of Ian Dubh, who lived at Achadh a' Mhadaidh in Glen Roy. He was a shepherd for Ian Ban of Inch. He was married to Catriana Currie, daughter of Moireach Currie. He came to Nova Scotia in the year 1816. He lived for a while on the Mam, or 'Ridge', in Cape Breton. He left it in 1847, and went to stay at Upper South River in Antigonish County.
>
> Allan was a true Gael, and a well-informed man. He had many old Gaelic songs at the tip of his tongue. He died in 1868. He was often called 'Allan the Ridge'.

Angus Ridge recorded fourteen songs for us when we visited him in 1937. All belong to the traditions of Lochaber. The tunes of eleven were transcribed by Séamus Ennis. In the spring of 1949 or 1950 the Rev. P. J. Nicholson and the Rev. Malcolm Macdonell visited Angus and recorded twelve Gaelic and three English songs from him on wire for St Francis Xavier University. Of these we had recorded five Gaelic songs in 1937.

It is interesting that in 1932 the Rev. Angus Bryden, parish priest of Lochaber, wrote me that Gaelic was practically dead there, but was kept up by a small community at nearby Giant's Lake in Guysborough County.

223

21. Angus 'Ridge' MacDonald, Upper South River, Antigonish County

49 'S MULADACH A THÀ M 'S MI NOCHD AIR STRÀID LE M' CHÉILE

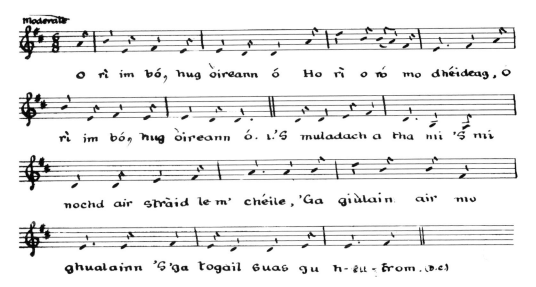

O rì im bó, hug òireann ó   Ho rì o ró   mo dhéideag, O

rì im bó, hug òireann ó. 1.'S muladach a tha mi 'S mi

nochd air stràid le m' chéile, 'Ga giùlain air mo

ghualainn 'S 'ga togail suas gu h-eu-trom. (D.c)

Fonn: O rì im bó, hug hòireann ó.
     Ho ri o ro, mo dhéideag,
     O rì im bó, hug hòireann ó.

     'S muladach a thà mi,
       'S mi nochd air stràid le m' chéile,[1]
     'Ga giùlain air mo ghualainn,
       'Ga togail suas gu h-eutrom.

5.   'S fhad' bho fhuair mi 'n Glaschu thu,
      Le t' *articles* 'gan leughadh;
    'S diùmbach dha na Frangaich sinn,
      'San amm seo tighinn do dh'Éirinn.

    Gun caill sinn ar cuid caileagan,
10.   'S ar gealladh gu bhith breugach,
    Mo shoraidh do shlios Mhórair,
      Far bheil m'eòlas agus m'éibhneas.

[1] An gunna aige.

Far a bheil mo chàirdean
   A dh'àirdeadh air an fhéill mi,
15. Chuireadh airgiod 'nam phòca,
   Agus òr, nan cuirinn feum air.

Mo cheist air na h-Earraghaidhealaich
   'S neo-chearbach théid 'nan éideadh,
Bidh féile cruinn am pleatadh orra,
20.   'S breacannan-an-fhéileadh.

Translation

1. Sorrowful tonight am I walking with my mate
[his gun], carrying her in my shoulder,
lifting her up lightly.

2. It is long since I found you in Glasgow
with your articles [military regulations] being read;
we were angry with the French,
coming to Ireland at this time.

3. We lost our own lasses and our chance of making them
false promises (of marriage);
my farewell to the slopes of Morar, where my
happiness and my acquaintances are.

4. Where my relations are, who would greet
me at the fair, who would put money
in my pocket, and gold, if I needed it.

5. My regards to the Argyllshiremen,
who are smart in their equipment;
they wear the neat pleated kilt, and
the tartan plaid.

Recorded at Upper South River in late October 1937. Tune transcribed by Séamus Ennis; words transcribed by J. L. Campbell.

Note

Verse 2. There was an unsuccessful expedition to Ireland under General Hoche in support of Wolfe Tone and the United Irishmen rebellion in December 1796, and another in October 1797, after which Napoleon was left supreme in France, and gave up any belief in the idea of such an expedition succeeding.

SE 136; Mode, G, Pentatonic, 4:7.

50 ÒRAN DO DH'AONGHUS MAC ALASDAIR

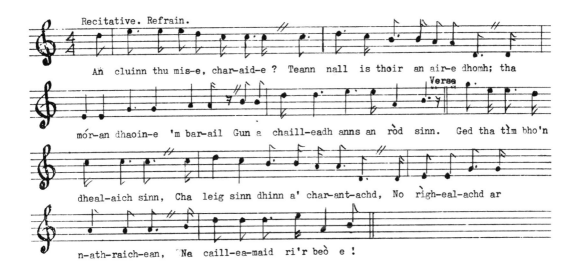

LE AILEAN AN *RIDGE,* AIR DHA BHITH 'GA FHAICINN 'NA CHADAL, IS E AN DEIREADH A LAITHEAN

An cluinn thu mise, charaide?
Teann nall is thoir an aire dhomh;
Tha móran dhaoine 'm barail
   Gun a chailleadh anns an ròd sinn.

5. Ged tha tìm o'n dhealaich sinn,
Cha leig sinn dhinn a' charrantachd,
No rìghealachd ar n-athraichean,
   Na cailleamaid ri'r beò e!

An càirdeas is an rìghealachd
10. A b'abhaist bhith air ar sinnsearach,
Gur tràth dhuinn bhith 'ga mhìneachadh,
   'S 'ga innse dha'r cuid òigridh.

Gu brach na leig air dìochuimhn' e,
Bha là 's b'e 'n càirdeas fiachail e,
15. Bu dàicheil, làidir, dìonadach
   Bha mhiar ud de Chlann Dòmhnaill.

227

Mo dhùil gun dig thu shealltainn orm,
'S gu faic mi 'n taobh seo Bhealltainn thu,
'S ged tha mi fàs 'nam sheann duine,
20.   Gun gabhainn dram is òran.

Ach 's fada leam gun tighinn thu,
'Gad fhaicinn, siod bu mhithich dhomh,
Bu chàileachd bidhe 's dibhe dhomh,
    'S a thoirt dha'm chridhe sòlas.

25.   Bho'n tha a' chùis cho iarguineach,
'S nach fhaigh sinn nì mar dh'iarras sinn,
Bho'n chaidh ar sunnd gu cianalas,
    A bhean, nach lìon thu 'n stòp dhuinn?

Translation

A SONG TO ANGUS SON OF ALASDAIR

By Allan of the Ridge after seeing him asleep at the end of his days

1. Do you hear me, friend? come over and pay heed to me;
   many people think that we have been lost on the road.

2. Though it is a while since we parted, we will not renounce fellowship,
   or the royalism of our forefathers; let us never lose it.

3. The relationship and the royalism that our ancestors used to have,
   it is time for us to be explaining and imparting it to our young folk.

4. Never let it be forgotten, there was a day when it was a
   worth-while relationship; that branch of Clan Donald was a
   handsome, strong, protective one.

5. I hope you will come to see me, and that I'll see
   you on this side of May day; and though I've become an old fellow,
   I'd take a dram and sing a song (with you).

6. But I feel it long since you came; it's high time for me to see you;
   it would be choice food and drink for me,
   to give my heart consolation.

7. Since the situation is so difficult, and we won't get
   what we ask for; since our happiness has turned to sorrow;
   wife! won't you fill a stoup for us?

Recorded from Angus 'Ridge' MacDonald, Upper South River, Antigonish County, in late October 1937. Tune transcribed by Séamus Ennis.

Text communicated by Mgr P. J. Nicholson from Bishop Alexander MacDonald's notebook. Mgr Nicholson writes 'Bishop Alexander MacDonald got the song from Murdock (*sic*), son of Allan, who learnt it from his father the day it was made. The bishop annotated Alexander Ridge's MS, which has in its very first line *Bi nall* and not *Teann nall*.'

Mgr Nicholson says that Murdock's renditions of lines 13, 15 and 16 were:

> *Gu brach, cha dean sinn diochuimhn' air*

and

> *'S ann aluinn, laidir, dionadach*
> *Bha mhior ud de Chlann Domhnuill*

Mgr Nicholson adds that 'the second last stanza appears on the MS in Bishop MacDonald's hand and (was) apparently added comparatively recently. The last stanza, the Bishop remarks, was added to the original by a hand other than the poet's.'

See Calum I. MacLeoid, *Bàrdachd a Albainn Nuaidh*, p. 23, where the text of this song is given as communicated by John Berry, a grandson of Bishop MacDonald's sister. In the letter written on 8 February 1922, the Bishop says in Gaelic that he got the song from 'Muireach', presumably the same person whom Mgr Nicholson calls 'Murdock', though 'Murdock' is normally the anglicised form of 'Murchadh'; Allan Ridge's father-in-law was named Moireach Currie; Currie itself is in South Uist the usual anglicisation of 'Mac Mhuirich', the name of the famous family that provided the hereditary bards and historians of the MacDonalds of Clanranald.

The Angus son of Alasdair to whom Allan made this song must have been Angus Ridge, Allan's older brother, who still lived in SW Mabou. Bishop Alexander MacDonald (1858–1941) was descended from Alasdair Ruadh, great-grandfather of our Angus Ridge, in the female line. He was popularly known as 'Bishop Sandy'. Catherine, one of Alasdair Ruadh's daughters, was his grandmother. I am obliged to Maureen Williams for this information.

SE 134; Mode, A, Hexatonic, no 6.

51   O DIÙRAM, É DIÙRAM

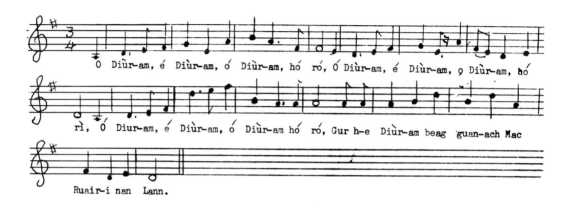

Fonn: O Diùram, É Diùram, O Diùram, ho ró,
          O Diùram, É Diùram, O Diùram, ho rì,
          O Diùram, É Diuram, O Diùram, ho ró.
          Gur he-e Diùram beag, guanach, Mac Ruairidh nan Lann.

O m'eudail, O m'aighear, chaidh dha'n abhainn an dé
Bha mise 'gad amharc, 's bu neo-shleamhainn do cheum,
Le d' chuilbhear caol glacte, chuireadh stad air na féidh,
Thug thu 'n dùthchas o t'athair a bhith tathaich 'san fhéinn.

Bha triùir de chlann Iarla 'gam iarraidh an dé,
Le 'n eachaibh, le'n gillean, le'm pillean, le'n stréin,
Le'n sporannan troma tighinn dhachaidh o'n fhéill,
'S gum b'annsa leam Diùram na 'n dùrachd gu léir.

Ged a gheibhinn-sa gille, is coileach is cearc,
'S na tha de chrodh guaillfhionn 's tha eadar seo 's Peairt,
Gum b'annsa leam Diùram air chùlaibh nam cnoc
Gur h-e fear nan gruaidh mìn, dearg, dh'fhàg m'inntinn fo sprochd.

Translation

Refrain: O Diuram, e Diuram, O Diuram, ho ro,
It is little light-hearted Diuram, son of Rory of the Swords.

1. My darling, my joy, went to the river yesterday,
    I was watching, your footstep was steady
    With your slender gun grasped, that would slay the deer,
    Your nature came from your father, who hunted on the hill.

2. Three of an earl's children were seeking me yesterday
    With their horses, their grooms, their saddles and their reins,
    With their heavy purses, coming back from the fair.
    I'd sooner have Diuram than all their good will.

3. Though I got a lad and a cock and a hen,
    And the white-shouldered cattle between here and Perth,
    I'd sooner have Diuram behind the hills,
    He's the fine red-cheeked man who left my mind sad.

Recorded at Upper South River in late October 1937. Tune transcribed by Séamus Ennis. Words communicated by Mgr P. J. Nicholson.

A lullaby. The only other version known to us is that in *Folksongs and Folklore of South Uist*, pp. 138–9 where Margaret Fay Shaw took it down from Mrs Currie 'Peigi Nill'. 'Diùram' is probably a pet name for a baby. Compare a song of the same type to 'Giuran' in *Carmina Gadelica* V, p. 330. The name of the reciter is not given.

Note

Verse 1. *'san fhéinn* according to the reciter = *'sa bheinn sheilg,* in the hunting hill. One would expect *'sa bheinn*, with long *e* as in Glengarry.

There is no need for the C# in the tune signature.

SE 143; Mode, D, Hexatonic, no 7.

52 'S TRUAGH NACH ROBH MI'N RIOCHD NA H-EALA
(COISICH, A RÙIN)

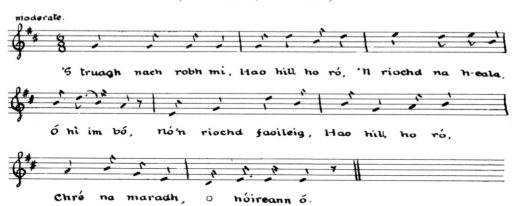

'S truagh nach robh mi, Hao hill ho ró, 'n riochd na h-eala,

ó hì im bó, nó'n riochd faoileig, Hao hill, ho ró,

Chrè na maradh, o hóireann ó.

'S truagh nach robh mi, 'n riochd na h-ela,
 hao ill ho ró, ó hì im bó,
No 'n riochd faoileig, *chrin* na mara,
 hao ill ho ró, o hoireann ó,
No 'n riochd faoileig, *chrin* na mara,
 hao ill ho ró, o hi im bó,
Shnàmhainn an caol, rachainn thairis,
 hao ill ho ró o hoireann ó,
Ruiginn am baile 'm bheil mo leannan,

5. M'aighear 's mo ghaol 's mo chiad leannan;
'S tric a laigh mi ghaoil, fo d'fhalluing,
Siaban nam beann bhith dol faruinn,
Deathach nan stùc bhith 'gar dalladh,

Banais anochd 'sa Chill' Uachdraich,
10. Nam bithinn ann dheanainn fuadach,
Nam biodh té eil' ann bhith 'ga luadh riut,
Sgathainn bun is barr a cuailein,
Dh'éireadh mo shròn àird nan stuaidhean,
Dh'fhalbhadh m'anail 'na cheò uaine.

15. 'S trom an naidheachd 'n diu chualas,
Thug Clann Nill druim a' chuain orr',
Chaidh iad fodha anns an fhuaradh,
Luchd nan seol àrd 's nan long uaibhreach,
Luchd nan leadan troma, dualach.

Translation

Sad that I had not	the shape of a swan,
Or of a seagull	of the sea,
I would swim the sound,	I would go o'er,
I would reach the townland	where lives my lover
5. My joy and my love,	my first sweetheart;
Often as I lay, love,	beneath thy mantle,
The showers of the hills	passing over us,
The mist of the crags	leaving us sightless.
There's a wedding-feast tonight	in the upper Cill,
10. If I was there,	I would clear it,
If another girl there	were with you connected,
I would cut off her hair	top and bottom,
My nose would rise	as high as the gables
My breath would go	in green vapour.
15. Sad today	the news we're hearing
Clan Neill have taken	to the high ocean,
They have gone down	beating to windward,
The folk of white sails	and proud galleys,
The folk of heavy	locks a-curling.

Recorded from Angus 'Ridge' MacDonald, Upper South River, in late October 1937. Tune transcribed by Séamus Ennis; words transcribed by J. L. Campbell.

See A. MacLean Sinclair, *Mac Talla nan Tur*, p. 119, previously printed in *Mac Talla* ix, 352, April 1901. The song is a version of *Coisich, a rùin*, see that sung by Mrs Patterson in this book. *See also Hebridean Folksongs* II, 144–50.

Note

Line 2. Mac Talla nan Tur has *Chrin na mara*. My transcript (line 37) has *Chré*. I can remember the long nasal vowel distinctly; *Chré*, long *e* marked nasal.

SE 140; Mode, E, Pentatonic, 2:6.

53   DH'ÉIRICH MI MUCH

Dh'éir-ich mi much, Na ha hó hì hò, Dhìrich mi mach, Na hì 's ì ri

ri rì ho, Na ho ho ro éil-eadh, Na hao hó hì hó.

<table>
<tr><td>Dh'éirich mi much</td><td>. . . . . .</td></tr>
<tr><td>Na ha hó hì hó,</td><td></td></tr>
<tr><td>Dhìrich mi mach,</td><td>'m beul nan stùcan,</td></tr>
<tr><td>Na ha hó hì hó,</td><td>Na hì 's i rì ri ri hó,</td></tr>
<tr><td></td><td>Na hó hó ro éileadh,</td></tr>
<tr><td></td><td>Na hao hó hì hó.</td></tr>
<tr><td></td><td>'m beul nan stùcan,</td></tr>
<tr><td></td><td>Na ha hó hì hó,</td></tr>
<tr><td>Chunnacas bàta</td><td>. . . . . .</td></tr>
<tr><td>E dol timcheall</td><td>Rubha 'n Dùnain,</td></tr>
<tr><td>5.   'S e mo leannan</td><td>tha 'ga stiùradh,</td></tr>
<tr><td>Dh'aithnghinn t'fhaileas</td><td>'sa chuan dùbhghorm;</td></tr>
<tr><td>An dig thu nochd?</td><td>am bi mo dhùil riut?</td></tr>
<tr><td>An dian mi 'n dorus</td><td>ort a dhùnadh?</td></tr>
<tr><td>An dian mi a' choinneal</td><td>bhàn a mhùchadh?</td></tr>
</table>

Translation

<table>
<tr><td>Early I rose</td><td>. . . . . .</td></tr>
<tr><td>Out I climbed</td><td>toward the cliff tops</td></tr>
<tr><td>I saw a ship</td><td>. . . . . .</td></tr>
<tr><td>Going around</td><td>Rubha an Dunain</td></tr>
<tr><td>5.   It is my lover</td><td>who is steering,</td></tr>
<tr><td>I'd know your shadow</td><td>on the dark blue ocean!</td></tr>
<tr><td>Will you come tonight?</td><td>can I expect you?</td></tr>
<tr><td>Or shall I shut</td><td>the door upon you?</td></tr>
<tr><td>Shall I put out</td><td>the white candle?</td></tr>
</table>

Recorded at Upper South River in Late October 1937. Tune transcribed by Séamus Ennis; words transcribed by J. L. Campbell.

The song is of the type of an eight-syllable line divided into halves, with penultimate syllables rhyming. On that basis it is clear that the second halves of the first and third lines have been forgotten.

Notes

Line 1. Much is a dialect form of *moch.*
Line 4. The second half of the line as sung was *Rubha'n Dùin*, 'the point of the fort'. This is a syllable short; the place must be *Rubha'n Dùnain*, 'the point of the little fort', a well-known promontory on the Isle of Skye, often mentioned in old songs.

SE 137; Mode, D, Pentatonic, 4:7.

54 O, CHA DÉID, CHA DÉID MISE

O, cha déid, cha déid mise
Hoireann éile, hó ró,
Chùl gàraidh 'n sgàth pris leat,
Hoireann éile hó ró na bhó
Hì ri rì éile,
Hoireann éile hó ró.

Chùl gàraidh 'n sgàth pris leat,
Hoireann éile hó ró
Mu'n éirich mo chriosan
Hoireann éile hó ró na bhó
Hi ri rì éile
Hoireann éile hó ró.

Ma dh'éireas, gur misde,
5. Gura lughaide mo mhios air,
Gura mothaide mo dhrip air,

Mìle beannachd dham' leannan,
Dh'fhalbh an dé as a' chaladh,
Air a' bhàta dhubh dharaich,
10. Siùil chneamhte ri crannaibh,
Buill chorcach 'gan tarruing.

Chuirinn péide 'nad chòmhdhail,
Chuirinn Alasdair òg ann
A chur nan Gall o'n òrdugh

15. Bha mi raoir air a' bhanais,
'S bidh mi nochd aig a' bhaile.

236

Translation

O, I'll not go, I'll not go
In the shelter of wall or of bush with you,
Lest I become pregnant,
If I do, I'll be the worse for it,
5.   My esteem will be the less,
My trouble will be the greater.

A thousand blessings to my lover,
Who yesterday sailed from the harbour
On the black oaken vessel
10. With sails hoisted to masts,
And hempen ropes hauled.

I'd send a page to meet you,
I'd send you young Alasdair
To put Lowlanders in disorder.

15. Last night I was at the wedding,
Tonight I'll be at the townland.

Recorded at Upper South River in late October 1937. Tune transcribed by Séamus Ennis; words transcribed by J. L. Campbell.

Note

Line 10. My notebook has *siùil chnefte*; I have not been able to identify the adjective.

SE 128; Mode, E, Hexatonic. No 6.

55   GURA MULADACH MÌ

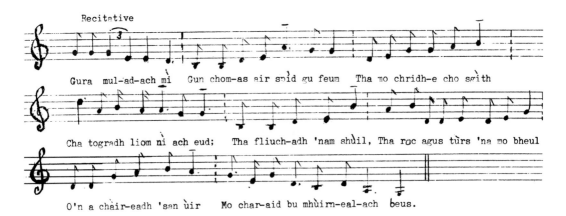

Gura mul-ad-ach mì   Gun chom-as air spìd gu feum   Tha mo chridh-e cho sgìth

Cha togradh liom nì ach eud;   Tha fliuch-adh 'nam shùil,   Tha roc agus tùrs 'na mo bheul

O'n a chàir-eadh 'san ùir   Mo char-aid bu mhùirn-eal-ach beus.

Gura muladach mì,
   Gun chomas air spìd gu feum,
Tha mo chridhe cho sgìth,
   Cha togradh liom nì ach eud;
Tha fliuchadh 'nam shùil,
   Tha roc agus tùrs 'na mo bheul
O'n a chàireadh 'san ùir
   Mo charaid bu mhùirnealach beus.

    Bu tu rìgh nam fear réidh,
10.   Thug mi fhìn dhut mo spéis ro-mhór;
   Cha rogh e fo'n ghréin
    Na bheireadh dhut beum 'na bheóil;
   Sàr-chompanach fial
    Nuair shuidheadh tu dian mu'n a' bhòrd,
B'e do chòmradh mo mhiann
    Gum bu tairis liom rian do ghlòir.

   'S ann thu cumha 'nad dhéidh
    Mar a bhuin riut an t-eug cho òg,
A liuthad deòiridh fo éis
20.   A nis o'n rinn thu bonn feum dha d' stòr;
Bhiomaid earbsach nan déidh ort
    Gun cuireadh tu 'n céill an t-òr,
Tighinn o sheòmbar nan creuchd
    Fhuair thu 'n t-urram gu léir, 's b'e a' chòir.

238

The do bhràithrean fo phràmh,
  Do mhàthair 's do chàirdean gu léir,
Gun do chaill iad gu bràch
  An deagh-charaid blàth unnad fhéin;
Nam b'e 'n nàmhaid am bàs
30.   A b'urrainn daoine 'ga smàichd le euchd
Bhiomaid uil' ann an sàs,
  'S gum biodh buil aig luchd ghràidh o'n ghéilt.

Translation

1. Sorrowful am I, without power of useful
   speech; my heart is so tired, I have no
   inclination but jealousy, my eyes are wet,
   my speech is hoarse and sorrowful, since my
   friend of great qualities was buried.

2. You were the king of even-tempered men, to
   you I have given very great affection; there
   was no one beneath the sun who would find fault
   with you; a true hospitable friend when you'd
   eagerly sit at the table; I wished for your
   conversation, I loved the manner of your talk.

3. There is a lamentation for you, touched so
   young by death; there are so many wanderers in
   distress, as you made good use of your wealth;
   we used to depend on you, that if you were
   approached you would reveal gold; coming from
   the room where you lay wounded, you
   were honoured everywhere, as was right.

4. Your brothers are distressed, your mother
   and your relations also, since they have lost
   for ever a good warm friend in you; if death were
   an enemy whom men with valour could control,
   we would all be involved, and those who love you
   would have victory over fear.

Recorded from Angus 'Ridge' MacDonald at Upper South River around 1949 by
Mgr P. J. Nicholson and Fr Calum MacDonell, on wire. Tune transcribed by Margaret

Fay Shaw and words transcribed by J. L. Campbell. Nothing is said on the recording to indicate who made the song, or on whom it was made.

The basic melody is given. The normal metrical structure of the song is $6^1 + 8^1$, but as this constantly varies by a syllable more or less in each case, the tune likewise constantly varies. It must also be noted that long vowels in the singer's dialect are not pronounced at such length as they are in the Hebridean dialects.

56 ÒRAN MU LATHA BHOTH FHLOINN

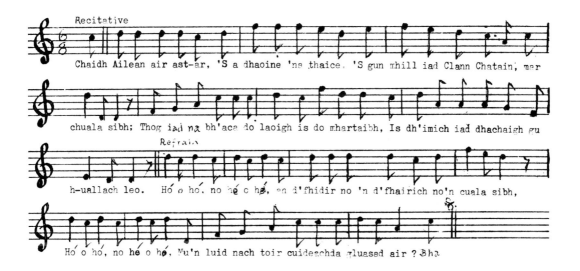

Bha an latha seo eadar Clann Dòmhnaill na Ceapaich agus na Camshronaich mu'n bhliadhna 1590. B'e Mac an Tòisich bràthair màthair Mhic 'is Raonuill, agus air an adhbhar sin, dhiùlt e (Mac 'ic Raonuill) dol a chuideachadh Mhic Dhomhnaill Dhuibh (ceann-fheadhna nan Camshronach) a thogail creach Mhic an Tòisich. Ach chaidh na Camshronaich ann, agus thog iad a' chreach.

Air an dol dhachaigh leis a' chreich sin, rinn iad stad air Both-Fhloinn mu choinneamh na Ceapaich. An sin chuir Mac Dhòmhnaill Dhuibh fios gu Mac 'ic Raonuill gu robh creach bràthair a mhàthar a' dol seachad air a shròin. An sin chuir Mac 'ic Raonuill a mach a' chrois-taraidh. Chruinnich e a chuid daoine, agus thug iad uapa a' chreach, agus chuir e air ais i gu Mac an Tòisich.

Fonn: Hó o hó, no hé o hé,
           An d'fhidir, no 'n d'fhairich, no 'n cuala sibh
           Hó o hó, no hé o hé,
           Mu'n luid nach toir cuideachda gluasad air?

           Chaidh Ailean air astar, 's a dhaoine 'na thaice,
             'S gun mhill iad Clann Chatain, mar chuala sibh;
           Thog iad na bh'aca do laoigh is do mhartaibh,
             Is dh'imich iad dhachaigh gu h-uallach leo.

241

5. Bha gnothach beag eil' ann air comhnard Bhoth-Fhloinne,
      'S gun innis mi soilleir 'san uair seo e;
    Bha creach Mhic an Tòisich aig muinntir Strath Lòchaidh,
      'S na gaisgaich Clann Dòmhnaill, thug uapa i.

    'S math 's aithne dhomh 'n t-àite 's na choinnich na h-àrmuinn,
10.   Fir ùra Bhràghad 'san uair sin iad,
    Bha iubhair Loch Tréig aig na fiùrain nach géilleadh,
      'S bu shunndach 'nan déidh fir Ghlinn' Ruaidh leatha.

    Tha còmhdach air fhathast far am beil iad 'nan laidhe,
      Gun d'fhuirich Clach Ailein gun ghluasad as,
15. Gu robh iad 'nan sléibhtrich aig ianlain an t-sléibhe,
      'S na chaidh dhachaigh le sgeul diu, bu shuarach e.

    Ceann-feadhna air meathaibh Iain Mór Sliochd an Taighe!!
      'S iomadh ceann bharr na h-amhaich a dh'fhuadaich e;
    Ma's fhìor mo luchd-sgeòil-sa, chuir e thairis air Lòchaidh
20.   Am beagan bha beò dhiu, 's an ruaig orra.

    B'e gaisgeach gun athadh, ceann stoic nam fear flathail,
      B'e Ailean a chreannaich 'san uair ud air,
    Gun a ghearr e 'm b- -l rò- -ch bho rumpuil a thòine,
      'S gun dh'fhàg e 'na sgonnan a' fuarachadh!

Translation

A SONG ON THE BATTLE OF BOLYNE

This battle was fought between the MacDonalds of Keppoch and the Camerons about the year 1590. The chief of the Mackintoshes was the maternal uncle of MacDonald of Keppoch, and for that reason Keppoch refused to go to help Cameron of Lochiel to make a raid on Mackintosh's cattle. But the Camerons went there, and lifted the spoils. On their way back with the cattle, they stopped at Bolyne opposite Keppoch. Lochiel then sent word to Keppoch that the cattle belonging to his mother's brother were going past his nose. At that Keppoch sent out the fiery cross, collected his men, recovered the cattle, and sent them back to Mackintosh.

    Refrain: Ho o ho, or heigh o heigh,
           Did you ask, or notice, or hear
        Ho o ho, or heigh o heigh,
           About the oaf whom a company can't make move?

THE SINGERS AND THEIR SONGS

1. Allan Cameron went on a journey with the help of his clan,
    they robbed Clan Chattan (the Mackintoshes and their friends),
    as you heard, they took all their cows and calves,
    and came home ostentatiously with them.

2. There was another small business on the plain of Bolyne,
    about which I will now tell you clearly;
    the folk of Strath Lochy (Camerons) had the cattle stolen
    from Mackintosh, and the heroes of Clan Donald took them from them.

3. Well I know the place where the warriors met,
    the young men from the Braes (MacDonalds) met them there then;
    the unyielding valiants had yew bows from Loch Treig,
    and the men of Glen Roy were happy with it.

4. There is proof of it from where we are lying,
    Allan's Stone (a boulder on the hillside where Allan Cameron was killed)
    has stayed there without being moved, the corpses of his men
    preyed on by the birds of the hill; only a miserable remnant of them
    got home with the tale.

5. Iain Mór of the Folk of the House a chief of weaklings!!
    many a (Cameron) head he severed from its neck;
    if the story told me was true,
    he drove the few survivors over the Lochy in a panic.

6. The chief of the noble race (MacDonalds) was a man without fear ;
    it was Allan Cameron who paid for it dearly that time;
    Iain Mór left him a mutilated corpse growing cold.

Recorded from Angus 'Ridge' MacDonald at Upper South River, Antigonish County, in late October 1937: text supplied by Mgr P. J. Nicholson; tune transcribed by Séamus Ennis, who did not set the words to it or include the refrain, which has been done by the Editor. The tune is a version of the air to which the late Seonaidh Caimbeul of South Lochboisdale in Uist composed his song *Òran Cearcan Dhòmhnaill 'ic Ailein*, 'The Song of the Hens of Donald son of Allan', a neighbouring crofter who alleged his hen-house had been raided and six of his hens stolen; a good example of the use of a pretentious air for a mocking song by a Gaelic poet. The refrain given is *Hó ró, idir na dh'fhairich no 'n cuala sibh, Na haoi ho ró, có idir a nis ris an stuaidhear iad?* 'Ho ro, did you perceive or hear at all, Na haoi ho ro, to what at all will they now be compared?' (p. 25 of *Òrain le Seonaidh Caimbeul*, 1936). I do not know to what song this version of the refrain was sung in South Uist, or whether Seonaidh had ever heard the Lochaber one. Angus Ridge would have sung at a lower pitch than is indicated here.

243

The story of this clan battle is told by the Rev. Somerled MacMillan on page 146 of hy *Bygone Lochaber*. It is clear from both this song, and from his account, that the MacDonalds owed their decisive victory to their superior bowmanship. The whole incident, and others that occur in the history of the Keppoch clan, leave one with the feeling that one is sometimes reading the story of competing Mafia families in Sicily.

Angus 'Ridge' himself, as has been related, was a descendant of Iain Mór and one of *Sliochd an Taighe*; so, it is said, was Fr Allan McDonald of Eriskay.

In translating this song, which I have done rather freely at times for the sake of readability in English, I have frequently introduced the names of the clans and their leaders involved, to make things clearer.

The background of this song is the wild and beautiful countryside north and north-east of Ben Nevis, between Loch Treig and Loch Lochy, the ancestral land of the MacDonalds of Keppoch, and scene of their feuds with the Mackintoshes and the Camerons, and with each other.

K. N. Macdonald prints a version of this song in his *MacDonald Bards*, 1900, pp. 89–90, but omitting the first and last verses here, and with *maithibh* for *meathaibh* in the fifth, entirely losing the point of the sarcasm. The Camerons had taunted the MacDonalds by daring them to attack them.

Note

The Battle of Bolyne is referred to in a taunting poem by Alasdair Odhar, 'Dun Alister', made to 'Lotti' (man) Cameron who offered Alister a bottle of whisky if he could make a song which made him, Lotti, angry. Alasdair, a son of Gill' Easbuig of Keppoch and brother of Silis the well-known poetess, made a song which contains the following verses:

Latha Bhoth-loinn rinn bhur leònadh,
Chuir Iain Dubh sibh an staid bhrònaich,
Dh'iomain e sibh null thar Lòchaidh,
 'S na bha beò agaibh 'nar breislich.

Tha Clach Ailein fhathast an làthair,
Far 'n do thuit ceann stuic ur pàirtidh,
 'S Leac nam Fachanan far am b'àbhaist,
 Far an d'fhuair bhur càirdean greadan.

'The day of Bolyne caused your wounding; Black John put you in a pitiful condition; he drove you across over the Lochy, with your survivors in confusion.

'Allan's stone is still there, where the leader of your party fell; and Leac nam Fachanan is where it was, where your relations got a pounding.'

Lotti Cameron lost his temper, and Alasdair won the bottle of whisky. This happened about a hundred years after the battle. A. MacLean Sinclair, *The Glenbard Collection*, p. 277.

SE 142; Mode, D, Hexatonic, no 6.

57 ÒRAN AIR BLÀR INBHIR LÒCHAIDH

O, gur mi a th'air mo leònadh,
Na hì ri ri ri hó hò;
O, gur mise th'air mo leònadh,
Na hì ri rì 's o ho ró.

Bho latha Blàr Inbhir Lòchaidh,
Na hi ri ri ri hó hò;
Bho latha Blàr Inbhir Lòchaidh,
Na hì ri ri 's ri o ho ró.

Bho ruaig nan eireannach dhoithte
Thàinig a dh'Albainn gun stòras,
5. Le bha dh'earras air an cleòcaibh,
Thug iad spionnadh do Chlann Dòmhnaill,
Mharbh iad m'athair is m'fhear pòsda,
'S mo cheathrar bhràithrean 'gan stròiceadh,
'S mo cheathrar mhacanan òga,
10. 'S mo naoinear chodhaltan bòidheach;
Mharbh iad mo chrodh mór gu feòlach,
'S mo chaoirich gheala 'gan ròsladh,
Loisg iad mo chuid coirc' is eòrna.

O, gur mi a th'air mo chlaoidheadh
15. Mu mhac Dhunnchaidh Gleanna Faochan,
Tha gach fear a's tìr 'gad chaoineadh
Thall 's a bhos mu Inbhir Aora,
Mhathan 's a bhasraich 's am falt sgaoilte.

O, gur mi a th'air mo mhilleadh
20. Mu mharcaich' nan strian 's nam pillein,
Thuit 'sa chaonnaig le chuid ghillean;
Thug Mac Cailein Mór an linn' air,
'S leag e 'n sgrìob ud air a chinne!

245

Translation

O, I have been wounded
By the day of Inverlochy,
From the charge of the grim Irish
Who came to Scotland without anything
5. But what they had on their cloaks;
They added strength to Clan Donald.
They killed my father and my husband,
They struck down my four brothers
They killed my four young sons
10. And my nine handsome foster-children;
They slaughtered my great cattle,
And my white sheep they roasted,
They burnt my oats and my barley.

O, I have been anguished
15. By the death of Duncan of Glen Faochan,
Whom all in the land are lamenting
Round about Inverary
Women beating their hands, dishevelled.

O, I have been devastated,
20. For the horsemen of reins and bridles
Who fell with his men in the battle;
The Earl of Argyll took to the water
And let that blow fall on his people!

Recorded from Angus 'Ridge' MacDonald at Upper South River in late October 1937. Tune transcribed by Margaret Fay Shaw from a disc copy of the original ediphone recording made early in 1938. See *Mac Talla nan Tur*, p. 92; C. MacPharlain, *Binneas nam Bard* (1908), p. 33. Words taken down from the singer by the Editor.

Each line is repeated with a slightly different meaningless refrain; the first two lines are set out to show how this is done. The tune is recitative *ad lib*.

Notes

Composed by a Campbell woman after the battle of Inverlochy, where the parliamentary forces under the Earl of Argyll were completely defeated by the Royalists under Montrose and Alasdair MacDonald.

See A. MacLean Sinclair, *Mac Talla nan Tur*, p. 92, where it is called *Cumha Mhic Dhonnachaidh Ghlinne Faochain*, 'Lament for the son of Duncan Campbell of Glen Faochan'. This song has been copied on to a disc. *See also* C. MacPharlain, *Binneas nam Bàrd* (1908), pp. 32–3, with a version of the air.

246

Line 2. The Battle of Inverlochy, near the present town of Fort William in Lochaber, was fought on 2 February 1645, when the Royalist army under Montrose and Alasdair MacColla MacDonald routed the Covenanters, led by Campbell of Auchinbreck for the Earl of Argyll, who took to the sea before the battle, which is described in the MacVurich writer in the Black Book of Clanranald printed in *Reliquiae Celticae* II, 184–5. After the Royalists, nearly all Highlanders and Irishmen, had made an incredible night march through the mountains of Lochaber, they surprised the army of the Covenanters at Inverlochy and routed them. Campbell of Auchinbreck was killed; 'all those of the kindred of MacCailin who were not killed on that day were taken prisoners', MacVurich says. According to MacVurich, the foreguard of Montrose's army was commanded by Magnus son of Giolla Dubh Ó Catháin. Giolla Dubh Ó Catháin had been on the Isle of Canna in the early summer of 1615 with Clanranald, when Coll Ciotach Macdonald called there on his way to St Kilda.

Glen Faochan is in Lorne, near Loch Faochan and Lochnell. On 5 July 1698 Duncan Campbell of 'Glen Feachin' and Dugald his eldest son gave a bond for £100 Scots to Colin Campbell, collector of the vacant stipends of Argyll (i.e. stipends payable to ministers of vacant parishes). This bond was witnessed by Colin Campbell of Braglen, and Patrick Campbell, younger son of Duncan. (The Clan Campbell, *Abstracts of Entries relating to the Campbells in the Sheriff Court Books of Argyll* ed. Rev. H. Paton, MA, 1913).

Line 11. Crodh mór, cattle, as compared to *meanbh-chrodh*, sheep or goats.

Line 21. The singer had *Mac Shimidh Mór;* but this was a slip for *Mac Cailein Mór; MacShimidh* is the patronymic of the Chiefs of the Frasers. Mac Cailein Mór, the Earl of Argyll, chief of the Campbells, left the scene of the battle in a boat.

SE 135; Mode, Hexatonic, ? E, no 3.

58 SLÀN IOMRADH DHA M' GHOISTIDH

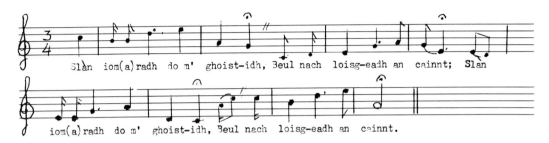

Oran le Dòmhnall Donn mac Fear Bhoth-fhiunndainn do'n
Phìobaire Chaimbeulach

1. Slan iomradh dha m' ghoistidh,
   Beul nach loisgeadh an cainnt,

2. Mo rùn an Caimbeulach sìobhalt,
   A thig le sgrìob thar a' Mhàim.

3. Rìgh! 's math thig dhut triubhas
   Gun bhith cumhang no teann,

4. 'S math thig dhut osain,
   'S bròg shocrach bhuinn sheang.

5. Brog bhileach nan cluasan
   Air a fuaghail gu seamh.

6. 'S ro-mhath ghabhainn thu romham
   Ann an domhladas blàir,

7. Bhiodh do phìob mhor 'ga spreigeadh,
   Pairt do h-eagal le càch,

8. Nuair a chluinninn fuaim t'fheadain
   Nàile! ghreasainn mo làmh.

9. 'S ro-mhath 's aithne dhomh nighean,
   'S cridh' ort an geall,

10. Ann an gleannan beag laghach,
    A dheanadh do thadhal fos n-àird;

11. Pòsar bean leat o'n Bhreugaich
    O'n cluinnear beucadaich mheang.

248

Translation

A GOOD HEALTH TO MY GODSON

By Donald Donn, son of the tacksman of Bohuntin

1. A good health to my godson,
   who does not talk sarcastically.

2. I like the civil Campbell,
   who makes the journey across the Ridge.

3. My word! the trews well become you,
   without being narrow or tight.

4. The hose well become you,
   and the comfortable, well-fitting shoe.

5. A welted shoe with lappets, carefully sewn.

6. Very well would I take you before me,
   in the thick of the fight.

7. The striking up of your great pipes would impart
   fear to everyone of the other side.

8. When I heard the sound of your chanter,
   indeed I'd hasten my hand.

9. Well I know a girl who has pledged you her heart.

10. In a pretty little glen, who'd visit you openly.

11. You will marry a wife from Breugach,
    from where can be heard the bellowing of wild deer.

Recorded from Angus 'Ridge' MacDonald at Upper South River, Antigonish County, in late October 1937. Tune transcribed by Séamus Ennis. Each two-lined verse is sung twice, making the full air. Text probably communicated by Mgr P. J. Nicholson, perhaps from Bishop Alexander MacDonald's notebook.

See A. MacLean Sinclair, *Glenbard Collection*, p. 274, where the text differs slightly. MacLean Sinclair writes:

'MOLADH A' PHIOBAIRE. Oran do Domhnall Caimbal (*sic*), Domhnall Mac a'

THE SINGERS AND THEIR SONGS

Translation

By Domhnall Donn 'Brown-Haired Donald', son of the tacksman of Bohuntin (in Lochaber), the night before he was put to death

1. 'Tis a pity, by God, oh brown-haired girl,
   that I am not over on Mull with you.

2. Where I'd get fish and venison, we would not,
   my love, want for anything.

3. Better the bellowing of the stags,
   than swarthy Duncan and his drumming.

4. Back and forth from street to street,
   with his empty 'sound-box' and his two (drum) sticks!

5. I would kill a roedeer in the bush,
   though very well she sees and hears.

6. I would kill a trout in a swiftly flowing stream,
   if my foot could wade it.

7. I would kill a blackcock off the branch
   ere many a man would have his shirt on.

8. I'll not eat food, I'll do no deed,
   nor kill a deer, I cannot do.

9. I'll be headless tomorrow on a mound,
   unless my friends are vigilant.

10. May God keep my sense to me,
    I was never yet in such danger.

11. May God raise my soul above,
    the ill-hour is now kept for me.

Recorded from Angus 'Ridge' MacDonald at Upper South River in late October 1937. Tune transcribed by Séamus Ennis, rewritten. Words taken down by J. L. Campbell. The song is sung in two couplets at a time, AB-CD etc.

Dòmhnall Donn, a Keppoch MacDonald, was a famous Highland reiver who flourished in the second half of the seventeenth century. Traditions about him are

252

numerous, and sometimes confused; a readable account of them is to be found in William MacKay's *Urquhart and Glenmoriston, Olden Times in a Highland Parish* (1893), p. 187: 'Donald who was a son of MacDonald of Bohuntin, in Brae Lochaber . . . looked on cattle-lifting as legitimate warfare, and on the reaver's trade as a gentleman's calling . . . although his deeds brought him at the end to the headsman's block, he died with the reputation of never having injured a poor man, or imbued his hands wantonly in human blood. The scenes of his adventures extended from Breadalbane to Caithness, and his custom was to make rapid journeys, with a few kindred spirits, by the least known mountain tracks, and to swoop down upon the cattle of the lairds and tacksmen (big tenant farmers) where he was least expected.'

Adventures attributed to him, it might be better to say. The occasion of this song is said to have been his love affair with Mary, the daughter of the Laird of Grant, who then lived in Glenurquhart Castle, and who forbade the marriage. After a row with the laird, who was furious at Dòmhnall Donn for leaving cattle lifted in Ross-shire, on a farm on the Laird of Grant's estate, Dòmhnall Donn had to go into hiding, from which he was lured by a fabricated message from Mary asking him to meet her at the house of a certain neighbour, to which Dòmhnall went. While waiting for her expected coming, his treacherous host plied him with whisky, and when he was inebriated, called in a party of the Laird's men to arrest him. He was imprisoned in Urquhart Castle and shortly afterwards executed.

See the work quoted; also Somhairle MacGill-Eain, MA, 'Domhnall Donn of Bohuntin', *Trans. Geal Soc. Inverness* XLII, 91–110; Hector MacDougall (ed.), *Clàrsach na Coille*, pp. 225, 291; *Hebridean Folksongs* No. CVI (Vol. III, 108–13 and 258–60); *Gesto Collection*, p. 5 (tune has only a slight resemblance).

Notes

Verse 1. Somhairle MacGill-Eain suggests that Dòmhnall Donn might have felt safer among the Campbells and MacLeans on the Isle of Mull than amongst the Grants. He had MacLean relations, and was less unfavourably disposed to the Campbells than most of his clan.

Verse 3. Presumably the drummer announcing his execution. *Bolgan fàs*; One of the meanings of *bolg* in Irish is 'the sound-box of a harp' (Dinneen). Here it is a drum.

SE 139; Mode, F, Pentatonic, 4:7.

60 'S ANN LIOM FHÌN NACH 'EIL TLACHDMHOR

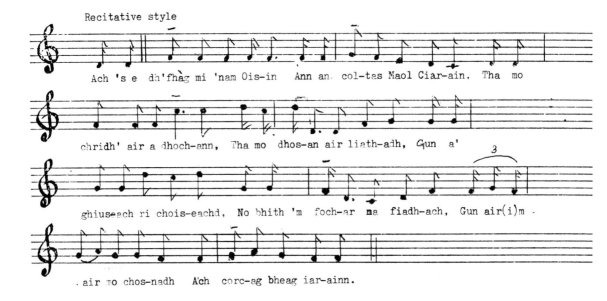

Recitative style

Ach 's e dh'fhàg mi 'nam Ois-in Ann an col-tas Maol Ciar-ain. Tha mo

chridh' air a dhoch-ann, Tha mo dhos-an air liath-adh, Gun a'

ghiuseach ri chois-eachd, No bhith 'm foch-ar ma fiadh-ach, Gun air(i)m

. air ro chos-nadh Ach corc-ag bheag iar-ainn.

ORAN AN DÉIDH BLÀR CHUIL-LODAIR

Le Iain mac Theàrlaich Òig

'S ann leam nach eil tlachdmhor
An t-Achd a rinn Deòrsa,
Thug ar n-airm bhuainn 's ar n-aodach,
A bhiodh daonnan 'gar còmhdach,
5. Am breacan 's a' féilidh,
Leis bu ghleusda fir òga;
Gun ach briogais is casag,
Agus bata 'nar dòrnaibh.

Cha b'e cadal 'san smùraich
10. 'S na chuir mi ùidh an tùs m'òige,
Ach éirigh gu sunndach,
'S dol air ionnsaigh le m' mhórghath;
Bhiodh a' choill' air gach làimh dhomh
Cur deagh-fhàileadh 'nam phòran,
15. 'S mi dìreadh nan creagan,
'S tric a leag mi damh cròiceach.

254

THE SINGERS AND THEIR SONGS

Nuair a thigeadh an t-àmhgar,
   Cha b'e chlàrsach bu cheòil dhuinn,
Ach bùirein an làn-damh
20.   Anns na h-àrd-bheanna ceòthar;
Bhiodh ar mìol-choin 's ar gadhair
   Cur faghaid an Conaghleann,   ? Corraghleann
Bu tric agh is damh cabrach
   Anns na faisrichean gorma.

25. Gheibhteadh cuach anns an doire,
   Cabar-coille, 's boc earba,
'S am bradan cho lìonmhor
   Air na linneanan garbha,
Snàmh air bhoinnean struth fìor-uisg',
30.   'S e gu h-inntinneach, tarra-gheal,
'S e gu cama-ghobach, ullamh,
   Ceapadh chuileag 'san anamoch.

Ach 's e dh'fhàg mi 'nam Oisin,
   Ann an coltas Maol Ciarain,
35. Tha mo chridh' air a dhochann,
   Tha mo dhosan air liathadh,
Gun a' ghiusach ri choiseachd,
   No bhith 'm fochair na fiadhach,
'S gun do dh'airm air mo chosnadh
40.   Ach a' chorcag beag iarainn.

Ann an àite nan dagaibh,
   A' chlaidhimh, 's na sgéithe,
'S a' chuilbheir chaoil ghlaicte
   Chuireadh stad air mac éilde,
45. Cha chluinn mi air gaisge
   Guth aca, no sgeula,
Ach cuibhlichean factoraidh,
   Glagraich, is Beurla.

Gun iomradh air dualchas,
50.   Air cruadal, no tapachd,—
Chuir a' chuibhle mun cuairt dhi
   Car tuathal is tarsuinn;
Sìol nam bodachan giùgach
   A bhiodh 'sna dùnain 'gan cartadh,
55. Seòladh àrd os ar cionn-sa
   Bho'n a thionndaidh a' chairt ud.

THE SINGERS AND THEIR SONGS

Mìle marbhaisg ort, a shaoghail,
   Tha thu caochlaideach, cealgach;
Bha mi uair cha do shaoil leam
60.   Tighinn as aonais a' gharbhlaich;
    'S mise chleachd bhith 'n Aird Ghobhar
    An cluinnteadh boc earba,
An diu an Sòrnan beag, odhar,
    Ann an todhar a' mheanbh-chruidh.

Translation

SONG AFTER THE BATTLE OF CULLODEN
AGAINST THE DISCLOTHING AND DISARMING ACT OF 1746
John Maclean of Inverscadale

1. Displeasing to me is
    This Act which King George made,
  That took our arms and clothes from us
    Which had always equipped us;
  For their plaids and their tartans,
    In which young folk were active
  We must now wear trousers and long coats,
    And carry sticks in our hands.

2. It was not sleep in the peat-dross
    That I preferred in my young days,
  But happily arising
    To set out with my fish-spear;
  From the forest around me
    Came sweet scents to my nostrils,
  As I climbed up the crags,
    Oft I killed the red deer.

3. At times of depression
    No harp was our music,
  But the bellowing of stags
    On the mist-laden hills;
  Our terriers and greyhounds
    Would be hunting in Conaglen
  Hinds and stags were found often
    Around the green hills.

4. In the oak-grove were found
   Cuckoo, roebuck, capercaillie,
   And many white-bellied salmon
   In the rock pools,
   Merrily swimming
   In streams of pure water,
   Hooked-mouthed and ready
   To catch flies in the dusk.

5. Like Ossian I'm left
   And like Maol Ciarain mourning,
   My heart is wounded.
   My hairs have turned grey;
   With no pine-woods to walk in,
   Far from the hunting,
   With no arms to win it,
   Except a little iron knife.

6. In place of pistol,
   Of sword and of target,
   And fine barrelled gun
   To check the red deer;
   I don't hear a word of
   History, or old stories,
   But of factory wheels,
   English and noise.

7. There's no word of heredity,
   Or of hardiness or heroism,
   Perverse and unlucky,
   The wheel of fortune has turned;
   A race of churls, cringing,
   Whom we'd dump on the middens,
   Now sails high above us
   Since the cards changed.

8. A thousand curses on you, world,
   You're deceitful and fickle,
   Once I never imagined
   That the mountains I'd leave;
   And I who'd lived in Ardgour
   Where oft heard was the roe-buck,
   Now am in drab little Sornan,
   Mucking with sheep.

THE SINGERS AND THEIR SONGS

Recorded from Angus 'Ridge' MacDonald on ediphone in late October 1937, but the tune was not transcribed by Séamus Ennis in 1948. Text and tune here were both transcribed from a wire recording which Angus 'Ridge' made for Mgr P. J. Nicholson around 1950, the tune by Margaret Fay Shaw.

The song is against the legislation of the government of King George II (1727–60), forbidding both the possession of firearms (even for hunting) and the wearing of Highland garb by the Highlanders of Scotland, alike to those of the clans which had risen for Prince Charles and those who had abstained or fought against him. The Act caused immense resentment in the Highlands and Islands, as is attested by songs against it made by Alexander MacDonald, Duncan Ban MacIntyre, and Iain MacCodrum.

A. MacLean Sinclair, who published a version of the song in his *Gaelic Bards from 1715 to 1765* says that the author was Iain mac Theàrlaich Òig, John son of Young Charles, the fifth MacLean of Inverscadale in Ardgour, by his second wife, a daughter of Archibald MacLean of Ardtun. The MacLeans of Inverscadale were an offshoot of the MacLeans in Ardgour, a mountainous district in north Argyll. Sorn, where Iain mac Thearlaich Oig went when he had to leave Ardgour, is on the Isle of Mull.

I have three versions of this song; one transcribed from the wire recording of Angus Ridge made by Mgr Nicholson around 1950 (AR); one from Bishop Alexander MacDonald's (MS) notebook communicated around 1937 by Monsignor Nicholson (AMcD); and that printed by A. MacLean Sinclair in his *Gaelic Bards from 1715 to 1765*, published in 1890 (AMS) (p. 193). MacLean Sinclair did great service to Gaelic literature, but is known sometimes to have 'improved' his texts.

Notes

Line   1. AMcD *'S ann leam fhin.*
Line   9. AMS *Smur*; AMcD *Smurach.*
Line 12. AMS *air mor-ghath*; AMcD *le m' mhoirghadh*; AR *le m' mhórghath.*
Line 14. AMS *am phoribh*; AMcD *am pollain*; AR *'nam phòran.*
Line 16. AMS *'n damh croic' ann*; AMcD *damh croice*; AR *damh cròiceach.*
Line 17. AMS *thigeadh an damhir*; AMcD *thugadh an dangar*; AR *thigeadh an dangar.*
The word must be *an t-àmhgar*, 'anxiety, depression' rhyming with *chlàrsach*. Whoever substituted *damhir* 'rutting season' overlooked the rhyme. What the poet is saying is that when depression came on him, it was not harp music that cheered him, but the bellowing of the red deer stags in the hills. Compare Irish *amhgar* pronounced *amhngar*, see Dinneen's Dictionary.
Line 22. AMS *Conaghleann* (is the present name for the estate of Inverscadail); AMcD *chorra-ghlinn*; AR, indistinct, sounds like *corra-ghleann* or *corra-bheann.*
Line 24. AMS *h-aisrichean*; AMcD *fasaichean* (defies rhyme): AR *faisrichean*, plural of *faisir* or *aisir*, defile or pass.
Line 25. Angus 'Ridge' telescoped the fourth and fifth verses of the other two versions, taking the first line of the fifth verse as the first line of the fourth, where it makes better rhyme, and omitting the fifth verse otherwise. The original first of the fourth verse in the other versions was:
> *Gheibhte broc ann is taghan*
> Badger was found there, and pine marten.

The pine marten is not known in Nova Scotia. In the original first line of the fifth verse, the cuckoo was 'heard' not 'found'. The fifth verse then reads:

Chluinnteadh cuach ann ad choille,
'S bu bhinn a ghoireadh an smudan.
A' toirt teistinis laidir
Mar bha nadur 'gan stiuradh,
Gheibhte liath-chearc 'san doire,
Is bu toil leam a ciuchran,
Is a coileach m'a coinnimh
Air toman a' durdail.

'The cuckoo would be heard in your wood,
and the ring-dove called sweetly,
showing how Nature directed them;
the grey-hen would be found in the grove,
her call pleased me; and her mate
would be answering on the hillock before her.'

Line 33. Oisin and Maol Ciarain are stock figures of the solitary bereaved mourner, Oisin as last survivor of the Fiann (see song No. 48 here), Maol Ciarain as mourning for his son Fearchar killed in Ireland. In a song to his brother Alasdair, Anndra mac an Easbuig has:

'S mi mar choltas Mhaol Ciarain
No mar Oisein gat iarraidh,
'S gum bi mise gat iargain ri m' bheò.

'I am like Maol Ciarain
or like Ossian, in search of you;   I shall bewail your loss as long as I live.'

Bàrdachd Chloinn Ghill-Eathain, p. 69, Colm Ó Baoill. *See also* William Matheson, *The Songs of John MacCodrum*, p. 158:

'S bochd a chrìochnaich ar n-aimsir
Mar Mhaol-Ciarain gun Fhearchar.

'Wretchedly have our days ended,
like Maol-Ciarain without Fearchar.'

See also Bhàrdachd Ghàidhlig, pp. 296–7; *Reliquiae Celticae* II, 332, prints Maol Ciarain's lament for his son Fearchar.

'Bás Fhearchair a shearg mo shúil
Mar cheard gun teanchair atáim
Rug tu m'aithe 's m'eagar bhuam
'S truagh, a Mhic, do dhol le dán.

'The death of Fearchar has withered my eye,
Like craftsman without tool I am
You took from me reward and my art,
Sad, o son, was your going with poems.'

Fearchar had been killed while on a 'poetic circuit' in Ireland.
Line 38. AMS *an fhiadhich*; AMcD *an fhiadhaich* AR *na (m) fiadhach.*
Line 39. AMS *chum mo chosnidh*; AMcD *air mo chosdsa.*
Line 41. AMS *na daga*; AMcD *na deige.*
Line 42. AMS, AMcD *ghlaice*; AR *ghlaicte.*

Line 45. AMS *Is nach cluinn mi guth aca | De dh-eachdridh, no sgeulachd*; AMcD *Cha chluinn mi air gaisge | Gath aca no sgeula.*

Line 47. AMS *cuibhlichean 's factori | Beairtean is Beurla.* AMcD *culbhlichean factoraidh | Glagadaich is Beurla.* After 1745 evicted Highlanders could only emigrate, or go to work at the looms in Glasgow.

Line 49. AMS *Cha n-fheil iomradh.*

Line 51. AMS *Chuir a chuibheall*; AMcD *Chuir cuibhle.*

Line 52. AMS *tuathal*; AMcD *tuathar.*

Line 53. AMS *Sliochd*; AMcD *Siol.*

Line 54. AMS *'Bha 'sna dunibh gan cartadh*; AMcD *Bhiodh 's na dunain 'gan cartadh.*

Line 56. AMS *a chairt oirnn*; AMcD *á chairt ud.*

Line 57. AMS *O, marbhphaisg ort*; AMcD *Mile marbhaish ort.*

Line 59. AMS *Bha mi uair nach do shaoil leam*; AMcD *Bha mi uair 's cha do shaoil leam.*

Line 60. AMS *Teachd as aogis*; AMcD *Tigh'nn as aonais.*

Line 62. AMS *'M bu tric gleadhar bhoc*; AMcD *'S an cluinnte gleodhar buic.*

Line 63. AMS *Tha an diugh an Sorn odhar*; AMcD *An diugh an sornan beag, odhar.*

BIBLIOGRAPHY

BENNETT, MARGARET, *The Last Stronghold. Scottish Gaelic traditions of Newfoundland.* Breakwater Books, Canada, and Canongate Press, Edinburgh, 1989.

BUMSTED, J. M. *The People's Clearance*, 1770–1815. Edinburgh, 1982.

CAIRD, Professor James B. 'The Creation of Crofts and New Settlement Patterns in the Highlands and Islands of Scotland', *Scottish Geographical Magazine*, Vol. 103, No. 2, pp. 67–75, 1987.

CAMPBELL, J. L. 'Scottish Gaelic in Canada: an Unofficial Census', *The Scotsman*, 30 January 1933.

——With Compton MacKenzie and Carl H. Borgstrom. *The Book of Barra*. London, 1936.

——'Scottish Gaelic in Canada', *American Speech,* Vol. XI, April 1936.

——'A visit to Cape Breton', *Scots Magazine*, September and October, 1938.

——With Annie Johnston and John MacLean MA, *Gaelic Folksongs from the Isle of Barra* (booklet accompanying set of five twelve-inch records). London, 1950.

——'Highland Links with Nova Scotia', *Scots Magazine*, October 1953.

——'Some Notes on Scottish Gaelic Waulking Songs', *Eigse* VIII, 87. Dublin, 1956.

——'More Notes on Scottish Gaelic Waulking Songs', *Eigse* IX, 129, 1959. (Cape Breton versions mentioned.)

——*Tales from Barra, told by the Coddy*. Edinburgh, 1960.

——'More Notes on the MacNeils of Barra', *Scottish Genealogist* VI, No. 4, p. 8. Printed at Hawick, 1960.

——With Francis Collinson. *Hebridean Folksongs*, Vol. I, 1969; Vol. II, 1977; Vol. III, 1981. Oxford. Vols II and III contain some texts from Cape Breton.

CROFTERS' COMMISSION: *Minutes of Evidence*, four vols., and *Report*, Edinburgh, 1884.

CRAIG, K. C. *Orain Luaidh Màiri nighean Alasdair*. Glasgow, 1949. (Texts of 145 waulking songs).

DAY, J. P. *Public Administration in the Highlands and Islands of Scotland*. London, 1918.

DUNN, Professor C. W. *Highland Settlers: a Portrait of the Gael in Nova Scotia*. Toronto, 1953.

GRAHAM, I. C. G. *Colonists from Scotland: Emigration to North America, 1707–1783*. Ithaca, New York, 1956.

HUTCHINSON, Roger, *Camanachd! the story of Shinty*. Edinburgh, 1989.

BIBLIOGRAPHY

Jackson, Professor Kenneth, 'Notes on the Gaelic of Port Hood, Nova Scotia' and 'More Tales from Port Hood' (*Scottish Gaelic Studies* VI, 89 and 176).

MacArthur, Dugald, 'Some Emigrant Ships from the West Highlands. (Paper read to the Gaelic Society of Inverness on 6 November 1987.) *Transactions,* Vol. LV, 1988.

MacDonald, Colin S. 'Early Highland Emigration to Nova Scotia and Prince Edward Island, 1770–1853. (Paper read before Nova Scotia Historical Society on 4 November 1932.)

MacDonald, Keith Norman. *The Gesto Collection of Highland Music,* including the second part of Appendix of 67 pages. Leipzic, 1895.

——The MacDonald Bards. Glasgow, 1900 (reprinted from the *Oban Times*).

MacDonell, Sister Margaret. *The Emigrant Experience.* Songs of the Highland Emigrants in North America. (No music.) Toronto, 1982.

——and John Shaw. *Luirgean Eachainn Nill: Folktales from Cape Breton.* A Collection of Folktales told by Hector Campbell, transcribed and translated from the original Gaelic. Stornoway. 1981.

MacDougall, J. L. *History of Inverness County, Nova Scotia.* Sydney, N.S., 1922.

MacKenzie, A. J. *The History of Christmas Island Parish with an Introduction by Rev. Patrick Nicholson, Ph. D., Professor in St F. X. College.* Privately printed, 1926.

MacKinnon, J. G. 'Na Gaidheil an Ceap Breatunn' (the Gaels in Cape Breton), *Mac Talla* XI, 52–4, 1902.

——*Fear na Ceilidh, Miosachan Gailig,* 1928–30.

——(ed. and founder) *Mac Talla,* weekly, began 28 May 1892; became fortnightly with the issue of 1 November 1901, after a fire in Sydney put a number of advertisers out of business; ceased publication with the issue of 24 June 1904, though not with the death of the editor-owner as is wrongly stated in *Typographia Scoto-Gadelica* in 1915.

MacLean, Sinclair, Rev. A. 'Clann Neill Bharra', *Mac Talla,* 2 June 1984, and 17 November 1894.

——'The MacNeils of Barra', *Celtic Review,* Vol. III, pp. 216–23, 1907.

——*The Gaelic Bards from 1411 to 1715.* Charlottetown, 1890.

——*The Gaelic Bards from 1715 to 1765.* Charlottetown, P.E.I. 1892.

——*Comchruinneachadh Ghlinn-a-Bhaird,* the Glenbard Collection of Gaelic Poetry, Charlottetown, 1890. Abridged, 1901.

——*Mac Talla nan Tur.* Sydney, N.S. 1901.

——*Clàrsach na Coille.* Glasgow, 1881 Second edn, revised and edited by Hector MacDougall, Glasgow, 1928.

MacLean, Sinclair, Rev. D. 'Gaelic in Nova Scotia'. Paper read to the Humanities Conference at Halifax, N.S. on 10 June 1949.

MacLennan, Gordon W. 'Some Anomalies in the Gaelic Dialects of Scotland and Canada', *Scottish Gaelic Studies* XIV, 128–137, 1986.

MacLeod, C. I. N. 'The Gaelic Tradition in Nova Scotia', *Lochlann* I, 235.

——and Helen Creighton. *Gaelic Songs in Nova Scotia.* Ottawa, 1964.

——*Bàrdachd a Albainn Nuaidh.* Glasgow, 1970.

MacMillan, Rev. A. J. *To the Hill of Boisdale.* Sydney, N.S., 1986 (Boisdale in Cape Breton).

MacMillan, Rev. S. *Bygone Lochaber.* Privately printed, 1971.

MacNeil, Neil. *The Highland Heart in Nova Scotia.* New York, 1948.

MacNeil, R. L. *The Clan MacNeil.* New York, 1923. (Neither this book, nor the Rev. A. MacLean Sinclair's articles, make any mention of the MacNeil of Barra Deed of Entail of 1806, or the Deed of Settlement of 1820.)

BIBLIOGRAPHY

MACPHAIL, Margaret. *Loch Bras d'Or*. Windsor, N.B., 1970.

NICHOLSON, Rt Rev. Mgr P. J. (formerly President of St Francis Xavier University, Antigonish). *Achadh nan Gàidheal* ('The Highlanders' Field'), the Gaelic column in the *Casket*, weekly paper published in Antigonish. Contained many folktales and words of traditional songs taken down in Cape Breton.

RANKIN, Rev. D. J. *A History of The County of Antigonish*. Toronto, 1929.

SELKIRK, Earl of. *Observations of the Present State of the Highlands of Scotland*, with a view of the causes and probable consequences of Emigration. Edinburgh, second edition, 1806.

SHAW, John. *Tales until Dawn*. Sgeul gu Latha. The World of a Cape Breton Story-Teller. Montreal, 1987.

SHAW, Margaret Fay. *Folksongs and Folklore of South Uist*. London, 1955. (Contains references to Cape Breton.)

——Margaret Fay. *Gaelic Folksongs from South Uist* (in *Studia Memoriae Belae Bartók Sacra*, Budapest, 1956).

LIST OF FIRST LINES

CLÀR NAN STREATHAN-TOISICH

265

INDEX OF PERSONAL AND PLACE-NAMES IN THE SONGS

CLÀR AINMEANNAN AGUS DHAOINE A THACHRAS 'SNA H-ÒRAIN

References are sometimes to lines, sometimes to verses. 3/4 = the fourth line of the third song; 48 v.8 = the eighth verse of song No. 48, for instance.

Abhainn Mhiadhaineach, Middle River in Cape Breton, 3/4.

Achadh nan Gall, the Scottish Lowlands, 18/12.

Ailein Donn, 7/1, refrain; 16/1, 3, 5, refrain; *Ailein* gen. used for nominative.

Àird Ghobhar, Ardgour, part of Argyll in Scotland formerly possessed by the MacLeans.

'*Alasdair Og*', 54/13.

Alba, dat. *Albainn* Scotland, 57/4.

Ameriga, 2/5.

'*Anna*', 34/7

Anna bheag, daughter of Iain Mùideartach, *c.* 1590–1670, Chief of the MacDonalds of Clanranald, 13/3

'*Annag*', 1/refrain.

Barraidh, the Isle of Barra, home of the MacNeils, 13/1, 17/25, 28/11.

Beinn a' Cheathaich in Barra, 28/1.

Beurla, the English language, 60/48.

Blàr na Féithe, the Battle of the Bog, between the MacLeods and the MacDonalds of Sleat, in North Uist, in 1603.

Borghraidh, Boreray a small island in the Sound of Harris, formerly held by a MacLean family, 40/13.

Both-fhloinn, Bolyne in Lochaber, scene of a battle between the MacDonalds of Keppoch and the Camerons, 56 foreword, and 1. 5.

Bràighe, gen. *Bràghad* the Braes of Lochaber, 56/10.

Bràighe Liantaidh, 31/6.

Bràighe Rainich, the Braes of Rannoch, 39/6.

Bran, Fionn mac Cumhail's dog, 48 v. 8.

Breugach, Am B., a place in Lochaber, 58 v. 11.

267

INDEX OF PERSONAL AND PLACE-NAMES IN THE SONGS

Caimbeul, Caiptein, Captain Campbell, 10 v. 4.
Caimbeul, Iain, 15/3.
Caimbeulach, a Campbell, 41 v. 11, 58 v. 2. *Caimbeulaich* Campbells, 3/13, 30/18.
Caisteal Dubhairt, Castle Duart in the Isle of Mull, seat of the MacLeans of Duart, 27 v. 5.
Caitriana, daughter of Iain Muideartach, Chief of Clanranald, 13/2.
Cameron, Allan, of Lochiel, 56/1, 22.
Camshronaich, the Camerons, 30/14, 56 foreword.
Caol Ìle, the Sound of Islay, between the islands of Islay and Jura, 9 v. 10, 19 v. 3.
Caol Muile, the Sound of Mull, 9 v. 2.
Ciosamul, Kismul Castle, seat of the chiefs of the MacNeils of Barra, 28/11.
Conaghleann, Conaglen in Ardgour, 60/22.
Cill Uachdrach, 22/3.
Cinn-tàile, Kintail, 2/17.
Cinn Tìre, Kintyre, 40 v. 10.
Clach Ailein, the boulder where Allan Cameron of Lochiel was killed at the Battle of Bolyne, 56/14.
Clann Dòmhnaill, the MacDonalds, 50/16, 56/8, 57/6.
Clann Dòmhnall na Ceapaich, the MacDonalds of Keppoch, 56 foreword.
Clann Chatain, the Clan Chattan, a confederacy led by the Mackintoshes of Moy, 56/2.
Clann Ghill' Fhinnein, the MacKinnons, 3/11.
Clann 'ic Leòid, the MacLeods, 30/17.
Clann Nìll, the MacNeils of Barra, 15/7, 28/17, 30/19, 52/16. *See also* the chapter on Emigration.
Cnoc nan Seanach, 34/5.
Coire Bhreacain, the whirlpool between the islands of Jura and Scarba, 23/1.
Coire Riabhach, the Brindled Corrie, 33 title, 1. 2.
Coirneal Grannda, Colonel Grant, 10 v. 5.
'Coirneal Iain', 10 v. 4.
Colbhasaigh, the island of Colonsay, 29/14, 31/9.
Colla, the isle of Coll, 27 v. 8; *C. creagach* 'rocky Coll', 27 v. 10; *Tighearna Cholla,* the Laird of Coll, MacLean of Coll, 27 narrative.
Cuan na h-Éireann, the Irish Sea, 30/4, 32/6.

Deòrsa, King George II, 60/2; *Rìgh Dòrs'* King George III, 2/16.
Diùraidh, the island of Jura, 29/13; *Diurach* adj., pertaining to Jura, 19 v. 10, 35/1.
'Diùram', subject of No. 51.
'Dòmhnall', 32.12.
Dòmhnall Donn', member of MacNeil of Barra's crew, 28/26.
'Dòmhnall dualach', 32/1.
'Dòmhnallan dubh', 32 refrain.
Dòmhnallaich, the MacDonalds, 3/9, 30/15.
'Donnchadh bàn', 19 v. 9.
'Donnchadh ciar', 59 v. 3.
Dunnchadh Gleanna Faochain, Duncan Campbell of Glen Faochan in Argyll, 57/15.
Dùnbheagain, Dunvegan Castle in Skye, seat of the Chiefs of the MacLeods, 27 v. 10.
Dùn Éideann, Edinburgh, 10 v. 3.
Dùntuilm, seat of the chiefs of the MacDonalds of Sleat, 27 v. 10.

INDEX OF PERSONAL AND PLACE-NAMES IN THE SONGS

Earraghaidheal, Argyll, 3/14; *na h-Earraghaidhealaich* the Argyll men, 49/17.
Eige, the isle of Eigg, 9 v. 9, 17/21, 31/8.
Éireannach, an Irishman, 57/3; pl. *Éireannaich* 13/28.
Éirinn, Ireland, 9 v. 11, 17/33, 19 v. 12, 40 v. 6, 48 v. 4, 49/8, gen. *Cuan na h-Éireann,* 32/6.

Fear an Tùir, 27 refrain, must be MacDonald of Clanranald; the Tur would be Mingarry Castle in Moidart.
'Fearchar', steersman of MacNeil of Barra's galley, 28/30.
Féinn, the heroic band under *Fionn mac Cumhail,* the feats of whom are the subject of Ossianic ballads, 48 v. 1, 2, 3, 4, 5.
Fionn, (mac Cumhail) leader of the *Feinn,* 48 v. 7.
Frangaich, the French, 49/3.

Gàidheil, na, the Gaels, 19 v. 1.
Gall, a foreigner to the Highlanders, a Lowlander, 54/14. *See Achadh nan Gall.*
Gill', Eóghanain Og young Gilleonan, heir to MacNeil of Barra, 13/20.
Gille Anndrais 47 v. 4.
Glaschu, Glasgow, 49/5.
Gleann Éite, Glen Etive in Argyll, 40 v. 16.
Gleann Faochan, in Argyll, 57/15.
Gleann na Géige, 31/1.
Gleann nan Dearcag, 28/26.
Gleann Ruadh, Glen Roy in Lochaber, 56/12.

Iain mac a' Phearsain, John MacPherson, father of two members of MacNeil of Barra's crew, 28/25.
Iain Mór, MacDonald of Bohuntin, 56/17.
Iain Og mac Dhubhghaill, Iarla Chluainidh, presumably a MacPherson of Cluny, 15*b*/6.
Ile, the island of Islay, 37/7, 40 v. 6.
Inbhir Aora, Inverary in Argyll, seat of the Chiefs of the Campbells of Argyll, 57/17.
Inbhir Lòchaidh, Inverlochy in Lochaber, 57 title, 1. 2.
Innseanaich, (American) Indians, 2/13.
Iseabail Bhuidhe Nic Neacail, 42 v. 14.

Leathanaich, the MacLeans, 30/20.
Lìte, the port of Leith, 19 v. 8.
Lòchaidh, Loch Lochy in Lochaber, 56/19.
Loch Tréig, in Lochaber, 56/11.
Loch Aoillte, Loch Eilt in Arisaig, 17/10.
Loch Aoineart, Loch Eynort in Skye, 18/29.
Loch Ròdhaig, Loch Roag in Skye, 18/32.
Lùngaidh, the isle of Lunga, Argyll, 29/13.

'Mac a' Mhaoir', 29/1, 21, and title.
Mac an Tòisich, the chief of Clan Chattan, 56/7, foreword.
Mac Cailein Mór, patronymic of the chiefs of the Campbells of Argyll, 57/22.

INDEX OF PERSONAL AND PLACE-NAMES IN THE SONGS

Mac Colla, Alasdair MacDonald, *Alasdair mac Colla Chiotaich* Alasdair son of left-handed Colla, 31/10.

Mac Dhòmhnaill Duibh, patronymic of the chiefs of the Camerons, 56 foreword.

Mac Dhòmhnaill 'ic Ruairi 'ic Dhubhghaill, 47 v. 6.

'Mac Eachainn', 35/11.

Mac Iain 'ic Sheumais, the MacDonald hero at the Battle of Carinish, 8/1.

Mac 'ic Ailein, patronymic of the chiefs of the MacDonalds of Clanranald, 27 v. 12, narrative, *'Mac Ailein an Tùir',* 28/9, 30/1.

Mac 'ic Raghnaill, patronymic of the chiefs of the MacDonalds of Keppoch, 56 foreword.

Mac 'ill' Eathain, MacLean of Duart, 28/9.

Mac 'ill' Onfhaidh, a small clan in Lochaber, 47 v. 8.

Mac Leòid, the chief of the MacLeods of Dunvegan, 30/11.

MacNeils of Barra: see *Gill' Eóghanain Og, Niall Gruamach; Ruairi an Tartair; Ruairi Og;* and the chapter on Emigration.

Mac Rìgh Lochlainn, the son of the King of Norway, 48 v. 7.

Maighdeanan Mhic Leoid, MacLeod's Maidens, rocks off the north-west coast of the Isle of Skye, 18/3.

'Màiri', 38/1, 5, and refrain.

'Màiri', 19 v. 11.

'Màiri', 40 v. 6.

Màm, a ridge in Lochaber, 58 v. 2.

Manainn, the Isle of Man, 37/7.

Maol Ciarain, a stock figure of woe, 60/34.

Mòirthir, in south Hebridean Gaelic the mainland properties of the MacDonalds of Clanranald. i.e. Morar, Arisaig and Moidart, 17/1, 3, and title.

Mórar (Mór-dhobhar), 49/11. Means 'Great Water', referring to Loch Morar.

Mùideart, Moidart, 17/19.

Muile, the Isle of Mull, 41 v. 11, 59 v. 1.

'Murchadh', 47 v. 3.

'Murchadh Beag', little Murdo, member of the crew of MacNeil of Barra's galley, 28/28.

'Murchadh Ruadh', auburn-haired Murdo, another member of MacNeil's crew, 28/27.

Na h-Earradh, the Isle of Harris (means 'the Heights') 15/2.

Na h-Innsean, the (West) Indies, 42 v. 6.

Nighean Mhic 'ic Ailein, Clanranald's daughter, 27 narrative.

'Ni Lachlainn', Lochlan's daughter, 28/28. (Lochlan was a MacLean name).

Niall Gruamach, 'Gloomy Neil', MacNeil of Barra, 28/23.

Oisin, son of Fionn mac Cumhail, prominent member of the *Féinn,* dialogue with St Patrick, 48; 60/33.

Òlaind, Holland, 40 v. 8, 42 v. 7.

Pàdraig, St Patrick, 48 v.1.

Peairt, 51 v. 3. Perth.

Port an Aisig, the Ferry Port, 41 v. 3. Compare *Aird an Aisig,* on Loch Awe in Argyll.

INDEX OF PERSONAL AND PLACE-NAMES IN THE SONGS

INDEX OF ENGLISH CHAPTERS

INDEX OF ENGLISH CHAPTERS

INDEX OF ENGLISH CHAPTERS

GLOSSARY

CLÀR NAN CRUAIDH-FHACLAN

aorabh, 40 v. 24, nature, constitution

adhraic, 35/7, dialect for *adharc*

àmhgar, 60/17, dialect for *amhghar*, sorrow. *See* note

amm, 'time'. In this spelling K. C. Craig's *Orain Luaidh Mairi Alasdair* is followed, as it is the *m* which is long, not the *a*

an-uair, 57 v. 11, unfortunate time. Pronounced with stress on first syllable

banchag, 33/5, the woman in charge of a dairy.

bàth, 48 v. 2, = *baoth*

bioran, 59 v. 4, a drumstick

bula, 44 v. 3, a bowl

cnèamhte, 54/10, *siùil chneamhte*?

coisridh, 46/15, a chorus

creannaich, 56/22, pay dearly for

crìn, 52/2, ?

cuach, 34/10, *c. air chrannaibh*, probably a bunch of rowan or mountain ash berries, bright red when ripe

cùl, back or inland country in Cape Breton

cuman, 45 v. 4, a wooden bowl

cumha, 42 v. 6, missing a person of the opposite sex. (The usual meaning 'lamenting' also occurs, e.g. 55/17.)

dòithte, 57/3, grim

dòmhladas, 58 v. 6, *d. blàir*, the thick of the fight

dòrlach, 48 foreword, a good many

drola, 44 v. 5, a pot-hook

earras, 36/16, 57/5, wealth, portion

faisir, pl. *faisrichean* 60/24, defiles

feannag, 36/22. a 'lazybed', old fashioned way of preparing land for planting potatoes in the Highlands

feurlaidh, 33/24, ? Scots ferly, a wonder

féinn, 51 v. 1, *see* note

fleòdradh, 13/4, washing, washing around

fraigh, 44 v. 3, an interior wall

giamanaiche, 38/17, a hunter

ialaidh, 44 v. 3, creeping

iollagach, 13/30, giddy

is, idom of, 41/6, *réidh 's do chomhradh*, clear of your conversation

làmh, *air do làimh*, 38/21, by your hand, asseveration

lì, *lighe*, 28/31, splendour, flood

lòghmhor, 40 v. 14, beautiful, brilliant

luaidh, 52/11, mention (one person in connection with another, in a sexual context)

minig = mairg, in the Gaelic of S. Uist and Barra

much = moch, (Lochaber)

mùgach, 17/9, surly

pòran, 60/14, nostrils

ròc, 55/6, a catch in the voice, hoarseness

ròisgeul, 30/17, ? eloquence

ruighe, 17*b*/3, to stretch out on a death-bed

sad, 14/15, a blow

seaghach, 19 v. 13, prudent, sensible. Compare *Hebridean Folksongs* I, 540, where the word

GLOSSARY

should be so spelt, and where it rhymes with *deaghaidh*(*deoghaidh*). Pronounced *seo'ach*

seanach, 34/5, *see* note

sgoltadh a' bhradain, 32/8, *see* note

sléibhtrich, 56/15, wreckage, dead bodies lying on the ground after a battle

spìd, 55/2, here = speech? usually considered a borrowing of 'speed' or of 'spite', 'energy', or 'an affront

stòpa, stòp, a can or stoup, about a pint

struth a dh'eòlas, 17/18, cf. Dinneen, *sruth eolais,* a ready fund of knowledge

sùgach, 13/31, merry from drink

tàileasg, 31/18, backgammon

teisteach, 45 v. 4, of good reputaion

truimeir, 45 v. 4, a strummer (?)

tuar, 15*b*/7, appearance

uiste, 15/19, = *uisge*, water, *see* note

umhail, 42 v. 12, *gun umhail*, without paying heed to

A' CHRÌOCH